THINGS I'VE LEARNT
WHILST WORKING IN
HOSPITALITY

Things I've Learnt Whilst Working in Hospitality

Some People Are Just Arseholes

EMMA ZETA SKINNER

At Your Own Whisk

CONTENTS

To everyone I've ever served,
Thank you for the inspiration.

To everyone I've ever worked with,
Thank you for the experience - whether it be
positive, negative, or constructive.

To the many people that
inspired the main characters in this book,
You really are a bunch of arseholes.

*** *** *** *** ***

To my mother, and also to
Mrs Buskin from school,
For encouraging me to write and
believing I could actually do it.

| 1 |

Prologue: A Victim of Customer Abuse

On a bustling Friday evening, diners chatted and laughed happily over the blaring music. There was the usual crowd in that night - not that anyone would *ever* stereotype a customer.

The boys were overdrinking the beers so they didn't get called 'soft'. They were half watching the game, every so often yelling at the screen, then discussing what the ref did to screw them this time.

The girls were posing on just the edge of the fine line between slutty and sexy. They took photos of their food, their boobs and their faces, instantly uploading them captioning each picture with things like 'besties', 'girls' night out' or something about love to the moon and back.

Speckled around the bar were the slightly sloppy office workers who had overstayed and would end up doing something they'd regret, whilst hiding in the corners were the awkward singles waiting for first dates to arrive.

Old Mate was spewing that some random stole 'his' seat, while the full-timers told him that was tough and he'd have to deal. It was petty revenge because he never said please or thank you. Even though he was a tool, we'd still serve him first, because locals always took priority. If the new girl served him by accident, he'd roast her, and then teach her how to pour a beer the proper way. There was no need; Tim who'd been there for years would scold her, then retrain her.

I cautiously watched the families with prams, assuming which would hide a dirty nappy under the table, whilst monitoring the women who would inevitably want to speak to the manager. I was pep-talking my staff and encouraging the bubbliest service to those who would surely leave a tip, then whinging discreetly when they didn't.

The chinking of cutlery scraping plates clean and the chiming of glasses during toasts enhanced the loud fun, as friends cheered, dates impressed and woo-girls squealed. Happy Friday indeed.

Then there was Nicki.

Nicki was shoving her way through the crowd, rage-glaring at the idiots who didn't keep to the left. She said, "Excuse me," then a bit louder, "*Excuse me!*" then violently bellowed, "*EXCUSE ME!!!*" at the top of her lungs to try to get the suits to move out of the way. They gave her rude looks for yelling and would include that in their online review. She really could have just politely said, "Excuse me."

She was already in a mood, but how dare our patrons have a drink and unwind while she needed to get through. She had a fire in her eyes, with tears threatening to ruin her makeup.

Actually, now that I've mentioned it, she'd put on way too much eyeliner, so crying would have probably improved it.

Nicki really needed to pull herself together, so I flicked her my 'don't you dare!' face and she got the silent but deadly message to take her rage to the cool room.

I watched her, to make sure she was off the floor, away from the prying eyes of customers who didn't give a toss about her emotions.

Speaking of silent but deadly, I'd let one slip out right near the woman with the hibiscus-covered fake nails and a bob haircut. She looked just like the kind of person who'd have random words plastered all over her walls and scented candles displayed all over her house. She was sporting activewear on a Friday night, therefore it was only a matter of time before she started complaining about something. I'd deliberately set the air con too cool and the music too loud, hoping she'd notice. People like that deserved a bad fart. If I didn't know why then, I'd soon find out.

Nicki barged straight into the fridge, yanking the heavy door closed behind her.

Even though she was over there and I was over here, I could hear her raging, hoping she wasn't taking it out on the innocent limes again.

Please note, in this rendition, Nicki was using far kinder words than the actual profanities common in the hospitality industry. Swearing was part of the job and an integral part of the language behind the scenes. I'll be kind to your ears, by substituting the rather quite offensive keywords throughout this story. There'll be no 'see you next Tuesdays' or ultra baddies like the F-bomb, however, 'non-sweary' swearies will still be included, because, you know, hospo. That's just how we roll.

Anyway, the bar was getting slammed, the pass was getting slammed, my butt was getting grabbed. "Oi!" I barked at the handsy civilian, "Do NOT touch me!"

"You can't speak to me like that! I'll tell the manager!" he arrogantly threatened.

I had so much hospo adrenaline in me. Any patron who'd dare grab me would live to regret it. A burning pit ripped through my abdomen. I wickedly threw my head back and laughed at him. "The manager? Do you want the manager? *I am the manager.*"

In another life, I'd dream of grabbing him back where it'd hurt, but my hospo conscience told me to rather hit him where it hurt emotionally. What was he going to do about it? If he admitted to grabbing me, he'd be affirmed he was in the wrong. I had every right to yell back at this one, so after my bold retort, I headed straight to the bar and told Tim to stop serving him. Handsy would either give up and leave when he realised he'd been shunned, or cause a scene so I'd kick him out. I was kinda still up for some non-guilt action, so I hoped he'd fight back.

Anyway, the bar was slammed, the pass was slammed, my butt was no longer getting grabbed, but the floor was a mess, the ashtrays were full and there were towers of stacked glasses on every table.

Someone had drowned a bread roll in a warm beer. There was gum stuck under table rims, packets of chips covered in spilled soda, and the floor was sticky.

I needed a glassy. I needed a glassy. I needed some help on the floor! Where's Nicki? *Where's Nicki?!*

That's right; she was still chucking a tantrum in the coolroom.

I marched straight in there, ready to kick her into shape, but she'd snuck out. I knew where to find her.

She was out the back sobbing, smoking, and huddling on a chef chair. You might call them 'milk crates' but to us, they were chef chairs.

I told her she had two minutes, but she argued she needed three. I let her have five because she was good. If she were useless I would have given her only one.

Before I left, I told her she had to put it on hold until the end of the shift. At the end of the night, she could whine and scream as much as she liked, but for now, she was at work, so she'd better slap on a smile. Five minutes. Please don't be late.

We were still getting slammed, but I knew she needed a time out, so I ran around on the floor as fast as I could to help get it clean. I understood what was wrong with her; sometimes we all just needed to remove ourselves from the situation to get better.

Nicki came in via the bar to sneak in a shot of vodka, which I of course, definitely did not see. She saw the man who made her rage - he was walking toward the door, so Nicki, being the good hospo girl she was, put her emotions on hold and got straight back to good old-fashioned customer service. She did the right thing and farewelled him.

Remember that thing I said about hospitality being really sweary? Remember how I said I'd substitute *some* words to protect your ears? Well, she called out something along the lines of, "Eff you! Have a great evening! See you next time!" only 'Eff' began with an F, ended in K, and it sure wasn't 'firetruck'.

"Eff you! Have a great evening! See you next time!" she farewelled nice and loudly with a big smile.

He turned to her, with confused anger. *What did she just say?*

I hoped he didn't cotton on. Pretty daring for Nicki, but if he made her cry, he probably deserved it. I was still bitter about Handsy and the glutes grabbing that I pretended she said the right thing all along.

She smiled and repeated the exact same thing, just like I thought she did. "Thank you! Have a great night! See you soon!"

The man shook his head and kept walking because he must have misheard her the first time over the background noise. He swore she told him to eff off... but, well, it *was* loud in there.

Her perfect smile confirmed it. "Thanks so much! Have a great night!" she confirmed.

See? I told you Nicki was good. She was resilient and obviously knew the survival skills of work in hospitality. Resilience was key when you were on the front line.

It was so easy to spot a newbie in the industry. Their charming efforts to prove 'the customer is always right' eventually got squished into a vague interpretation of a soul, merely surviving for a meager paycheque and discounted booze. Hospitality was a fickle industry, accepting those who couldn't find work elsewhere; those who were too stupid to do anything else; those who needed work 'in the meantime'; and the remaining few who glued the rest together: the passionately creative types, who lived it, breathed it and loathed it - but were infatuated with it.

I wish I'd figured it all out earlier, for when I was new, I too used to take everything to heart. Resilience was not something I was taught - it was plain old experience. As a veteran beer wench, I felt like it was my duty to pass on my wisdom to the newbies of the hospo world. Surely my experience in the behaviour of the public was worth something to the young impressionable faces of the future - even if they only stayed with the job temporarily, as so many of them did.

Nicki got it, and I got it too. You had to be resilient and you couldn't take it to heart because there was no excusing their behaviour. The number one thing I've learnt whilst working in hospitality is that *some people are just arseholes.*

| 2 |

PART 1: Rutherford, a Fancy-Pants Hotel

I realised pretty quickly into adulthood that I needed a job to fund my social life, and it was a little bit dumb to quit my supermarket gig before I had anything else lined up. I still had one year left of my degree, and so a year to work in the meantime before landing a real job. What was the only thing I could do without experience? Hospitality.

Hospitality - the scavenger industry, collecting hopeless souls to serve the privileged since the beginning of food.

One more year and I was out. I'd never serve another person again after this job. I kept my eyes open for something, then one day I saw an ad for a hotel. I leapt at the chance of working at a hotel definitely not named Rutherford. Reading the description of the job advertisement, my heart melted: *Rutherford is seeking experienced Food and Beverage attendants to join their team. Applicants must be well presented, able to work both independently and as a team, and have experience in both food and customer service.*

I was well presented (sort of). I could work independently and as part of a team (if I *had* to). I had experience in food and customer service!

Ding ding ding! We had a winner! I *had* to apply for this role! It was still customer service, it was in food, but five-star hotels portrayed the creme de la creme of the service life.

I immediately applied, then sat fantasising about getting the role. Rutherford was everything my old job at Clarkson was not. It was the only five-star hotel in the suburbs, and everything about it depicted pure class.

The white edifice towered on the top of a hill. The sheer enormity of it drew attention as a place of importance, cleanliness, and sharp edges. The perfectly manicured hedges and lawns, decorated with twinkling fairy lights, embraced the exterior, offsetting its threatening glare.

Inside, glossy cream tiles clacked beneath the heels of executives. They led to the bar to greet men gathered in the piano lounge, nibbling on olives in between sips of neat scotch.

The staff wore crisp white collared shirts, with ankle-length black aprons. Instead of appearing flustered and sweaty like the Clarkson staff, they presented as calm but firm. Their hair was pulled back in perfect high buns, cemented with spray until it became one solid piece. They wore nude lipstick, sheer stockings, and brassy name tags.

Behind the front desk, a fierce-looking woman perched, typing whilst speaking into her headset. The concierge nodded curtly to all passing guests while the porters assisted with their luggage.

To work there, I dreamed, would be the next step in my career. It was clean, respectable, and reputable. If one were to be stuck in hospitality, one had better work in the swankiest of places.

I was thrilled when I received word of my acceptance. No more freaky mystery meat, no more beeping timers, no more corporation bull-shit, and no more stress.

The morning I was due to start, I woke excitedly. My heart pounded as I dressed in my new clothes. Of course, once I arrived I would be issued a proper uniform, but for now, I was in the industry-standard 'formal uniform': Plain black slacks, free from any embellishments, a crisp plain white collared business shirt, black cotton socks, and fully enclosed, black non-slip shoes. I figured out I could claim the shoes on tax because they were 'safety wear'.

I spent time perfecting my makeup. The look I was going for was classy, yet understated. I longingly admired a glittery bubble-gum pink lipstick I'd bought on a whim. That day, I knew, I'd better err on the side of conservative, so I opted for the boring fawn shade.

I gazed at myself in the mirror. I looked like no one. Like myself, but I was now also the image of every hotel worker. Friendly, but forgettable. Just as they wanted. Just as I should be. I was ready.

I arrived early on my first day, eager to prove my excellent customer service skills and job technique. It was still dark and the cool morning breeze made me shiver as my little bomb of a car pulled up. It looked decidedly out of place against the sleek luxury models in the car park. They told me I wasn't allowed to park my car there, and the spots were reserved for guests. I parked there anyway.

I spent some time trying to be brave enough to get out of the car. I was experiencing nerves; keen to get in there and show them what I was capable of, but hesitant due to the looming unknown.

At ten minutes to start time, I decided it was a good time to brave my jitters and head inside. I boldly moved toward the building, feeling intimidated by its enormity. I kept saying important things about my excellence in my head.

The concierge giggled. He'd caught me giving myself a pep talk.

I focussed on him, mildly embarrassed, but drew a breath and put on my customer smile, "Hi, I'm Alexandra. I'm due to be starting work in the restaurant this morning."

"Ah, new meat," he smiled. "Lauren is waiting for you." He pointed toward the left.

I thanked him and headed in.

"You're late!" snapped an unfamiliar voice. What a greeting.

"Oh." My confidence faltered. "Hi, I'm Alex... Sorry, they told me on the phone I needed to be here by five, and it's," I glanced at my watch, "five to. Sorry I didn't realise..."

"No you didn't," Lauren cut me off. "We *open* at five. Thanks to you, we're not set up properly."

"Oh, sorry, I misunderstood," I apologised. "What can I do?"

"Well, I've already *done* almost everything without you. Go set up the espresso machine. You *do* know how to make coffee, don't you?"

"Yes," I replied shortly, shocked at the mood of my trainer. Lauren didn't need to know that I made terrible coffee and anyone I made would surely be sent back. I chose not to mention it.

"Well?" Lauren barked, causing me to jump.

"I'm doing it," I said, trying not to be defensive. I pushed the bar door open. The first bar I'd ever walked behind and I'll never forget the awe I felt.

It was sleek, dimly lit, and spotless. A chandelier of cocktail glasses dangled, framing the walls and softening the stainless steel panels. A mirror hid behind shelves, giving the illusion of a deeper room. There was *alcohol* on the shelves. I recognised some bottles, but others held mysterious liquids in beautifully intricate vessels, labelled with enigmatic descriptions. My beef with Lauren was immediately forgotten, as I grew excited about the contents of the bar.

I shoved my bag in a cupboard under the counter and began to set up. I ground coffee beans, stocked the fridges with milk, and put together the steel pieces of equipment until I was satisfied it was ready to be used. I even remembered to put out cloths for cleaning and wiping the steam wand. I was fairly proud that I knew all of these steps after only doing a short barista course. I was even prouder that I managed to locate all of my stock for mis-en-place without bothering Lauren, who seemed to be pointlessly straightening chairs frantically.

Just as I looked at her disdainfully, Lauren barged into the bar.

"Are you ready? We need you on the floor!" she barked, without bothering to hear a response.

Startled, I moved out, toward the entrance of the restaurant. I took a moment to appreciate the beauty of the set-up, in a way that only a worker could truly identify with. The tables lined up in perfect rows, each dressed with a crisp white tablecloth. The cutlery lined up to an exact tee, ensuring that any guest who glanced down a row of tables would see all of the settings impeccably aligned.

The cereal stand held canisters with seemingly useless generic labels: *Corn Puffs, Breakfast Flakes, Muesli,* and *Wheat Biscuits.* I had to wonder if those vessels actually retained the brand-name contents or if they skimped on no-name products.

The continental breakfast station offered yoghurts, fruits, Danishes, bread rolls, and croissants all meticulously arranged to appear effortlessly draped.

All of these offerings surrounded the most sought-after of breakfasts: the hot buffet. A sixteen tray steaming bain-marie decorated with tongs and chrome labels soon became my most hated position to work with.

Before working at Rutherford, I didn't mind a buffet. It was never my first choice, but it was a party staple. Always a queue, and I always seemed to get with the dregs. From the day I began work at Rutherford, I felt more strongly about buffets: I loathed them.

It could have been that buffet or perhaps the uselessly labelled cereal canisters that fuelled my hatred, but it first stemmed from Lauren and her foul disposition.

"We're open!" barked Lauren from the floor. "You're on buffet. Just keep filling the trays from the kitchen!"

I looked up, and the empty restaurant was full. The thick silence had suddenly transformed into loud chattering, as people seemed to infiltrate from every direction. Groups surrounded every table, each person vying for a hint of when the hot buffet would be ready. Right about... now!

I lifted the lid off the first tray in the bain-marie, and a gush of hash-brown scented steam engulfed me, blinding me by fogging up my spectacles. By the time I wiped them, the people were there!

They seemed to grab at the buffet from every direction, lunging to snatch the last chipolata, and arguing over who deserved the limited amount of scrambled eggs.

"Hurry up! Your trays are empty!" Lauren snarled at me, whilst standing importantly and uselessly instructing people how to serve themselves.

Well, it would be faster if you actually did something to help! I thought to myself. I pasted on a smile to conceal the nasty thoughts I was thinking about Lauren.

I tried to push through the line, but it was too crowded. People stood everywhere, fighting to get to the front.

A frail man stared intently at nothing.

My eyes wandered to where he was looking. There was nothing there.

He was staring through space, with great concentration, his head aimed at the scrambled eggs.

Oh no, you don't! I thought desperately.

He opened his mouth and hovered with it half-open then closed, focussing on the eggs.

No...

He took a breath and leaned back forcefully.

"No!" I cried.

"Ahhhhh-CHOO!" the man sneezed. Right into the food!

I pushed in and went to remove the tray, but Lauren scolded me and pulled me back.

"We can't leave an empty spot with just the boiling water! What if someone burns themselves? Plus it *looks* so *unprofessional!*" she shuddered.

"So you want me to just leave it?" I asked, disgusted at the thought of anyone eating snot-covered scrambled eggs.

"Go ask Chef for another tray of eggs, *then* take this one away," Lauren directed.

I cringed at the thought of leaving the contaminated eggs there.

Lauren shooed me away.

I made my way through the clawing crowd into the brightly lit kitchen.

"Ah!" I tried to get any of the chef's attention, not knowing any of their names. I'd never spoken to a chef before, so I didn't know what to do.

"Ah!" I tried again. I stuck my head out to the restaurant to see if another girl could help me.

They all seemed to turn their backs at the sight of me. Great. As if I didn't feel useless enough.

Desperate for attention, my polite little voice found a thriving crescendo, "EXCUSE ME, CHEF! MORE EGGS PLEASE, CHEF!" I yelled to no one in particular.

A young chef near the front responded, not even looking at me. "Four minutes! Come back then!"

My heart sank. Was he even speaking to me?

"Chef? Can I please get more eggs?" I tried again.

"FOUR MINUTES GET OUT!" he screamed, throwing a deathly stare.

Turns out he was speaking to me.

I barged my way through the mob to meet Lauren. "They're on their way," I told her, as I clambered around checking the contents under the lids.

"No, you tell Chef I need them *now*," Lauren pushed.

"They'll be ready in about four minutes," I repeated.

Lauren stopped and glared at me, daring me to speak again. The look was enough for me to wince and return to the kitchen.

"Sorry, Chef, I need eggs please!" I pleaded.

"Four minutes!" the chef replied.

"But-"

"Four minutes!" he cut me off. "I have other meals to make!"

I gagged when I realised the contaminated eggs had by now all been taken by the crowd. I looked around the restaurant, guessing who had eaten them. Already, on my first day, I knew who I wished had.

The ones wearing business attire were the nicest. Some held a slight air of entitlement, but mostly, they kept to themselves and were polite when addressed. The few guests in casual attire were chatty and happy – clearly enjoying their holiday. Some were in awe of the facilities. The guests I despised, however, were the tour groups.

It never mattered their country of origin, their ages or their genders; they were equally pushy and disgusting. They massacred the buffet.

During that first breakfast, I witnessed that man conduct an open-mouth sneeze onto food that people consumed. Plates were piled higher than any stomach needed – or were able to fill, and serviettes wrapped up extra bacon and sausages for later. Fashionably large handbags were utilised as food storage containers, smuggling out as much food as they could carry, along with complimentary butter, sugar packets and even silverware. Hands were used despite tongs being clearly available. Tasters were nibbled, then returned, then taken again before I could confiscate them. The tour guests burped loudly, and some didn't consider concealing their farts.

I saw an old lady hock up a goey and spit it on the tiles near the entrance; I avoided the area hoping no one would notice it or make me clean it.

I rescued one idiot about to use her fork to pry stuck toast from the electric toaster. I was rudely shunned as a thank you. They were society's scumbags. They'd paid for an all-inclusive tour and used that as an excuse for their gluttony and sordid manners. What dirty people! What a taste of the general public.

| 3 |

Mini-Bar

At nine o'clock, I was relieved to hear I'd be moving to the mini-bar. I did a little dance of excitement that I would be learning how to actually serve in a bar. A miniature bar, but still, a bar with drinks and glasses and people!

Imagine my disappointment when I was dumped in a cupboard of tiny spirits, micro cans, snack-size chocolates and overpriced spring water. I wasn't serving in a mini-bar! I was stocking the hotel room mini-bars!

"So all you do is check off the rooms and items you filled and come back when you're finished," Lauren pointed to a clipboard. "Here's the key – it'll open any of the rooms. Oh, and don't go in if there's a sign on the door. When you're ready to enter, knock and call out, 'guest services' then open it. Like this, 'GUEST SERVICES'," she sang loudly. "Now you practice," she directed me.

"Like, right now?" I asked her.

Lauren rolled her eyes. "Yes, *now*."

I imagined a cartoon princess knocking on the door, and charmingly smiled and sang out, "GUEST SERVICES," to Lauren. I must have passed the test, for I was soon on my way.

I opened the first fridge and checked the chart. I replaced a tiny beer and a tiny wine and marked them on my list. This was easy. By the end of the first floor, it became tedious.

Open fridge. Soda can missing. Soda can replaced. Check. Next room. Open fridge. Scotch opened and refilled with what we assume is tea. Charge guest. Replace. Check. Next room. Open fridge. Nothing to replace. Check. Next room. *TESTICLES?!*

"Er, sorry!" I called out, as I hastily kept my eyes to the floor and backed out of the room. Note on the clipboard: *Saw balls!*

I opened the next door, shocked to find Lauren waiting for me.

"Have you done Room 214?" she demanded.

"Um, I, er..." I stammered, unsure of whether I had in fact visited Room 214.

"Check your sheet!" she snapped as if it were the most obvious thing ever.

"Yes."

"Yes? Are you sure?" she looked me up and down fishily.

Was I sure? I checked my notes again, feeling guilty, but not knowing what I'd done wrong. "Yes."

"Let's go for a walk," Lauren said, walking away.

Yep. This meant I'd done something wrong.

I followed her, panicking about what I could have possibly done to upset her. Was it the buffet? Was it because of the snot eggs? Did she see me roll my eyes at her? Did she know about me seeing that guy's penis?

Lauren swung open the heavy door marked 214 and greeted the freshly cleaned room, "Look familiar?"

Yes. It looked just like every other room. They were all the same room, over and over and over. I decided silence was the best answer.

Lauren strode across to the mini-bar, and opened the fridge and stood back. "Can you tell me what is wrong with this?" she asked as if I were in kindergarten.

I peered into the fridge. I checked off the list that all items were there. I checked they were all in the correct place. I checked the fridge was clean, it was turned on and there weren't any expired items. I was stumped.

"This!" Lauren pointed to a beer I had replaced.

I looked at it, still unable to detect a fault. Unless? Could it really be that? I queried my thoughts. "The label is slightly off-centre?"

"YES!" Lauren cried, amazed it took me that long to figure out such a blatantly obvious error.

"Really? That's it?" I asked in disbelief. A slightly off-centre label.

"That's it? *That's it?*" Lauren articulated dramatically. "*That,*" she said, twisting the bottle five degrees to the left, "is a *big no-no,*" she wagged a pointed finger in my face.

"A big 'no-no'?" I repeated to be clear Lauren had actually used the term 'no-no'. Yep. A grown-up food and beverage manager told me that that was a big no-no.

"It's not good enough," she lectured. "All of the labels must face the front. Make sure they're all aligned from now on."

I nodded. As Lauren went to leave, my bladder reminded me I needed something, "Sorry Lauren," I called out. "What time do I-"

"When you're finished!" Lauren snapped.

"But can I just-?" The door slammed in my face. I looked at my watch. Six hours I'd been on. I'd only done three of the ten floors. My heart sank. My stomach growled. I longingly looked at the candy on display on the trolley but decided against it for fear of repercussions. I hadn't been there long enough or made any alliances to risk eating their food yet. My bladder would have to wait too. I tried to turn off the niggling feeling, which was slowly growing more persistent.

Then I became sad. It was only my first day and a feeling of melancholy swept over me. This was supposed to be my big break from the supermarket scene, but I felt as if I'd moved back to square one.

I'd dominated my deli at Clarkson. I knew everything and everyone. I knew where things were, what procedures entailed and what the expectations were. In the lonely few hours I'd been at Rutherford, I had crumbled from being an optimistic recruit to feeling worthless, stupid and unsure of myself. I had looked forward to starting there, but now I wondered if this job was some mistake. A hint of paranoia ate at me, and I speculated that this was just a cruel joke, for I did not belong. I was not one of them, and never would be. I sniffled, forcing myself to shut off the emotions driving behind the tears welling in my eyes. *Six months.* Six months was the minimum acceptable time to remain in a role without a résumé looking bad. I needed this job for at least a year though, while I studied. I would have to suck it up.

Several gruelling hours later, I returned to the foyer, proud I'd managed to succeed. The mini-fridges did not destroy me.

My dishevelled appearance, however, more closely represented what I was attempting to hide for the sake of my career.

I was sweaty from pushing the enormous trolley down the corridors, lugging boxes around to restock it, then continually squatting then standing. Despite the workout, the air conditioner was icy, and goosebumps revealed themselves, making the fine hairs on my arms stand on end. I'd become both burning and freezing, hinting that the day's duties may make me ill. My voice became raspy after the constant blasting of chilled air knocked me in the face as I entered each room. My stomach gnawed on itself; I hadn't eaten since early in the evening before. I stood awkwardly clenching my leg muscles, praying that no liquid seeped out, as I actively thought of suppressing the blaring reminder that my bladder was at capacity. On top of all this, I was exhausted. I'd barely slept the night previous out of excitement and anticipation for my new role, and I hadn't woken this early in... ever?

Nevertheless, I'd done it. The first day was over. A sense of victory surrounded me, that despite all of the challenges of that day, I could go home (and urinate and have a nap) and know that I'd learnt things (like straightening labels) and tomorrow would be a better, and hopefully easier day.

Lauren greeted me as I returned from the mini-bar shift.

"Ok, so I've filled out your timesheet so you can see how we do it here; all you have to do is sign it," Lauren informed me, holding out a pen.

I read my timesheet. "No, sorry, this is incorrect," I said. "It says here I took a break but I didn't. I worked through."

"Oh, well. Payroll will just insert one anyway. We have to. Don't worry, they'll usually change it so it says you'll finish half an hour later instead so you'll get paid the right hours," Lauren replied casually.

"No, but I *didn't* have a break," I said more persistently.

"Yes, but they'll add one in any way, then pay you for an extra half an hour to cover it." Lauren was growing frustrated with my lack of understanding, and her tone grew more condescending.

"No, but I didn't have a break, so please don't write and say that I did!" I snapped. "I'm dying to go to the loo, I'm starving, and now you want me to lie too?" I'd had enough of that day, and my exhaustion and bodily desperation were catching up with me.

"Look, if you needed to go to the loo, you should have gone before you started mini-bar," Lauren insisted.

"No! That's not fair!" I cried. "No one told me how long the shift would be! You needed to give me a break!"

"But mini-bar doesn't get a break," Lauren started.

I was not having a bar of it. I knew my rights and knew I was entitled to a break that shift. I *knew* I was entitled to access to a toilet at any time needed. They were taking advantage of me, and it was wrong. I decided a different approach: to give Lauren the benefit of the doubt.

"How long does the mini-bar shift usually take? Maybe I was slow because I'm still learning," I suggested quietly.

"They usually all finish about now," Lauren replied.

I was enraged! "So you've made me work a buffet shift, then straight onto a six-hour mini-bar shift, without a break, knowing full well that I'd work for ten hours straight without so much as a sit-down, let alone a break or access to a toilet! Then you're trying to make me sign, saying I was given a break when I wasn't! This is ridiculous!"

Lauren was taken aback by my explosion. She stood dumbly, then seemed to remember she was the supervisor, and matter-of-factly put me in my place.

"Look, that's just the way it is. Payroll will automatically enter a break for you, so you may as well write one yourself. You can leave your sheet in this folder when you are finished. I have other things to do, so unless there's anything else?"

I shook my head, betrayed by the face of my big break into a fancy hotel.

Lauren walked away.

I took a pen and scribbled over Lauren's timesheet and signed, noting it was incorrect. I took a fresh timesheet and wrote in my actual hours, sans break. I then found a thick, black marker and wrote a large note in capitals: DID NOT TAKE A BREAK. WORKED TEN HOURS

STRAIGHT. Then signed my curly signature next to it, and shoved it back in the folder.

The next day, I arrived at twenty-five past four in the morning. I followed Lauren's lead in setting up the restaurant – turning on and filling the buffet with water, setting up the espresso machine and switching on the lights - and guessed I could have done all that in half the time that Lauren did.

Lauren seemed to waste time on tasks that didn't need doing.

I watched her straighten up straight chairs, tidy paperwork that was in a drawer, align cutlery on tables and brush table skirts that already fell perfectly straight.

During buffet service, I learnt to run to the kitchen (barging through the thick crowd) and grab a new tray of food when the first became half-emptied. My timing became spot on. It didn't stop Lauren from commanding me to fill the trays (as they were already being filled). I ignored her and kept on being fantastic at my job. I managed to anticipate customers' needs, and search for tasks that needed doing. Today was a good day.

At nine, Lauren informed me that I would be moving to mini-bar again. Great.

"May I please go to the bathroom first?" I asked, possibly too quickly.

Lauren eyed me off but believed it was a reasonable request. "You have exactly three minutes. Don't be late!"

I scooted out of the restaurant and then plummeted down the back corridor toward the staff room.

A woman came around a corner, walking toward me.

I slowed. I pulled my shoulders back to seem more professional. Everyone's always mentioned I slouched. From a distance, I could see this woman was smiling at me with enormous intent. I could hear the clacking of her heels on the cold concrete. I strained my eyes to see if I'd recognise this woman.

Clack. Clack. Clack. Clack.

What did she want? Satisfied she was a stranger, I kept wondering why this woman was smiling at me so purposefully. I discreetly glanced over my shoulder. No one was there.

This perfect stranger was positively beaming at me, eyes fixated with mine. As she approached, I admired her flawless makeup. Nude lipstick and natural tones, paired with dark dramatic lashes. She strutted toward me as if she were on parade. Determined, with a slight swagger. The stark concrete may as well have been a runway.

As she drew closer, I slowed even more, curious as to what this woman was going to say to me.

The woman entered the desirable zone of approachability. It was the golden instant where she could pass me and say something important. Keeping eye contact, she had a clear expression of purpose. What this woman needed to say was of great significance. Her mouth opened into a wide smile, exposing her beautifully whitened teeth. "Good morning!" she sang out enthusiastically. "One team, one dream!" Her voice echoed against the bare walls, causing me to flinch nervously.

"Er, morning," I mumbled, confused at the woman's intention.

Clack. Clack. Clack. Clack.

The woman passed me and continued on her mission.

I shook my head, grappling at what just happened. That was it. This model specimen of a hotel worker had wished me a nice day. It was common to be polite, but how this woman made her greeting, I felt as if she were a salesperson, or perhaps a game show host. How bizarre.

I remembered my deadline and hurried to the staff room. I used the facilities, then found a muesli bar and an egg salad sandwich from my bag, and shoved them in my apron. I was disappointed nothing else would fit. A piece of fruit would have been nice to keep me going. It was a perfect crime: If they weren't going to give me a break, I would take one myself in the luxury of a five-star hotel room. It was illegal not to, I reminded myself.

I sprinted back down the long corridor and ran straight into Lauren's coffee, which spilt down her front. Of course it did.

"I'm so sorry!" I cried.

The cup couldn't have been full. I examined the damage, and only a few noticeable drops seeped on Lauren's front. According to Lauren, this was a disaster.

Watch where you're going! Look at this mess! This will stain! You're so lucky I keep a spare shirt in my office!"

"Look, I'm really sorry, I just didn't see you."

"Well that worked out for you, didn't it?" Lauren reprimanded me. "You've just wasted my time. You'd better hurry up and get the trolley, or you'll be late."

Late for what? I asked myself. There was no finishing time for this shift. Maybe I'd be late for my after-work beer. Late for my escape from this shithole?

My plan worked. I began filling the fridges and cupboards with an array of tasty treats, carefully angling the labels so they exactly faced the front. I left no reason for Lauren to find any fault. No big no-nos.

As I grew hungry, I locked myself in a guest's bathroom (praying the guest would not return during my visit) and munched on my sandwich. I went to throw the cling wrap in the bin, then thought it was best to keep the evidence in my apron.

The routine went well for a few weeks. I took my time doing mini-bar. If they were paying me unsupervised and deducting breaks I hadn't been issued, then they could pay me the extra hours for 'being slow'. It was good revenge.

| 4 |

First In, First Out

It didn't take long before I hated my job.

I hated the filthy international tour guests. I hated the smell of bacon and eggs mixed with self-loathing and a bit of snot. I hated the easy listening background music. I hated the spelling mistake in the menu describing pinot noir as 'pinot nior'. I hated stocking those stupid tiny fridges with their stupid tiny bottles and their stupid tiny perfectly aligned labels.

I hated the staff – even the people I'd never met. They seemed as if they were manufactured in a plastic smile factory. None of them displayed any personality, except that it was their duty to perform exemplary customer service. No matter how unique they appeared as individuals, they had all been cast from the same mould. They might have had varying ethnic and cultural backgrounds, but all I could see was artificial compliance to a set of unspoken standards. They were all the same person. They had no unique distinguishing features. Everything from their hair to their polished shoes matched a recipe for model behaviour.

After the people, I hated the exploitation. I knew my rights but suspected – no, knew – I would be punished for standing up for them. A casual worker was expendable, and I had to keep my job for the money.

I hated the intellectual capacity of the team. As a collective, they could perform duties flawlessly. When it came to actually thinking, they failed miserably, searching for direction in procedures, and not questioning the dangerous concept of 'but we've always done it this way.'

One afternoon, Lauren asked me to stock up the bar fridges - the actual bar fridges - for a change. I happily obliged, as I prefer working alone. Anyone who said that thing about teamwork making the dream work was lying. Teamwork sucked.

I began by rotating the stock that was already in the fridges and was surprised to find several bottles out of date. For an establishment that prided themselves on hospital corners, they'd left quite a mess of their itinerary.

I grabbed the milk crate I was sitting on, and flipped it over, putting all the expired bottles in it. I then rotated the cola so the older bottles were at the front. *First in, first out,* I reminded myself.

The next product – bottles of lemonade – was the same. There were a dozen out of date bottles.

When it was time for the next product, I pulled *everything* out of the fridge. It was easier to just start again.

Lauren decided to come and visit me at the moment the bar floor was covered in bottles. Perfect timing.

"Did you use the toilet in Room 318?" she asked. She was always so good at greetings.

"No," I said, completely lying to her face. Of course I had - when else did she expect me to have a wee?

"Are you sure?" Lauren asked fishily, her eyes narrowing.

"Yes," I said.

Yes, I used it because she wouldn't give me a break.

"Because the man in 318 says that his toilet has been used. I looked at the key scans and the only other key used today was the mini-bar key. So I'm going to ask you again, did you use his toilet?"

"No."

I knew I couldn't be pinned on this anyway. Also, going to the toilet is not a crime. Also – how would he know his toilet had been used? Also, *they could run key scans?!* I'd better remember that!

One year left. Only one year left in hospitality until I could get a real job.

"So you didn't use the toilet in his room then?"

I knew she was onto me, but I refused to budge. "Nope."

Lauren needed something else to throw at me. She looked at the floor at all the bottles strewn around, the milk crate, and the empty fridges.

"Just what do you think you're doing here?" she demanded.

I winced – caught in the act. Only I wasn't doing anything wrong.

One year left. I just had to stick it out for another year. Lauren was not worth getting upset over.

"I asked you to stock the fridges, not pull everything out of them!" Lauren cried as if the world were falling apart.

"Well, I began to check what we needed, and noticed that a lot of stock was out of date, so I thought I'd rotate it and then see what we needed," I rambled, still feeling like I was in trouble. I was right. One year left.

"No. Clean this up immediately! How dare you make such a mess in my bar?" Lauren scolded me.

I should have left it at that, but I was a bit unclear on what she wanted me to do. I asked her if I should keep rotating it? Should I waste the out-of-date ones? Did she still want me to refill the fridges?

"Just put it all back in the fridge!" Lauren snapped.

Sometimes I couldn't help but argue with people. Yes, she was my manager. Yes, I was a junior food and bev attendant. But what she was doing was flat-out wrong. I took a deep breath and tried to negotiate a solution.

"But, they've expired - and a lot is about to. I thought maybe the short-dated ones could go on special and-" ...there was no point.

Lauren was furious – as she usually was toward me.

"I *said* put them back in the fridge!" Lauren screamed.

One year left. One year left. One year left.

I stopped to wonder if they really intended on selling expired stock. Then I realised the part of the job I hated the most was Lauren. The staff as a whole were plastic and thick, but at least they were polite. I hated the fact that they refused to roster me a break, but I accepted that that was a regular occurrence in hospitality. Lauren, however, was just plain nasty. She never had anything nice to say and preferred to be critical and demanding. She was set in her ways and had no room for flexibility and no space for new ideas. It was her way or the highway.

Lauren's face was red and sweaty. She held her arms crossed in front of her chest, in a stance, daring me to make one more wrong move.

I accepted. I stood by my ethics, and spoke up, "You're not really going to sell out of date stock?"

"Just shove them at the back; we can't leave the fridges empty! Of course we won't sell it, but it needs to *look* full," Lauren brushed me off, tired that this conversation was still happening.

One year left. One year left. One year left. One year left.

"No, they need to be wasted," I said firmly.

"Just put them back!" Lauren screamed again.

One year left? That's it. I was over this. "No, *you* put them back! I'm out of here!" I shouted.

"What?" Lauren was taken aback.

"I quit!" I spat.

Lauren did not see this one coming. "Is there a reason why?"

There sure was a reason!

"Yeah, because you're a bitch and this job sucks."

Lauren stood dumbfounded as I collected my bag, threw my apron on the floor, and walked out of the bar. I left her with all the bottles and a look of disbelief. It was over. I vowed never to work in premium accommodation again. It was time to move on.

| 5 |

Petit Four: Pumpkin Soup

"What would you like?" I asked the woman.

The woman knew what she'd wanted before she'd even sat down, for she enjoyed her meal so much last time.

"I'll have the pumpkin soup please," she requested.

"I'm sorry," I told her, "the soup of the day today is broccoli. Would you like to try the broccoli soup?"

Broccoli soup? Broccoli... soup? Soup - with broccoli? The woman was stunned with this absurd suggestion, for she knew they had pumpkin soup on the menu; she devoured it last time. She had been looking forward to having the pumpkin soup all day. Surely, this girl must be mistaken. "Sorry, but I thought your 'soup of the day' was pumpkin!" the woman blurted.

"It might have been last time you were here, but today it's broccoli," I informed her. "The broccoli soup has had some fantastic feedback from other guests. I'd highly recommend it. What do you think?" I offered again, confident that the broccoli soup was just delightful.

The woman, however, wouldn't let it slide. She *knew* there had been pumpkin soup on the menu last time. "But I thought your 'soup of the day' was *always* pumpkin!" she exclaimed desperately.

I took a deep breath, pondering the best way to explain the soup situation without sounding rude. "The soup of the day changes every day. Otherwise, it wouldn't be named the 'soup of the day'. It would simply be named the 'soup'."

| 6 |

PART 2: Silvermans, Your Favourite Restaurant

As much as I knew I'd be out of the game soon and into a new job (a 'real' job) I still had one year left of temporary work whilst studying, and decided to have a crack at restauranting. The hours were perfect for a student, with shifts at night and on the weekends, and the days free to continue studying and network.

Only one year left in hospitality, promise.

I arrived at work scathingly close to being 'late' (which was actually fifteen minutes – unpaid – before my rostered start for the shift prep). As I jogged into the back of house area, I tied my sauce-stained apron around my waist, hoping it passed the cleanliness test.

I fumbled to check all necessary items were in there – several pens, a notepad, change purse, breath mints, lip-gloss, bar blade, and the decidedly *un*necessary oversized laminated cheat sheet, which Mavis the Manager forced us all to carry.

This cheat sheet came in handy for such emergencies such as forgetting how to write down an order or being unsure of how to answer the phone. In those instances of utter panic, never fear: the oversized laminated cheat sheet was here to save the day!

Still huffing, I arrived just in time for Mavis to call out my name.

"Alex? Alex!" she glared suspiciously.

"Yes!" I raised my arm to be seen. "I'm here!"

Mavis frowned. "I didn't see you before. Thought you were late," she dared.

"What?" I said innocently. "I've been here since twenty to."

She shrugged. "You're on Section Five."

Excellent! I was a little bit chuffed I'd gotten away with being 'late' (ok, I was still yet to begin getting paid, but anyway) and now I was allocated the best section too!

"Nicole?" Mavis looked around.

"Here!" My friend Nicki wheezed breathlessly behind me, gently patting my hand as if to ask me to cover for her tardiness.

"You're late," Mavis frowned.

"No?" I piped up. "We came at the same time," I lied.

Nicki nodded assuring.

We must have been convincing enough, for Mavis shrugged again, and allocated Nicki to, "Section One, Nicole."

Section One: the worst section. Near the door, in an awkward layout, just out of reach of the cutlery station, and just close enough to the host that she'd constantly be flagged down by people at the door - and there's always a line waiting at the door.

Silvermans was an icon in Lonsdale. It had only been there for five years, but in that time had earnt a well deserved reputation of being the funnest restaurant in town.

We were miles away from being called 'fine dining' yet the food was all made from scratch - even the sauces - and we were known for our big portions and delicious cuisine. We weren't branded with a particular style of food, and grabbed meals from all sorts of culinary backgrounds to showcase a blended amalgamation vaguely branded as 'modern', unless the chefs accidentally plated it up a bit sloppily, in which case it was deemed 'rustic'.

According to our licence, you didn't have to eat to be able to drink there, so we were as much a bar with a restaurant in it, as we were a restaurant with a bar. There were always people there to party, as well as those who went just to eat.

The decor was inviting enough to entice you in, yet quirky enough to get you to stay. Some people took photos of odd idols and eclectic pictures, while others scrawled words of wisdom on the backs of the toilet doors.

It was the dive bar live music venue, but with outstanding food. A restaurant with personality and entertainment. The place where you wanted to go to be fed, go to party, or go to get laid.

The doors opened.

Ding! The pass bell! I grabbed the docket and checked the order.

"Mushroom sauce please, Chef!"

"Charge them extra!" he scowled.

"It's on the docket! *Already charged!*" I retorted bossily.

Chef snatched the docket and read it. He dumped sauce in a ramekin.

"Thanks!" I called sweetly.

He glared at me, then let out a sly smile.

Sleeping with him every so often to get my way was a fantastic idea. I had no idea if he knew I was just using him to both get myself off, and get preferential treatment at work. Maybe he wanted me to be his girlfriend, or maybe he just loved a bit of casual sex too. Either way I wouldn't be surprised, nor would I have minded.

None of the other cooks were looking, and in a fleeting moment there was a millisecond of eye contact, and we silently agreed to meet in the dry-store after close.

Two plates in the left hand and one in the right to Table 54. "Follow me to 54?" I asked Nicki, who barged into the kitchen as I was leaving.

Nicki grabbed three more plates and followed me out.

I had a mean game I'd play whilst carrying plates of food out: make eye contact promises with every table on the way, and watch them smile expectantly… then smirk at their crestfallen faces when they realised the food was not for them.

As we arrived at the table, the customers looked up expectantly, just like all the others on the way.

"Ok, so here we have the penne marinara, the stuffed chicken and the medium rare eye fillet," I announced as I dropped the plates in front of the allocated seats.

"I didn't order this," a young woman whined.

"That's the stuffed chicken… I have it here that that's what was ordered…" I checked the crumpled docket in my hand. "I'm sure that's right, but what did you say you ordered?"

Naturally I questioned myself and had to recite the seat numbers I already knew off by heart to reinforce that I was right. Ass to the pass and clockwise from the left.

"I ordered the eye fillet and my sister ordered the chicken," she whined.

"Ah, you must have swapped seats. No problem," I switched the plates.

Whiney woman's sister had a turn next. "You're still wrong! I didn't order this. I ordered the prosciutto wrapped chicken with asparagus."

I looked at the plate. It contained a prosciutto-wrapped chicken with asparagus. "Yes, that's correct," I smiled.

"But you *said* it was the stuffed chicken," the whiney woman's sister continued.

"Well, it's stuffed with sundried tomato and ricotta, so that's what we just call it for ease."

"But I didn't order the stuffed chicken; I ordered the prosciutto-wrapped chicken!"

"Yes, and that's what you have been served," I replied through gritted teeth and a big fake smile. "'*Sundried tomato and ricotta stuffed chicken breast, wrapped in prosciutto on a bed of cauliflower rice with seared asparagus*,'" I quoted off the menu. "It's the correct dish," I sang out, smiled and backed away before she could argue again.

Nicki dropped off her three plates. "I'll just grab that last plate from the kitchen for you," she announced to the man sitting nearest to her and began to walk away.

A hand secured itself around my wrist. My heart pounded as my body went rigid. *HANDS OFF!*

"We're still waiting on my wife's food," the man sitting nearest to me snarled.

"I know." I yanked my arm free, looking at it pointedly. "That's why she said she'd be right back with it."

"Oh! Sorry!" he chuckled, lightening up suddenly. "Didn't hear you. It's coming?" he nodded, mirroring me.

Back to the kitchen.

"Hey-" Nicki tried to say.

"ARGH! Stupid wanker! He grabbed my arm!" I moaned.

"Yeah, just a heads up... He's a bit of a douche-canoe."

Back to the section. More napkins for table 51. Ketchup for 52. Water for 53. "How are you finding everything?" for 54.

"Mmmmmmm," they murmured.

I scanned my section, noting the timelines of the tables. *Eating mains. Mains away. Got the bill. Waiting on dessert. Need to clear glasses. Waiting to order.*

"I'll grab those plates off you," I smiled to the two young girls on 55. "Were you interested in having a look at our dessert menu tonight?" I queried.

"Oh no, we're so full! We might just sit here for a few minutes if that's ok?"

"Yes, of course," I replied. I made my way to the cashiers' station to print the bill and keep it in my apron, knowing it would be requested shortly. I returned to the section to check on other tables.

Eating mains. Mains away. Got the bill. Waiting on dessert. Need to clear glasses. Waiting to order. Nothing's changed. I'll just drop the bill to those girls...

There was only one problem. The girls were gone! *Gone!* It had happened instantly.

Oh, shit.

My heart sank as I tried to give them the benefit of the doubt.

Maybe they've just gone for a smoke.

I sprinted for the smoking balcony, startling the guests out there.

Not there.

Shit! Shit! Shit!

I bolted to the bathrooms, panic mode setting in. Not there either. If they're not smoking, not at the table, not at the bar, not peeing... that pretty much means they've left!

I scrambled to the front section, desperately hoping they'd be hanging around there waiting to pay. "Have you seen those two girls? Where did they go?" I spluttered to Nicki.

"What girls?"

"The girls!" I screamed. "The two on 55!"

What did they even look like? One was wearing a green dress. Which may or may not have been a red shirt. Or yellow. I'm sure they both had long hair....

"What? They've gone... wait, *did they pay?!*" Nicki's eyes widened as she realised what happened.

My frantic scramble out the front entrance answered her question. It was too late. The girls had vanished. They left without paying!

I flew back to the restaurant, determined to find the girls. They were gone! They deliberately left without paying! I was so screwed!

As I burst inside I ran straight into Mavis the Manager, who looked furious.

Mavis's beady black eyes clashed with her yellowed peroxided hair. In her angry stance, her sweaty cropped haircut made her look like a ferocious bumblebee.

"*Where* have you been?" she demanded in her tart accent, "Your tables have been neglected! Nicki has had to pick up your slack! Now get *back* to your section!"

"No, but you don't understand! Those girls have gone!" I stammered, pointing at a vacant space.

Mavis froze, then glared at me, and deathly quietly asked, "What do you mean *gone?*" This was the calm before the storm.

My chest pounded and there was ringing in my ears as I braced myself for what was coming.

Doom... Doom... Doom...

The noise of the busy night seemed to disappear as all I could focus on was the contorted look on Mavis's face and the pounding sound that dominated my ears.

Doom... Doom... Doom...

Mavis's starchy voice thrust into a thunderous rage, "**Where** have they gone?!"

I flinched as though I had been whipped. "They must have left without paying. I don't know. They were there. I went to get their bill and they were gone. I've looked everywhere. I can't find them," I was panicking now. Excuses poured out of my mouth rapidly, but they were all worthless. I knew what was coming.

"Well then," Mavis continued. Her tone had now morphed into being condescending. She directed explicit instructions, sneering at the stupidity of me for letting a table leave without paying. "You will return to your section. You will serve the remainder of your tables and be *extra* nice for inconveniencing them with your antics. Then you will cash in all of your tables and go home," Mavis smirked.

I knew I was in trouble. Tears pricked threateningly. I felt like a school kid awaiting the cane. Despite this, I still wasn't clear on how my float was going to balance at the end of the shift. I decided that being humiliated tonight couldn't get much worse, so I asked the obvious question, "What about the missing money? How are we going to balance the float?"

Mavis crossed her arms, and paused for what seemed like an eternity. There was a curious look of wonder that I could be so dumb.

Doom... Doom... Doom...

"Oh, there won't be any money missing at the end of your shift, will there?" Mavis forced evil eye contact and a crafty smirk, pressuring me to cave into inferiority.

I swallowed the lump in my throat. "No," I sadly whispered in agreeance. I returned to my section, trying to be brave. I knew it was not the time to cry. I drew in several deep breaths and forced my well-practised Customer Smile. I still had a job to do. I went back to work, I smiled, I was lovely and forgettable and the customers were none the wiser.

I knew it was illegal for the restaurant to force me to pay the bill. They couldn't ever recover money unless they could prove the staff member had been deliberately vindictive.

However, when a squat, beady-eyed angry little woman abused me, I got scared and cracked under pressure.

Mavis and I may have been the same height, but she reigned superior hierarchy over me via her nasty personality. For her to progress in her field, Mavis had confused leadership with dominance. Instead of empowering her staff, Mavis threatened them to conform. Instead of earning respect through trust and positive reinforcement, Mavis commanded it and preferred to remind staff members they were never good enough.

I marched down to the ATM to withdraw the cash that I so foolishly misplaced, thanking my lucky stars that there was enough money in my account (not by much) to cover it. I wondered how I was going to eat for the rest of the week.

I snatched the cash and stomped back into the restaurant, stopping by the staff change rooms to compose myself on the way.

I envisioned myself calling the workplace ombudsman and seeing Mavis getting ripped out of the office, handcuffed, screaming at no one in particular as she got dragged out of the restaurant.

I knew that was only a fantasy – no one in hospitality ever actually complained to the officials. We were easily replaced and easily blacklisted. I didn't need to be bad mouthed to the rest of the city. I didn't need to answer the dreaded question of why I left my previous position after only being there a few months. I needed to buy groceries next week. I needed to pay rent. I needed to stay at least six months to keep my resume looking good. I needed to pay for that table who left me so I could keep the income I needed from this job. I only had a year left and knew it might be difficult to get another job in hospitality right away. I couldn't go two weeks in between jobs without pay. I needed a reliable stream of money and knew I'd be punished if I didn't comply.

I'd only been here a while, but I still had university to finish. One year left, then that's it. No more hospo.

So I forked it out to keep the peace, and, more importantly, keep myself rostered next week. I knew that had I not paid, I could kiss my shifts goodbye. People had been fired for a lot less.

What those girls thought they were doing exactly, I didn't know. Did they deliberately sneak out? I thought so. Did they simply forget to pay? Doubtful, but I hoped so. Perhaps they thought it was a victimless crime? It certainly wasn't. I was the one getting hurt.

Despite their intentions, I could only imagine that the girls thought it was a write-off. I'll bet they never realised that I was forced to go to the ATM; that I paid for their meal out of my own pocket, and that was actually *more* than what I earned the whole shift.

The girls had participated in a carefully orchestrated heist known as the Dine and Dash. Who was responsible for their bill then? It wasn't a write-off. The manager didn't spread the items 'accidentally' to all the other tables hoping they wouldn't notice. It wasn't charged to a 'recovery account'. It was all on me. I was responsible for their bill. I paid the bill. I couldn't afford it, but I paid for their disgusting theft.

I felt like I had been fined, but without doing anything wrong. I actually paid to go to work. I would have been better off not working in the first place. In fact, I could have stayed at home and drank a fine scotch for that price.

I knew, as a server, I was forgettable. Unless there had been a life-changing incident, most people could not recall the names or faces of anyone who had served them once in the last year. It was part of the job – to be friendly but not familiar. We'd always remember the people who hurt us, but the odds were they'd never remember us.

I knew those two girls would not remember me, and would probably re-enact their performance once again in the future. They didn't care – why would they? It was a victimless crime for them!

I, however, would never forget them, and how they quietly etched away a small part of my soul.

I vowed to never let it happen to her again. If only I could really promise myself that – I knew deep down that working as many hours as I did, it would one day. I would fight to stop it.

| 7 |

The Guessing Game

I scooted over to the bar and picked up a black tray bearing a glass of chardonnay and a lager. *Wine for the lady and beer for the man,* I thought. I was right.

Today, I was rostered on the floor by myself, with only Mavis the Manager helping in the bar, making drinks in between doing the roster on her laptop. 'Skeleton staff' were used during quiet periods, typically weekday lunches when we projected limited sales. On this day, I was everyone, except for the chef of course. I would greet guests waiting by the entrance, guide them to a table, take their orders, run their meals and drinks, and process their bills. I was a host, a bar runner, a busser and a server (I've always hated the term 'waitress') in one.

It was slightly busier than expected – but not enough to warrant an extra staff member. Given the cost of labour, I would have loved that extra set of hands to run food and clear tables, but that extra person was too expensive. I was on my own.

I whizzed past a messy table for the umpteenth time, promising myself to clear it soon. The plates were attracting flies already. Other tasks needed prioritising first. The sticky, insect swarmed crockery would have to wait.

What needed doing next? I fished out my notebook and assessed my duties.

Table 40 has ordered. Table 51 has just been sat. Oh! That's right. Table 24 ordered drinks.

I scooted over to the bar, collecting the next tray of drinks: a juice and a red wine for Table 24. I glanced over at 24 and spied a bored-looking boy opposite a woman engrossed in her phone. I decided it would be fun to place the incorrect drinks in front of them to, well, break the ice. Kids always found this funny.

I approached the table, balancing a thick black tray on my left palm. I've always been amused by movies that depict servers carrying trays on their fingers – it's a simple matter of science. Using the palm of one's hand creates a greater surface area, meaning the pressure isn't as intense and the tray seems lighter. That, and using the palm gives greater control of balance.

Glancing at the docket to confirm it was in fact Table 24 I needed to deliver to, I looked and saw the boy fidgeting with the cutlery, and his mother still peering intently at her phone. Affirmed, I confidently strolled toward them, smiling at my plan.

I placed the plastic tumbler of orange juice in front of the mother, who grunted without taking her eyes off her phone.

The boy, however, was astonished! His eyes leapt up, widening as he questioned me – *Why has Mommy been given my drink?*

I was all over it, and proceeded to act innocent whilst exaggeratedly querying the child, "So this orange juice belongs to Mommy, is that right?"

A toothy grin accompanied a shake of the head.

"The juice is for Mommy, right?" I quizzically asked the boy. "It's *not*? But it says right here that this table ordered an orange juice and a red wine. *Who* ordered the wine? Did *you* order the wine?"

Obviously, this child thought I was hilarious.

I genuinely smiled adoringly. "Whose juice is this? Whose wine is this?" I cooed.

The young boy leaned over in fits of giggles and replied, "No! The juice is mine! Not hers! She has the other drink," he proudly informed me.

"The shiraz is mine!" snapped the mother, clearly irritated I was interrupting her relationship with her phone.

The boy jolted at his mother's reaction, bracing himself, but she returned to her gripping news feed, occasionally letting out a soft snicker.

I stole a quick smile from the boy.

This one was easy! Of course, the child ordered the juice and the parent ordered the wine! Where was this woman's sense of humour? I only wanted to get a laugh out of her. I bet Mama Shiraz was a right personality online.

"You ready to order?" I asked her lightly.

"I want the Caesar salad with no anchovies and extra dressing and he'll have the American ribs," the woman deadpanned without looking up from her phone.

"Sorry, I just want to clarify, there are anchovies in the Caesar dressing, is that ok?"

"No anchovies," the woman repeated.

"Ah... how about I put the dressing on the side then for you?" I suggested.

"Fine."

"Also..." I timidly continued.

A set of eyes flashed up, daring me to stay longer.

"I just wanted to confirm... the American ribs... that's a full rack... I'm wondering if it's too much food... did you see the kid's menu on the back?"

The woman took a deep breath, and painfully articulated, "Caesar salad, no anchovies and an American ribs."

Probably my queue to leave anyway if the mother didn't want me there. Service staff must never be too familiar. Caesar no anchovies and dressing on the side, and the full rack of ribs is what she'd get. I didn't want to hear shit about there being too many leftovers.

The little boy smiled a goodbye, pleased with my attention.

I scanned the dining room, wondering who the customers were when they weren't at Silvermans. Did they have jobs? What did they do that they could be here on a Monday? Then there was the biggest mystery of them all: What were their names? Even the regulars I knew by drink and small talk, but I never knew their names, and it was too far into our relationship to ask.

Every table I served, I played a game with myself, predicting who would order what, and the 'type' of guest they would be. Men rarely ordered sparkling wine for themselves. A large group of young guys were always the most fun to serve. Parents would either be extremely helpful and apologetic, or they'd let their kids run around like wild banshees and leave questionable wet patches and sticky rubbish.

I looked over at the little boy with the juice and his mother. They were eating. Mavis the Manager must have run their food to the table. The boy had just about cleaned up the entire rack of ribs! Whoa, you certainly can't judge an appetite based on a person's size!

Next table was ready to order. "Hi, I'm Alexandra. I'll be looking after you today. Have you been to Silvermans before?"

Two girls stared at me without answering.

I cheerfully continued my mandatory introduction, hating every second of my script, but beaming sunshine at the guests *('they're not our customers, they're our guests!')*, for it'd be just my luck that these teens would be secret shoppers, judging my every move.

"Ok," I continued, as forced to by my managers.

The girls sat with their eyes glazed over, hating this as just much as I was hating life right now.

"So we have a house speciality, a twenty-four-hour slow-cooked..." I brightly recited.

"Ok, that's enough, we're ready to order," one of them interjected.

Thank goodness!

Relieved as much as the girls were that I could stop that painfully uncomfortable spiel, I returned to my normal personality – which was actually a million times more genuine than that shit I was forced to recite.

"Can I get the..." the first girl scanned her menu one more time.

Chicken! I predicted chicken. She was going to order something chicken-y! Get the chicken! Get the chicken so I know I'm right!

"Ahhhhhm... The chicken parma, please," she finished.

YES!

"Sure can; and you, what would you like?" I asked her friend.

The second girl was scrunching up her nose, shaking her head at the entrée page. She was looking at the prices. No shopping bags like her friend. Drinking tap water, not cola. She'll order something cheap, like a side. Chips? Yeah, she'll get chips.

"Just a bowl of chips."

"Would you like gravy or tomato sauce with that?" I asked her.

"Does it cost extra?"

Of course she asked if it cost extra.

"No, it's included."

"Can I get both then?" she requested excitedly.

"Ah- sure."

Boom! Both orders right!

I was on a roll! I did a little victory 'whoop' then quickly came to my senses as I remembered I was still in public. If only there were some sort of token or recognition for my efforts. It wasn't a real game, so the confidence in my role serving would have to be enough accolade for now.

| 8 |

WhiteTeaTwoMilkChangetheCup

For a while, Silvermans had a policy that customers could get a free refill of tea or filter coffee, provided they used the same polystyrene cup (because what restaurant wants to pay for crockery when we rarely served tea or coffee to being with?).

Not many people took us up on the offer, firstly, because it was never advertised; we just did it because it was a thing, and secondly, because the coffee was so bad, very few people wanted a second cup.

I always had a gripe with charging for tea anyway. Tea was only two dollars and was presented as boiling water in a cup, a teabag, two packets of long-life milk and a stirrer.

If anyone just wanted some boiling water, we would give it out. Free. Do you want a stirrer? Free. Just a teabag? It's free. Some extra milk packets - they're free too.

So I asked my manager, Mavis, what constituted as a tea and therefore warranted a two-dollar charge if one could collect all the individual components free of charge. She told me it was the cup.

Just to be a bit cheeky, I told her that next time a customer came up and asked for an extra cup, I would charge them two dollars.

She wasn't impressed.

I must have been a decent food slave though - my roster never got cut even though I was a bit of a pain in the butt.

Anyway, my mother always warned me to be weary of little old men wearing hats, so naturally, I pasted on a smile and cringed as I saw one heading my way. "Hi, how are you today!" I beamed.

He ignored my greeting, gave me a cup, and mumbled, "Whiteteatwomilkchangethecup."

Heh? I sunnily asked him to repeat his order.

"White tea two milk change the cup."

I made him a tea, with two packet milks in a new cup. This was expressly forbidden - we were supposed to refill the same cup. Cups cost money you know. Day after day, I would serve the same little old man with a hat.

"Whiteteatwomilkchangethecup."

I'd make it and dump it in front of him. "You're welcome," I'd huff as he started drinking without acknowledgement.

He was a bit rude. Manners don't cost a thing but they certainly demonstrate character. There was never a hello, a goodbye or a thank you. Just whiteteatwomilkchangethecup.

I served him every morning, until one day I realised that I'd never actually seen him order his first tea for two dollars. Did he just happen to miss me every time? Then it dawned on me - this guy was taking home the cup and washing it! What a sneaky trick! He must have had free tea for years. Also, I was a bit of an idiot for missing this all this time. So the next day, I went on a power trip. That'd show him!

"Whiteteatwomilkchangethecup."

"Good morning, how are you today?" I rudely sneered with a fake smile.

"Whiteteatwomilkchangethecup."

"Just white tea?" I asked, like the brat I was. "That'll be two dollars."

"Whiteteatwomilkchangethecup."

"Look, mate," (yeah, I called him 'mate'), "You can't just bring back a washed cup from home! It's a free *refill*, not just a free drink!"

Looking back, I don't know why I was so frustrated by him. It might have been that I found out I got played. It might have been that he only said 'whiteteatwomilkchangethecup' to me. It might have been the fact that he was a little old man in a hat, and that just didn't sit right with me. It was only two dollars, but that was two dollars he never paid, and he needed to be stopped! I was obsessing over this enormous ordeal, so I decided to tell my manager. I stormed into the office, all red and flustered and passionately rattled off my story of theft and deception.

Do you think Mavis was as wildly infuriated as me?

No, no she wasn't. Instead, she taught me a lesson. As much of a mole she was on the floor, she was alright when it was just us. You might call her 'two-faced' but in the hospo world, I'd call that behaviour normal.

"He's an old man. He's going to die soon," Mavis shrugged.

"He... he's dying?" I was shocked. I felt awful.

"I dunno," she shrugged again. Zero cares for this guy.

I stopped feeling awful.

"Old people are closer to dying. Just give him the free tea, who cares?" Mavis didn't care. Therefore I shouldn't care. That was it. Fair enough.

Mavis's zen must have infiltrated my brain because I calmed down and thought about it. What was the harm in an old man getting a free tea? He was old, he'd done his time. I needed to respect my elders.

The next day when I saw the little old man and his hat in the line, I got his tea ready. "White tea, two milk, new cup," I said to him.

He took a sip, nodded at me, and said, "Thank you," then he left.

| 9 |

It's My Birthday!

"It's my birthday!" gushed Miss Thirty-Something. She really didn't need to mention it, for the gift bags and tiara had already indicated this to all the staff. "Do I get anything special for that?" she asked hopefully.

"Yes," I smiled warmly, "You get very sincere wishes of 'happy birthday'. Happy birthday!" I sang out, curtseying.

Miss Thirty-Something's face fell. "Oh, is that all?"

There was a house policy to offer free sundaes for birthdays. I hated it.

"And I'll grab you a sundae," I added grudgingly under my breath. Running a business should not involve giving away free food. Food was stock. Free sundaes were wasted stock.

As I started to walk away, a guy grabbed my wrist.

"Hey," he said under his breath, "It's my girlfriend's birthday."

"I realised," I said, attempting to twist my arm out of his hold. I could feel his fingers imprinted on my skin, tingling icely. "She just told me too."

"We'd really like it if you could all sing happy birthday to her," the guy said, making frightfully uncomfortable eye contact.

Let go. Let go! I wrestled my arm free from the boyfriend, giving it a good yank to make a point.

"Oh, sorry," the guy said, seemingly unaware that he had grabbed me.

I was very aware. "I'll bring out her sundae, but it's up to your group to sing to her, sorry."

This was not the right response. He shifted his weight uncomfortably. "Hey, I know the owner, you know?"

"So do I," I replied. "I'll tell him you say hi if you like?"

He stared at me, realising I wasn't succumbing so easily. Threats wouldn't work on this waitress. "Look. We come here all the time. I'd really appreciate it if you could sing for her. It would mean the world. Really."

I scanned his face. If he came here 'all the time', how come I didn't recognise him? He seemed genuine though. I begrudgingly agreed.

Ding! The kitchen bell rang, reminding me to collect my food.

Ding! The pass bell rang again, and a tall chocolate sundae, dripping with hot fudge sauce, dusted with freshly shaved milk chocolate flakes and decorated with a shiny maraschino cherry, appeared.

"I need singers!" I called out. I looked around and all the staff were suddenly busily cleaning, unaware I'd called them.

The fastest way to make front of house staff disappear is to ask them to sing. Customers love it, servers hate it. I looked around frantically, hoping to snatch an enthusiastic newbie who'd support me. Even they had disappeared. *Dammit.*

I stuck a sparkler in the sundae and lit it. The ice cream was already beginning to drip. I scanned the floor, searching for someone – anyone – to come to sing with me.

The staff were all too busy.

I had no choice but to go out now.

The group smiled in anticipation as I approached them, nervously smiling back.

"Haaaaaaaaaa..." I boomed, hoping they'd join in.

They didn't.

"Haaaaaaaappy birthday to you!" I sang, solo, to a group of strangers. Other guests watched on. The sparkler sizzled and flared.

"Happy birthday deeeeeeeear..."

WHAT IS HER NAME?

I scanned the group desperately looking for a hint. No one helped me out, so I belted out, "Happy birthday, dear... Arrrrrrblaaah!"

They fell over with laughter and began to clap, joining in the singing for the final line, "*Maddie!* Happy birthday to you!"

"Hip, hip!" I called to the entire floor.

Several tables stood up and clapped, calling, "Hooray!"

Well, I'd already made a fool of myself. May as well do it right. "I can't hear you!" I called. "Hip, HIP!"

"HOORAY!" the whole restaurant called and applauded.

I dumped the dripping dessert in front of the birthday girl and walked away, unnoticed, without so much as a thank you. Maddie's friends fawned over her and took selfies.

"Hey!" a youngster zapped right in my face. Bing! Customers seem to pop up out of nowhere.

"Ah- can I help you?" I asked.

"Yeah, you wouldn't believe it, but it's *my* girlfriend's birthday too!"

"Oh, no kidding. Happy birthday," I wished vaguely, trying to run away.

"Any chance you could sing for her too? She'd *love* it!"

"Ahhhh..." I looked around, it was quiet enough now, and he seemed so excited. "Sure," I agreed. "Who's looking after you tonight?"

"The blonde chick... You know, with the blonde hair..." he tousled his own hair, describing almost all of the staff.

"Was it... ah... Kristen?"

"She the girl? With the blonde hair?" he asked again, arms framing his head. Not Kristen then.

"You mean Nicki?" I asked.

"Yeah! Yeah, that's it! Blonde Nicki!"

"I'll make sure Nicki sings to you," I promised. If I went down, Nicki was going down with me too.

| 10 |

Fully Booked

The group approached the restaurant early in the evening; so early that we were just opening.

I flicked on the lights, then dimmed them to create an inviting atmosphere. The upbeat background music filtered down to the tables, each set to the number of seats requested in the bookings diary. I scanned the page, reviewing the bookings had been allocated correctly, for the fifth time. I looked up and smiled at the group approaching me, armed with balloons and a box presumably containing a cake.

"Good evening," I beamed.

The man of the family strode forward and requested a table for ten, "Now, please."

"Of course," I replied, "what name was your reservation under?" I asked sweetly, knowing full well, that this group had not – foolishly – booked.

"Well we haven't reserved, but that won't be a problem will it?" the man of the family asked me, looking at the empty tables in the restaurant hopefully.

"Oh," I said, shaking her head, "I'm sorry, we're fully booked tonight."

"But, Dan, you said it would be ok," the mother started, pleadingly looking up at her husband. This can't be happening. They'd all be planning Grammie's 80th birthday for weeks. Everyone had arranged to eat here. Everyone, except for the reservation maker, Dan.

"Really? We need a booking?" asked Dan in disbelief.

"It's recommended," I nodded, "that way you're guaranteed a seat."

"So it's *recommended*, not necessary?" questioned Dan. He was determined to get a table.

"If you choose not to book, you run a chance of either waiting for the first available table or missing out, I'm sorry," I explained.

Dan looked around the empty restaurant. Clearly I was being ridiculous – there were tables everywhere!

"Can we sit on one of these tables here?" Dan asked, gesturing at some vacant spots.

"I'm sorry," I stated, "those are reserved too."

"It's ok," Dan replied, "We won't be long. What about this table? We can fit here," he walked toward a table set with ten places.

"I'm sorry," I said again, trying to suppress my frustration, "it's reserved too." I drew another breath and counted to ten silently. "Look, I'm not lying to you. I would love to have you dine here this evening. It's a special occasion, and I want you to have a great time, but I'm really sorry," I paused to emphasise the last point, "we're booked out."

"But they're not here now."

"Yes, but they will all be here within the hour. There's no way you could eat and leave by then. I can't even shuffle people around for you because we're so fully booked," I replied, getting fed up by this point. I had been very clear – the restaurant was fully booked for the evening.

"What about that waitlist?" Dan asked, suspiciously. He was sure that I was being rude deliberately. He had arranged for his family to come out – and they would come out!

"Look, as I explained, we are fully booked this evening," I told them. "This means we can't use a waitlist, as I don't have any tables for you to wait for. Next time, I'd suggest you reserve a table, that way you're guaranteed a place."

"There won't be a next time! Not with that attitude, lady! We are *never* coming back here!" he threatened.

I stared at him silently, daring him to utter another word.

Dan and his family finally left, sighing and discussing alternative options amongst each other.

Just as they were leaving, the phone rang. I answered politely and waited for the caller to speak.

"Hello? Just wondering if I can get a table tonight for about half an hour's time?"

I apologised, "Sorry, we're fully booked."

| 11 |

Petit Four: Wild Mushroom Risotto

"Excuse me, does the 'Wild Mushroom Risotto' come with mushrooms in it?" a young woman asked.

I stopped in my tracks to process the query. I had to confirm that this idiot had actually just asked that.

"Excuse me, does the 'Wild Mushroom Risotto' come with mushrooms in it?" the young woman asked again, getting impatient.

I scanned the woman's face and body language, desperately trying to determine her motive. Was she actually being serious? Was this a bad joke? Or worse - a trap?

The young woman sat expressionless, waiting to be answered. Her friend mirrored me, also unsure of whether this seemingly obvious question was serious.

"Well? Does it have mushrooms?" she demanded, clearly upset that her valid question was not being taken seriously.

Still unsure of how to answer without making the idiot look even more stupid, I decided to err on the side of clarity, and simply answered, "Yes."

"Oh. Well, I won't have that then."

| 12 |

Becoming Hospo-For-Life

I never thought that working in hospitality could be a career. I never wanted to work in food and beverage and knew that I'd be out as soon as I finished studying. As soon as I graduated, I was shocked to discover that I just couldn't land a job - a real job - so in the meantime, I kept working in bars and restaurants, only now I'd gone from casual to full time.

My phone beeped and a short notification message popped up: *Jonathan Stevens is now a Senior Account Manager with BJD Lonsdale.*

I wondered how he managed that - he was always a bit thick wasn't he?

I closed the hospitality blog I was reading, suddenly engrossed in my professional newsfeed. I was compelled to know what my graduating year classmates were doing, and if it was better than my lowly restaurant job. I had always assumed, given how dumb Jonathan Stevens was, that he'd end up stocking shelves at Clarkson.

He was now a 'senior account manager'. Whatever that was.

I scrolled through my classmates, growing more so disheartened with where my life was going. My classmates were labelled big impressive-sounding titles: Senior Account Manager. Consultant. Executive.

I served food at Silverman's. Awesome.

I let out a deep sigh as I pondered what went wrong. Nothing did. I did everything right. I finished high school then studied at university, just like one was supposed to. When it came to looking for jobs, I wasn't sure how to apply exactly, and when I did, I was greeted with the same dreaded response: "We're actually looking for someone with experience."

It had now been five years of "one year left" – forever trying to get out of hospitality, but always, always being there. Wasn't it time to get a real job? When did life begin after waiting tables?

What do these people do? I envied their portraits in suits until I read deeper and one role popped out at me.

Katrina Evans, a former classmate at Lonsdale Grammar, was a 'Human Fulfilment and Relationship Expert'.

What on earth is a Human Fulfilment and Relationship Expert? I assumed it was some sort of psychiatry professional. I clicked on Katrina Evans' profile to learn more.

Katrina Evan's photo revealed a whimsical bare-foot dreamer, gazing into sunny nothingness, trailing a purple pashmina in her shadow. I was pleased to notice Katrina hadn't aged gracefully, and already possessed parched cracks along her leathery casing. Served her right for spending too much time in the sun.

I read her career summary. Katrina appeared to be a wanderer, moving between fillers and never remaining long in the one role. It appeared she procured money from others by advising them on how to be successful. She was a life coach. People paid this twenty-something year old to offer life and career advice. She may have been a decent one (I never wanted to find out, but living in Somerville was not cheap), but it seemed, with her flighty demeanour, she didn't believe in her own product.

Katrina Evans had designed a professional profile to present a reliable, dedicated free-spirited expert. In fact, she didn't have any qualifications and conjured this career from nothing. According to her social profile, she spent most of her time smoking bongs and banging on bongo drums.

I read the titles of my classmates carefully and guessed their actual jobs. Their titles were all bullshit euphemisms to make themselves sound more successful than they actually were.

There were content creators (writers), waste acquisition managers (garbage collectors) and frontline customer support facilitators (call centre operators). I had to wonder what an 'influencer' did and why their opinion mattered more than others did.

One classmate claimed he was a decorative technician. A closer look at his profile revealed he installed window blinds for a living. The whole network was a modern-day example of keeping up with the Joneses.

Maybe their careers were as terrible as mine was after all. Except for, you know, those who worked for their folks, slept their way to the top, or won the career lottery by being in the right place at the right time.

I tried to think of how I could label my job to make it sound better than 'beer wench', 'shit-kicker' or (my most loathed term) 'waitress'.

Beverage Consultant? Liquor and Culinary Advisor? I decided to type simply 'Hospitality Professional' and vowed to get a better job. One with an actual, real title, in an office, where I could wear a suit, have business cards and be proud of what I did. One where I could show them all, by being a raging success. What else could I possibly do with a useless science degree and no experience?

I wondered what I enjoyed doing... What was I good at? Well, there was food, but as if working in hospitality could ever be considered a 'real' job. Could it? If one quietly enjoys working in a restaurant, could one do that, like an actual job? Be a hospitality superstar?

I had always loved food, but I never understood that a career could be created out of love. Until I saw how successful my classmates were in their mundane jobs, I had never realised *how* much I loved my industry.

It was as if I was already doing well, but needed permission and approval (from who exactly?) to be a success.

I never realised that not everyone could do my job, and even less could do it well. Most people who work in various aspects of hospitality (as a career) are smarter; more dedicated and possess more versatile skills than the general public they serve. Anyone in management and will tell you they see their staff more than their families.

I thought about celebrity chefs and the judges on cooking shows. They were hospitality superstars – and I'll bet no one gave them shit about looking for a 'real' job.

Could I really do that? Could I be more than just a waitress? Could I... could I run my own place – run my own empire? Really? Was that a thing? Was that a real job?

I pondered about this plan. It was actually feasible.

Well, that's it. If no one wanted to hire me for my lack of experience in my useless degree, I'd just have to make it in hospitality. It would be tough and take dedication, but it was doable. At my ten year reunion, I wouldn't be the one they pitied, I'd be the one they'd envy. The only thing I needed to break through now was that looming glass ceiling.

| 13 |

Cashier Shift

Saturdays were the busiest nights at Silverman's. They were usually booked out the day before, but that didn't stop the phone ringing all day with the hopeful, the ignorant or the downright pushy seeking a seat at one of Lonsdale's most popular night-spots.

The roster was fully staffed with servers, floories, runners and hosts signalling each other, jogging and smiling, dodging the waves of hands vying for their attention. In the kitchen, at least one chef manned each section, with the hot larder, the fryer and the grill stations being controlled to the central exposition chef, who then handed completed orders to the pass. Timers blared, chefs swore and the fryers crackled as a new batch of frozen chips were dumped in them.

The two dishies sprayed searing water against the crockery, slammed the plates into the racks and shoved them into the washer. As soon as they were finished, the scorching hot plates appeared back on the shelves, and food appeared on them once again.

Near the pass, two young girls hurriedly polished cutlery with cloths. As soon as the forks were ready, they disappeared again to reset the tables.

The managers were split up to do the toughest roles: managing the floor, running the pass, or hosting the front desk. All required resilience, time management and immense pressure. Tasks screamed for attention, and time zoomed past as the managers juggled priorities. Dropping the ball was not an option, for if one area failed, the others failed too.

That night, I was on the front desk, meeting, seating and greeting guests, allocating reservations, prioritising walk-ins, settling bills and answering that eternally ringing phone.

It was ten o'clock and we were on the final stretch. Soon the restaurant part would be closed, and the bar part would be full with party-goers.

Gradually less people arrived to dine, and vacant tables appeared. I hid under the desk and drew a long drink of my water bottle. It was the first time I'd stopped all night.

Time to reassess where we were.

I was double-checking the balance in the till, when suddenly I felt as if I were being watched. The back of my neck tingled and I shuddered slightly. My eyes shot up, searching for the culprit.

A man from the table nearest to me stared.

I looked around – there was no one waiting to pay right now. It was getting late, and unlikely more food guests would arrive. It was an opportune time to leave my station – quickly. I shot out from behind the desk and smiled purposefully at the man, inviting him to speak.

He said nothing, then re-engaged in his conversation.

Well, that's great. He didn't need me; he was just staring.

I cleared some remaining glasses from his table, and the man fixated on me again.

"Can I get you a tea, coffee or anything else?" I asked the group, hoping the man would indicate why he was staring.

Another thought popped into my head. Did I have broccoli in my teeth? I panicked. I rubbed my tongue around my mouth. I hadn't actually eaten anything since that morning, let alone broccoli. I reminded myself. Why broccoli? If one were to have food stuck, it was almost always broccoli for some reason.

"Yes," the man said.

I was confused. What did I ask again? Maybe he misheard me.

"Would anyone like a tea or coffee or anything else?" I asked the group in general, slightly louder.

"Yes, thanks," a woman replied.

What?

I turned to her, and carefully asked, "Would you like a tea? Or would you like a coffee? Or would you like anything else?" with big pauses between each option.

"Thanks, that would be great," the woman answered vacantly.

What? I loathed being ignored.

This woman was doing that thing where they didn't listen, they just responded.

I still had to be the face of customer service, so I swallowed my feelings and tried again. "Ahhh... So... Just the bill then?" I delicately suggested, nodding appropriately.

The woman blinked and slightly shook her head, coming to her senses. "Oh!" she patted my arm, "Yes! The bill, I think. Thank you."

"Sure, just wait here and I'll be right back." I jogged back to the desk, shaking my head, muttering profanities under my breath. I considered releasing the fart I had been suppressing all shift, but decided against it. It was a gamble at this stage, whether it would be too noisy, or silent but deadly. Thankfully I held tight, for when I printed the bill, I looked up, sensing someone was watching me again.

It was the man from the table. He'd followed me back to the desk and was silently watching my every move.

Did he see me bitching about them in my head? What part of 'Wait here, I'll be right back' didn't he get?

"Hi," I said sheepishly.

"We'll need to split the bill."

Hello to you too!

"Sorry, we don't actually-" I started.

"Of course you do. So *this* card," he held up a red card, "needs to pay for… the barramundi, one of the steaks, that pasta…" he was reading the bill, searching for items.

"Which steak? There are four different ones on there," I questioned.

"The ahhh… the rib fillet."

"The medium one? 400 grams?"

"Yes? Look, can you do this faster, we're in a bit of a rush."

"Sorry, as I explained, we don't normally split bills. I'm happy to print off several itemised bills which you can take to sort it out later. There's an ATM over there," I pointed just outside the door, "which card would you like me to charge it to?" I asked, insisting the bill be paid in one amount. I didn't want the till to run short, and I knew – I *knew* - there'd be a mistake somewhere. There always was. Our till system just didn't split bills. Sure, if a table said they'd pay half and half, it was a no brainer. I, who is dreadful at basic maths, was not about to calculate eight different mains, plus entrees, plus drinks, under pressure. I certainly was not going to pay for leftover mistakes.

"I'm *not* paying for everyone," the man said firmly.

I sighed. What part of 'we don't split bills' wasn't clear? Looked like I was going to split the bill – I knew this would end in trouble!

"Ok, so the barra, the 400 rib, the tortellini…" I checked off. "Any entrees, sides, drinks or desserts?"

"Ribs? No, I didn't get any ribs!" the man snapped defensively. How dare I add items to the bill!

"Sorry," I took a breath, "I meant to say the rib *fillet*."

"So why did you say 'ribs' then?" he accused. "I've seen this on the news – you people sneakily add items to get better sales!"

"I must have misunderstood," I said coolly.

"Well you should know what you sell here," he snorted, amazed at my stupidity. Some waitresses would never amount to anything. "There better not be any ribs on that bill," he muttered.

"Ok, so just those three mains then – the barramundi, the 400 gram rib *fillet* and the tortellini on that card then? No other drinks, desserts, sides or breads?" I asked emotionlessly.

"That's it," he held the card up, just out of my reach, taunting me to take it.

I snatched the card and stuck it in the machine.

"Wouldn't hurt to smile, love."

I grimaced.

"Maybe one day when you get a real job, you could go out for dinner with your friends," he commented as it processed.

I ignored him, staring straight ahead, thinking about my new plan to become the best hospitality worker there was. Start at the bottom and work my way upward.

This man was a rock bottom douche-canoe.

I couldn't say anything; he was a paying customer, and I was serving him. It was always an excuse for people to be rude. They were being served so therefore they had the right to be rude. People were entitled to be as demanding as they liked, because The Customer is Always Right.

Right now, the man was getting on my nerves. I told him we didn't split bills and he insisted that they did. Arguing wouldn't end well. As far as society was concerned, he was the customer, so he had the right to be right at all times. So instead of arguing, I stared in silence, straight ahead into nothingness, wishing this ordeal would stop.

I processed the six other payments, much to my displeasure, and the guests from the man's table all went to leave. I quickly added up the six bills, and a pit of dread lumped in my stomach as I realised – as it so often worked out – that the bill totals did not match! There was still money left owing on the bill!

"Wait!" I called after him, "There's still money left on the bill!" I could see the remainder of his friends looking at us.

The man glanced back quickly and said deathly quietly, "Don't be silly."

I wasn't as quiet. He was rude, and there was no way I'd let him leave without paying what he owed! Mavis would make *me* pay.

I said loud enough for his group to hear, "As I asked before, there are still drinks, sides, entrees and desserts!" I was not about to get caught out owing for his food. If he refused to pay, I had witnesses. I was right.

"Well, I'm not paying for them," he stated matter of factly.

He had to. It was his bill. If the till was short money at the end of the night, it would be me to pay. I couldn't afford it! He was going to pay the money that he owed!

I stared at him.

"I'm not paying," he insisted. "If you can't do the math properly, that's not my problem."

"Look," I forced myself to at least try to be patient with this man, "I just did you a favour by letting you pay separately, even though it's against our policy. You're still obliged to pay the total bill amount." I concentrated on my breathing, begging to myself to keep calm. I had to convince him to pay!

He stood up taller and arched his shoulders back – the big man was going to put the little girl in her place. How dare she argue back to him?

I wasn't going to let that happen.

He leaned over the top of me, and quietly, but very forcefully, told me, "I will settle this tonight... but... you will *never* embarrass me in front of my friends again. We will *never* return, do you understand? Never. I've never been so disgusted – so *disappointed* with service until I spoke to you. We were having a great night, and you – your attitude just ruined it. We're never coming back here - never."

Eff you. I bent over, pulled a milk crate out from under the desk, flipped it over, and climbed on top so I towered over the man. "Thank you for your understanding," I boomed over him, so others could hear, smiling professionally.

"Calm down," he muttered aggressively.

A flame shot through my chest. He's telling me to calm down? I processed his payment, focussing every bit of will power I had on not screaming, not crying and not reacting. I couldn't get a complaint about this. Not this. He was picking on me!

I rigidly pulled out his card as the screen flashed 'approved' and shakenly thrust it forward.

He snatched his card back and stormed off, glancing back every few steps to remind me of my behaviour.

"Have a lovely night!" I called out to him waving happily but also in a crazy internal rage, as he muttered to his wife and shot me dirty looks. I was fuming. It was because I was a girl. He leant over me, questioned me, argued with me, then threatened me because I was young and female. If I had a penis, this would have never happened!

It was true. People often talked down to me because I was female and because I was young. Pretty girls couldn't be smart too. If I were a man, he wouldn't have taunted me as much. Customers could be rude to anyone, but the girls got the full brunt of it. It was like my skills were valued less – how could anyone treat a little blonde chick seriously? I reflected on the argument while observing the rest of the floor. Dozens of people were in deep conversation, oblivious to the attack at the cashier desk.

A younger man toward the back smiled and flicked his head with effortless cool, summoning me.

I took a breath and swallowed my anger. I had a job to do. Pasting on my Customer Smile, I forced the rage lump down, and ripped up the happy hostess who was hiding in the depths of my personality.

As I approached the table, I spotted the guy indiscreetly waving a bill folder. I stepped closer, and he enthusiastically flapped the black folder back and forth, eyes fixed on mine, with a broad smile indicating to the rest of the guests that he was trying to get my attention.

He nodded at me, not breaking eye contact, calling out, "Excuse me! Excuse me!" before making a sweeping gesture with his hand, resembling that of a person signing an invisible slip. I was baffled to predict what the young man could possibly be insinuating.

"Would you like me to fix that up for you?" I queried the table with perfect professionalism.

"Yes, please!" he smiled, "I'll come up with you."

I walked purposefully ahead of him.

His girlfriend joined him and they skipped together holding hands. They were so unaware of the previous guest and my mood from that. In fact, they were positively glowing with wine induced glee.

It was enough to rub off on me. I took a deep breath and reminded myself that this was a new table, and I couldn't let the grudge continue. I filed the awful man away in my mind for an after work rant, and by the time I reached the cashier desk once more, I was back in business.

"Hi," I beamed at them from behind the desk. "How are you?"

"Great, we had such a great night!" the girlfriend praised. She looked like a Sarah, so I'll call her Sarah.

Just as Sarah went to hand over her credit card, another woman leapt over her, pouncing and swiping at her hand, shoving it out of the way.

"What are you doing?" Sarah demanded.

"No, no, you always pay! It's my turn to pay this time!" her friend insisted, frantically waving her credit card in my face. Let's call Sarah's friend Amanda.

"No! I've already taken care of it – I was here first!" Sarah snorted back.

The boyfriend took a step back in surrender, raising his arms. "You two sort this out."

They two girls spent some time each leaning as far as they could over the desk, shaking their credit cards at me. They competed, with arms outstretched, forcing eye contact, daring each other to retreat. Blood rushed to each of their faces as they started sweating, forcing a glaring smile at me through gritted teeth.

"Take mine-"

"No! Mine-"

They fought, and I was forced against the wall, shaking my head at them pleading them to stop. It seemed to encourage them to move closer, their enormous bosoms knocking over the cup of pens on the desk and squashing the computer keyboard. This was enough!

I pounced forward, and swiftly snatched the card from Sarah's hand, grabbed the terminal and swiped it, turning my back on the argument, which had now switched to their native language, becoming more vocal as I punched in the numbers. Finally! I jumped a little happy-dance, relieved this was over soon, greeting Sarah again, gasping, "It's done, it's done!" to shut them up.

Amanda threw her hands in the air and stormed off.

"Sorry about that," Sarah apologised, "she always tries to pay, but, you know, they don't earn as much as us, and I like to do something nice for her," she sighed.

I smiled, "Of course. "Now, is that on cheque, savings or credit?" I asked.

"Better put that on spendings!" she replied.

I laughed loudly, while agreeing how hilariously true – and original – that joke was. "Well that's all done. Enjoy the rest of your evening."

Two different tables. Two vastly different experiences. One cashier.

I had to please them all, or I risked pleasing none. I was the face of the industry, able to morph into whoever the guest wanted to see. I predicted body language and behaved how they expected me to. I could be quiet and almost non-existent, or boisterous and friendly. I was expected to be subdued, but polite. I was expected to be bubbly but not overwhelming. Friendly, but never familiar.

For the most part, I succeeded. One day, I promised myself, I wouldn't be serving. I wouldn't be at their beck and call. I wouldn't smile whilst being yelled at, and I wouldn't be so diplomatic in my opinion. One day, I'd just be me. A superstar venue owner who would be fabulous in customer service, but wouldn't let them walk all over me. Start at the bottom, work upward. Tonight, I moved up one small step. Plenty more to the top. Until that day came, I was stuck here.

| 14 |

If You Like Piña Coladas

"Can I have... oh! Can I have a piña colada please?" the woman excitedly asked.

"Sure!" I exclaimed. Any chance for a cocktail enthusiast to show off some skills. A bit of rum, a bit of coconut, a bit of pineapple and there it was: a deliciously refreshing piña colada! Who doesn't love a good chilled cocktail on a steamy summer's night?

"There you go," I dramatically draped a square napkin on the high top, and presented the frosty glass to my guest. "One piña colada." I didn't need, or expect a thank you in this case; the jaw drop of awe indicated that the guests appreciated the effort that goes into creating a beautiful and delicious cocktail.

I loved the theatrics of mixology. Watching the cocktail being made is part of the bar experience. The anticipation of the glass chilling on the bar. The shots poured in. Watching the shake, the blend, the build or the muddle as flavours twist to create an unexpected masterpiece of delight. Creating the precise balance of flavours, carving and crafting a beautiful garnish and decoration, and perfectly presenting an amalgamation, often surprising and frequently pleasant is a true work of under appreciated art.

I genuinely wanted the piña colada lady to love her drink. Every cocktail takes time and skill to perfect, and a disappointed guest makes an offended bartender: We pour our soul into our craft, which is why I asked, "What's wrong?" worriedly, when Nicki stomped back over to the bar with said chilled cocktail.

"She won't drink it."

"Wh- why? I made it perfectly..." I moaned whilst flicking through my recipe rolodex to confirm my method was correct. I could remember most of the everyday cocktails, but it's that thing - when someone questioned me, I still had to double check that I was correct. I was. It was perfect.

"She said she can't have cream, so can you please make her one without cream," Nicki complained.

"Without cream?"

"I know."

"But it's coconut cream, not regular..."

"I know."

"But that's just a... really bad version of a rum and pineapple."

"I *know*."

"Um... ok... why don't you give her the menu and ask her if maybe she'd prefer another cocktail. One without cream? Or see if maybe she's happy with a rum and pineapple?" I suggested.

I watched as Nicki, the little trooper, walked back into the lion's den. I saw some frowns and serious words exchanged. Nicki shot a look toward the bar.

Time for me to go in.

"Hi, how are you tonight?" I asked innocently.

"Fine." Every time a customer said the word 'fine' things were not fine. Things were bad. Always be cautious when they say 'fine'.

"I understand we were looking for some cocktails... perhaps I can make some recommendations for you?" I politely and professionally offered.

The woman's face froze.

Apparently 'offering suggestions' was the wrong thing to do.

The woman turned to me and looked me dead-on in the eye. "No!" she huffed. "I just want a piña colada!"

Nicki went rigid. I could see her eyes twitch.

"Hey, would you be able to wait for me out the back in the manager's office?" I asked Nicki quietly.

Nicki understood the code and went out the back for a cigarette. There was no point in keeping an angry staff member on the floor – it would resonate, and that was not the image we were after.

"I understand you can't have cream, and that's one of the key ingredients in a piña colada, and if I take it out, it would be a boring old rum and pineapple. I can see it's a special occasion, so let's see if maybe there's another cocktail you might like," I suggested.

"So if I don't have the cream, you can't make it?" she questioned, despite Nicki and I both being pretty clear.

"Ahhh – no. No, sorry." I'd been trained to always try and say yes - do whatever I could to accommodate - but she was insisting we change the whole drink. I would more than happily make her a rum and pineapple, but this would affect the price and presentation - so I needed to be clear with her if that's indeed what she wanted.

"But I drink these all the time – I don't get why you guys can't do it here," she moaned.

I silently thanked every bartender in the world who'd served this chick in the past and probably just made a rum and pineapple and not told her because she was thick and it would save a further argument. Bartenders have a silent code where we back each other, and I had to believe this is how any other bartender would deal with her.

"Water then," she shooed me away.

Water. I failed that one. There went a sale. I'd lost fourteen dollars plus the cost of labour and ingredients, for water. *Water.*

Over an hour passed and Nicki was long back from her smoke and the piña colada lady was now up to considering dessert: an opportune time to make up for that sale, and bring the average cheque back up.

Nicki stomped over to me again. "Can you go talk to her? She's got the dessert menu, and I've tried, but she won't listen."

"Urgh... Sure," I agree.

I could see the woman frowning at her dessert menu. Lips pursed. Holding it at arm's length to see it better.

Time to break the ice. "I used to do that – but now my arms aren't long enough!" I chuckled. I thought it was small talk level funny. It fell flat. Nothing. Not even a smirk. Just awkward silence.

"Anyway," I quickly moved on, "Having any dessert this evening? The sticky date pudding is unbelievable," I recommended. Sticky date pudding was hands down my favourite dessert!

"No," she waved her hand down. "I think I'll try the crème brûlée."

"I'm sorry," I apologised. "Didn't you say you couldn't have any cream?" I lightly queried.

"You could just do it without the cream though?" the woman blurted. How obscene that I wouldn't get that.

"Ah, no sorry. It's a *crème* brûlée."

"So I can't have it without the cream?" she disdainfully snorted. Why was this waitress being so difficult? It's quite simple: make the dessert without the dairy.

I pondered how to explain without screaming. This woman was a special kind of stupid. Better take it slow. "Well, it's... it's mixed in. You know *crème* brûlée. Made with cream. If you didn't want the cream part, you'd just get a sheet of burnt sugar."

"This is ridiculous!"

"Did you want to try the sticky date pudding? That's the only one I can suggest without dairy," I offered, counting to ten in my head. Deep breaths. Focus on the uneven highlights in her hair, and breathe out slowly.

"What about this one?" the woman pointed to the bottom of the sheet.

Breathe in. Hold it. Breath out. "The sticky date is the only one I can do without the dairy component," I replied.

"But it's a banana split – just do it without the diary."

Breathe in. Hold it. Breath out. "Well, we *could*, but-"

"Then do it."

"I feel the need to mention that a banana split without cream or ice cream is essentially a decorated banana."

The woman rolls her eyes.

"If you're really keen on dessert, perhaps I could recommend the sticky date pudding?" I tried yet again.

"No, I'll just order the panna cotta. *Ok?*" she death-stared me.

Breathe in. Hold it. Breath out. "We can't make that without the dairy either. The sticky date is the only dessert you could order sans dairy. Would you like a sticky date?"

"*Why* can't I just get the panna cotta without the cream?" she demanded.

"It's *made* with cream? Do you understand what a panna cotta is? It's like a creamy custard-jelly! You can't have it because it's made with cream! Now, for the last time, I can assure you, the sticky date is absolutely the only one we can make without dairy! Nothing else! Just the sticky date. Would you like a sticky date?"

I took a deep breath and pasted on a huge smile.

"Are you sure it's good?" the woman sniffed.

"Yes."

"Well, I guess. Considering you won't make me anything else without the dairy."

"Excellent choice."

| 15 |

Cleaning the Bins for Mavis

I figured out that Mavis didn't like me.

I was dumb enough for a while to give her the benefit of a doubt. I tried to see the best in people, so in the beginning, the short and snappy words with eye rolling and huffs were put down to me being empathetic and nothing else.

I gave her every excuse I could think of. Maybe she was having awful marriage problems. Maybe she had anxiety and being mean was her way of coping. Maybe she was sick, or a family member just died.

It was a few months and confirmation from other staff that I finally acknowledged that no, there were no excuses for her behaviour, yes, she was singling me out, and generally, she was just a mole.

I could be quite gullible in believing there's a bit of good in everyone. Now I'd learnt that some people have no good in them, and are just awful for no reason.

One of the big hints I'd missed with Mavis hating me was the cleaning. Restaurants always had disgusting jobs that needed doing. There'd always be gum stuck under tables. There would always be spilt drinks. At least one person a week would have too much to drink and vomit.

Pee cups (yes, exactly what you think they are) were left sitting on top of urinals for a laugh. Meat juice would inadvertently spill onto the floor, and the wheelie bins gradually smelt worse and worse until the maggots arrived.

Any of these things were expected with the job. We spent half our shifts cleaning, and when it was quiet, we detail-cleaned things you'd never imagine needed cleaning, but they did. You'd be shocked how filthy ice machines got over time, even though it's only frozen water inside.

I kept thinking that everyone had their fair share of grotty work, but for some reason I always seemed to get the ickier and more frequent of the gross jobs. If there was a filthy job, it was me who was delegated the task. Not a glassy. Me.

Whether it were a front of house or back of house responsibility, if there was something that made everyone gag, I'd be the one putting my hands in it.

Mavis didn't like a lot of people who worked for her - or more to the point, very few people who worked there liked her. She was abrupt and commanding and just a bit unfair to some - including me. The staff turnover was high and the managers were in and out like a revolving door.

During one change of management at Silvermans, several jobs slipped through the cracks. They realised when the office girl left, that she actually did a lot of ordering - things that you never noticed coming in but were always there - things like stationery and wristbands.

One thing she used to - and I say *used to* - organise was the changing of the sanitary bins in the ladies room. As soon as the office girl (and I'm sure her title was actually something like Administration Manager or similarly important, but it turned out Mavis didn't like her either) left, some of the bills stopped being paid, so those everyday heroes who had the job of emptying those bins stopped coming.

Mavis had the wonderful idea that instead of paying a sanitation company to come and empty the contents, it'd be more beneficial to just pay one of her staff who was already getting paid anyway. Someone like... me!

The only thing is, she brainwaved this feral idea only after the things were overflowing. Of course the customers noticed the bins were over capacity and were grossed out by the smell, let alone the vision of someone else's used plugs and manhole covers!

I got busted standing still for ten seconds, so with a dreading warning of, "If you've got time to lean, you've got time to clean," she frogmarched me to the restrooms armed with some plastic bags and a set of gloves.

During service - in my full uniform that I still had to work in for the rest of the day - I had to empty those stinky bins. I'm not sure what was grosser - cleaning the bins out, or knowing I had to serve food later, in the same black dress.

I decided that food safety was paramount, so I crafted an apocalypse poncho out of one of the kitchen garbage bags with head and arm holes. There was no face shield, so I forced my mouth shut for fear of splashback. This proved to be problematic, as it exposed me to the odour of dead uterine lining, so bad I could taste it. I opened my mouth to gasp for air and dry heaved as I went.

I kept gagging the whole time, while disgusted customers kept saying, "Gee, you've got a glamorous job!" hilariously originally each time.

The first time, I fakely chuckled, as a hospo is expected. After that I wetly grimaced in a contorted trying-not-to-vomit sort of way.

If you can name a bodily fluid, I can safely say that I have cleaned it - and just to remind you, I have been on minimum wage my entire casual career.

I take my hat off to sanitation workers - they all need a pay rise for their humble duties. If you ever see a cleaner in a public toilet, greet them politely and thank them for their work. You'd never notice a job well done by them, but you'd certainly notice if it wasn't done. Not all super-heros wear capes.

After that day, I knew to tread carefully around Mavis. She was nothing but an arsehole. She had no reason to be, she just was.

Her bullying ways taught me some important things about how I would eventually manage a team: always earn respect and never command it, show appreciation and praise to your team where it's due, and never ask a staff member to do something that you wouldn't do.

I cleaned out those bins because they needed doing. I absolutely did not want to, but I also did not want to lose my job. I cleaned them because unlike Mavis, I chose to earn the respect of a team, rather than command it. She might have been a huge arsehole, but I was not. I was a sorta arsehole. Witty and likeable but still a bit of a turd, but in a good way.

Even today, I will always clean up vomit on the first shift of a new job, because I would never be that person who asked a staff member to do something I wouldn't do myself.

Also, if I could go back in time, I wouldn't have done it. I would have reported her and walked out. I'm a lot braver now about standing up to what's right and what's wrong in hospitality.

Back then, I was terrified.

| 16 |

Real Allergies

I get really angry when people tell me they have an allergy. Let me clarify - if you *actually* have an allergy, yes, you should absolutely alert restaurant staff. No one would get angry about that.

The people I hate are the people who *pretend* they have an allergy in order to get an alteration on their meal.

I get it. People make mistakes. I have no doubt that at some point, you've asked for no sauce, then, you've gotten sauce. It's not the first time. That waitress just doesn't get it - when you ask for no sauce, you mean NO SAUCE!

People make mistakes! So what's the one guaranteed way to ensure that you're definitely not going to get that sauce? Tell them you have an allergy. Right? WRONG. Here's why.

The hospitality industry has a lot of talent in it.

It also has a lot of dumb people.

Someone great once told me that not everyone can run a restaurant - some people can only pick up glasses. Service is the one job sector that accepts and applauds the lower end of the bell curve. Society will always need people to work in service - probably why so many of us get insulted when people treat us like idiots and tell us to get a real job. It is a real job, and it is a career for many people. Smart or not smart, as long as you have a great personality and work hard, the hospitality industry will embrace you.

So, let's continue with the sauce example. Why is it 'every time' you ask for no sauce, you get sauce? It's pretty simple. It was an accident. Whether it be the order taker forgot to write it down, or the cook added it automatically whilst making twelve other burgers - it happens. We're only human. I apologise on behalf of all hospos for causing this sauce crisis for you.

In saying that people make mistakes, one thing that we don't mess around with is allergies. No venue wants an incident on their hands that could result in injury or death to a patron.

If someone has a legitimate allergy, there is a protocol in place. Work stations need to be cleaned and sterilised. Equipment needs to be cleaned and sterilised. Produce needs to be isolated. Chefs need to wear gloves (FYI, chefs usually don't wear gloves unless really required. True story.). All this cleaning and careful procedure slows down the kitchen. Cross contamination is a real threat, so we have to be careful.

At the same time we're dealing with customers who are now complaining *their* meals are taking a while, because the kitchen is down a cook who is meticulously cleaning and sterilising and cooking you a safe meal. Instead of cooking five meals, it's one. The rest of the team is one cook down, just because you're so smug you can't scrape it off, so you lie, and blame the staff anyway.

What you're doing by saying you have an allergy when you don't is a spectacular waste of time. It's changing a procedure that we have to protect those vulnerable - and we are more than happy to accommodate - into an infuriating charade.

Now there are so many people out there saying they have allergies when they don't, just to get a specific meal alteration, that the people with real allergies have to fight to be heard.

I've had people call me days in advance to discuss menu options, research ingredients, and work out a system with the chef - which is great, by the way, so we can plan ahead.

Other times, some guests pre-arrange to bring in their own food, which of course is fine (but please *don't* do this without prior permission; there are all sorts of wrong things with that).

Sufferers have to be very clear when there's a real allergy, only because there are so many people who tell lies about it. Everyone who has a bad reaction knows of the lies other people spread to restaurant staff.

Customers will sit at a table and blatantly lie by telling their server they are allergic to onion, simply because they don't want any. Would it guarantee there'd be no onion? Yes. Would it slow down service because chefs are forced to clean and sterilise equipment when they don't need to? Yes. Will the customer with the 'allergy' complain about how long the meal takes to come out? Too right they would!

Allergies and dislikes are two different things. Hospitality staff are sick of the lies. By lying about an allergy, one is undermining the integrity of those who actually suffer. Enough bullshit; we can see right through it anyway.

| 17 |

Petit Four: There's Hair in my Burger

A man stormed up behind me and grabbed my shoulder. My blood boiled and I felt the urge to throw a punch or roundhouse kick him where the sun doesn't shine.

"Can I help you?" I asked sunnily. I reminded myself to kill him with kindness. For now.

"I want to speak to the manager!" he bellowed.

Bits of his spit speckled my cheek. "Yes, can I help you?" I say, wiping my face. Maybe I shouldn't have been so nice to him. I went for the middle ground. Robotic and soulless. Not nice, but not crabby enough to warrant a complaint.

He looked me up and down for size. This young girl was the manager? Fair enough.

"There's a haaaa-ir in my burger!" he howled loudly, hoping other customers might overhear.

I peer over at the hair, examining it, nestled in the bed of lettuce. "Yes, I'll agree with you. There certainly is a hair in your burger."

"*Well?* What are you going to do about it?" he sneered, demanding compensation.

I was not going to comp anything. That hair did not belong to us.

"I suggest that you pull it out, put it aside, and continue eating your burger," I calmly told him.

"*Excuse me?* I will not! You will make me a new burger right now!" he insisted, going quite red.

"No."

"No? *What do you mean no?*" he was irate now – first a burger with a hair, and now some snooty manager who thought she knew better!

"I mean that's *your* hair. It's not from here, so I'm not making you a new burger."

"EXCUSE ME?" he spat at me. "You calling me a liar?"

"Well, I have straight blonde hair, and the chef who cooked it has no hair,"

He looked at me suspiciously. What was she playing at?

"This hair in your burger is black and curly..." I continued. "*Your* hair is black and curly..."

Realisation crossed his face, and he stammered, "Yo-you're a bitch!" for he had nothing better to say.

"Thanks, you too," I told him.

"Excuse me?" he dared.

Without flinching, I emotionlessly deadpanned, "Thank you."

He hurled that burger at me, hitting me squarely in the shoulder. Did I deserve it?

Discuss.

| 18 |

The Gluten Free Scam

I approached a group of four, three of which sat chatting with their menus placed on the table in front of them. The fourth, a dashing young man with thick framed spectacles, however, continued to concentrate on the options.

I had allowed ample time, and the remainder of the group were indicating their readiness to order.

A woman beckoned me with eye-contact and a curt nod.

"Good evening, are you ready to order?" I queried.

Again, three of the four diners murmured affirmation, while the fourth, the young man with the spectacles, flinched with pressure to make a decision.

The first three chose their mains, and I paused and smiled at the young man, encouraging him to speak. The menu seemed to defeat him.

"What are some of the dishes you are tossing up between? I might be able to recommend a good one..." I gently began.

"No," he shook his head.

I was clearly not able to assist in this case.

The young man scanned the menu once more. The same, now familiar meals sprang up at him in the same order.

There were breads, entrees, share-plates and sides. There were some steaks, some seafood and a touch of poultry. But what this menu lacked was the one thing he wanted – *needed*. He fruitlessly searched for it one more time, hoping he somehow missed it the first eighteen times. How could a restaurant possibly fail to indicate which items were gluten-free? He had seen it many times before, the tiny GF symbol, neatly wedged between the meal description, and the V for Vegetarian, or the little leaf icon for vegan.

Other places he had dined at offered several gluten free dishes and substitutes. He was disappointed that this 'restaurant' failed to provide options supporting his lifestyle choice. That is, of course, unless this waitress knew of some 'secret menu' that was not presented. Surely, she would offer him a special meal for being gluten-free?

"Would you like me to come back?" I asked the group. Three of the guests groaned, indicating they were hungry, and were also getting impatient with the young man bearing spectacles.

He looked up to see three frowning faces, and decided to give the waitress the benefit of the doubt.

"Sorry, are there any gluten-free options available on this menu?" he asked me snootily, upset that they are not specifically listed.

His three friends huffed pointedly, for they'd heard it all before.

I pursed my lips and cocked my left eyebrow up. Side note, I just really wanted to include the word 'cocked' there. It's not sweary because it's a harmless verb.

Anyway, this man was full of shit. I admired his dazzling expression of puzzlement – eyes the colour of the espresso he was sipping on, framed by bold eyebrows which had been carefully waxed to follow the

exact curvature of his wide forehead. I glanced at the half-nibbled biscotti on his saucer, which gave him away.

Then he asked the biggest giveaway of the lot, "Are there any gluten-
free items on this menu?"

"That depends. Are you actually gluten free?" I dared him.

"Yes, my naturopath diagnosed me, actually," he replied preten-
tiously, disgusted that this waitress dare rudely question his lifestyle
choices.

"Well," I replied, "If you are *actually* suffering from coeliac disease,
you, *of course*, would *already know* to avoid anything with pasta or bread
and be weary of most sauces. Also," I looked down at the biscotti, "no
biscuits."

He looked at me, considering his options. "So you don't have anything gluten free then?"

I took a breath and continued, for he seemed too thick to understand.
"Most coeliacs would *already know* to order a plain bit of chicken or beef
with some fresh vegetables or salad - with the dressing on the side, of
course."

"No need to be rude," he jutted. "I just need to know what I can and
can't have."

Hmmm... perhaps I went a bit far then. Better put on the niceties.
I pulled my well-practised expression of polite concern and raised my
tone. "Oh, I'm sorry; I just wanted to make sure you knew what to order!
So did you want me to get you just a plain bit of chicken then? Maybe
with steamed vegetables?" I offered.

"Can I have chips?"

"No, sorry, they're cooked in the same vat as the crumbed chicken,
which is not gluten free."

"Oh, I'm sure that would be fine," he started.

I wasn't having it. This hipster represented a society of false allergies, special diets and fads. If he was going to be 'allergic' to gluten, I would make sure he got the full experience. "Sorry, I can't get you chips if you're allergic; there's quite a significant risk."

"Oh, the chips would be fine."

"No."

"No?" he questioned. "I'm the customer, and if I want to order chips, I should be able to. What happened to 'the customer is always right'?"

"I am not going to risk a customer suffering an attack over fried food, sorry. Do you even have an adrenaline shot with you?" I asked, knowing he was lying.

"Ok, ok, fine, no chips!" he agreed, probably guessing he'd been caught out.

The young man in the spectacles was not a real coeliac. I knew this the second he asked, 'Excuse me, are any of these items gluten-free?'

The half-eaten biscotti confirmed his lack of knowledge. He was a smug time waster. Did this man think it would be fun to have an allergy? Did he think that having an intolerance made him special? Did he think that a gluten-free diet was healthier for him? Was he currently under-taking tests to see if eliminating gluten would help his apparent symptoms? Or was he simply trying to be fashionable?

Whichever it was, this man lacked dedication to the cause. Either be intolerant or do not. Do not query the menu and request that the chefs provide a special meal, and then order a beer because it's ok to 'cheat a little'. Do not loudly proclaim you have an intolerance, but pick and choose times when it's an intolerance and when it's ok. Do not tell people you're allergic to coriander simply because you dislike the taste.

After the mains were cleared, I popped dessert menus in front of the first three guests. The man in the glasses reached to take one, but I regretfully declined him.

"I'm sorry, we don't have any gluten-free alternatives for dessert tonight," I told him.

"But I'm sure..." the man began.

"No," I looked at him, "we don't."

| 19 |

Why I Can't Go Back to the Pub

One minute I was fine and the next I wasn't. There I was, just like any other mid-afternoon, sitting in afternoon traffic, slowly creeping toward my destination. My mind was bored and I'd zoned out of the drive time radio show which I declared I listened to to be trendy – but, in actual fact, never really heard. As auto-pilot took over and my mind drifted away, I reminisced about my lunchtime close call, chuckling as I thought I got away with it – or had I?

It was a busy morning, and in between errands, before the first of a swing shift, I spotted a sushi shop – you know, the dodgy kind with handwritten signage and dim lighting – and thought, "Yum! That's going to hit the spot."

I approached the counter and placed my order, "One chilli crab roll, please." I grabbed the roll, devouring my first bite before I even retrieved my coins to pay.

"$2.50," the sushi guy says.

I glanced at the sign saying '$3.50' and in my gluttonous chilli crab roll massacre, I shot the guy a look of confusion.

He's told me a price lower than the one advertised.

With mayonnaise dripping out the crease of my lips, I muffled through the sticky rice and gargled, "Nah, free-fiddy?"

I was all for a discount at faceless corporations, but I wasn't about to rip off a small family business.

"It's ok," the sushi guy said, "Happy hour price!" he proclaimed proudly.

I whooped a little whoop of victory, for a one-dollar saving was a huge deal to my mundane life. I celebrated by stuffing my face with the rest of my chilli crab roll. Just imagine: with all my savings, I could have splurged out, treated myself and maybe bought two for that deal.

In my little happy-dance, I overheard the sushi guy selling to the next man in line. "$2.50," he told him. "Happy hour price!" he said with the same trusting smile. What a nice sushi guy.

But *this* customer, this customer was smarter than me and questioned the sushi guy. Surely happy hour would *not* fall during lunch, presumably the most profitable time of day?

"Well," the sushi guy shrugged sheepishly, "We discounted the price because the fridge broke."

I turned in horror to confirm what he'd just said.

He shuffled uncomfortably and owned up. "We put on a discount because the fridge broke."

I pointlessly slammed the small remainder of my germ-ridden chilli crab roll to the pavement and my eyes widened as I came to the startling conclusion that I was done for!

Not only had I risked the dodgy-looking place, then ordered the crab, but I'd risked the dodgy-looking place, ordered the questionable crustacean, and now had to live with the fact that it was probably contaminated too! That saying, 'she'll be right' came screaming into my head.

I glared at the sushi guy, in the dodgy shop, peddling his hazardous food to idiots like me.

He was now looking more sinister than friendly. That welcoming smile was now a churlish push for selling salmonella to unsuspecting victims.

I boldly admitted the truth to myself: No, I would *not* be right. I would not be right at all. A small part of me was afraid as I wondered when my moment would come.

Well, fate chose the right time, here, in traffic, listening to drive time radio, with nowhere to pull over and no toilet in sight.

I went from cool, calm and collected to a panicky sweat in no time. That tell-tale boiling down deep in the guts started to stir and I knew that my time was limited.

I put on my indicator, desperate to move to the other lane, closer to the side of the road. I could always pull onto the footpath if needed. It wasn't ideal, but I might have to forget my shame.

My muscles cramped up as I began to actively clench.

Nope, not happening! Hold on, hold on! Screw the indicator, I was forcing my car across! I had to pull over... RIGHT NOW! I could always mow down pedestrians if need be.

My pulse was racing and I was sweating, both hot and chilly at the same time. My hair was a wet mop against my neck and I was frantic. I was actively concentrating on holding on tight, and my fingers gripped the steering wheel in support of that. My knuckles were stretched white but I had to cling on. If I let go, I let go of everything!

Deep breath. Hold on... *HOLD ON!*

I pleaded into the rear-view mirror and saw a friendly hand wave me in.

"Thank you!" I saluted and swerved over.

Now what?

My eyes zapped electronically to points of interest over the landscape. Where were the toilets? *Where were the toilets?*

Up ahead there was a servo. Ummmmm? Desperate times…

I imagined the stainless-steel bowl lined with urine and stains and shuddered. I was mortified at the thought of asking a man to use a toilet. My stomach growled again and I silently screamed to myself that beggars can't be choosers.

I was not going to make the wait in line for the key!

What's next?

I was searching for a fast food joint, a shopping centre, or pretty much anywhere I could blend into the background and also know there were toilets there. Everything that could go wrong was running through my head.

"Customers only."

"Staff only."

"Out of order."

Why was it so hard to find a toilet?!

Then, it appeared. A bottle-shop, and then right behind it, a giant flashing sign that said, *Guaranteed trading hours until 4am.* It was a pub. A PUB!

I screamed with glee, in a contorted frigid sort of way, daring a drip to escape. I couldn't even trust a fart now, I was so on edge.

IT WAS A PUB! A giant pokie room with lavish toilets and anonymity! If one were to hit the diarrhoea jackpot, this would be it!

I flew out of my car toward the entrance, not even closing the door and burst inside. I saw the flashing lights and tell-tale songs of a gaming room, knowing the loos would be close. I saw the little girl sign and rushed in.

I had to consciously tell myself, "not yet, not yet" while I was unzipping my pants (*Dammit, pants! I'm never wearing pants again!*) when I heard the horror of the main toilet door opening again.

NO!

There was someone else! *Someone else was here when I needed to poo!*

I froze, stomach burning and anus threatening leakage, defensively glaring at the cubicle door.

I couldn't go now! There was someone else in there!

I silently screamed every swear word I knew, tears pouring down my blotchy face, urging her to hurry the eff up and get the eff out of the effing bathroom so I may explode with some sort of dignity still.

I heard the toilet flush and gleefully encouraged her to wash her hands and leave – in my head though. No one must know I was there.

Get out. Get out. Get out. GET OUT!

I was stealthy but at the same time I was freaking out.

Hurry up. HURRY UP!

The firey sensation flared around my exit hole, and I braced myself, clenching for dear life. This was going to be a burny-stinky one!

Then, it happened: A swing of a door and a world of wonderful solitude: the other person left the restroom.

A euphoric smile and a waterfall gushed out of me at the same time. Oh, sweet relief! I leaned forward in tears of joy as my bottom exploded into a steaming fountain of release. I gasped and quivered as the liquid fell out and hoped it wouldn't splash out of the bowl. Briefly, it ceased, but I took a breath and anticipated the next round. One spasm, and a slop and the rest was evacuated in a swift orgasmic spurt.

I giggled in celebration, shaking excitedly in my blotchy, teary hot mess, and grasped the toilet paper. I dabbed the ring of fire gently, twinging at the roasted parts.

I fumbled for my water bottle and squirted some on some toilet paper.

The cool sensation tingled. Such sweet relief!

Then I sat and just breathed.

When it was time to stand up, I gingerly turned to observe the evidence. I swallowed and defiantly assured myself that it was a lie, and no one needed to know the truth. No woman would ever be capable of such a thing.

I flushed and thought, "byeeeeeeeee," confident that no one would ever know. I unhooked my handbag, and collected myself, ready to leave and deny – the lady-like way.

As I opened the door, I looked in horror at the queue which had formed outside my cubicle. I passed the first person and silently apologised for the embarrassing smell. I saw her recoil, as the other women were relieved they didn't have to go in after me.

Well, that's it. I'd have to disguise myself and I could never go back there. I would now be known as that woman who produced that stench that women don't produce.

I hopped into my car and vowed to never return – to the unfortunate pub, or the dodgy sushi place.

As I was about to pull out, a familiar face screeched in. There was a man with a desperate need about him.

I knew that need.

He gritted his teeth in concentration and grimaced when he saw me again. I unwound my window and smugly informed the dodgy sushi guy, "The toilet's broken mate! Might have to try somewhere else.

| 20 |

A Medium Rare Eye Fillet

"Hi there. Are you ready to order?" I asked to silence.

I moved to the first woman. She was forty and had her haircut in a bob, slightly longer in the front. Her pink hibiscus bejewelled nails matched the pink hibiscus bejewelled cover on her phone, which she showed off while ordering. I know you know what her name was - I'm going to call her Sharon. She looked like a Sharon.

I should have known then, but I was still innocent enough to believe there weren't any stereotypes in customers. I was wrong.

"Hello. What would you like?"

"Good thanks. Eye fillet," Hibiscus Sharon asked me, peering over her menu.

"Yes, how would you like that cooked?" I queried automatically.

"On a grill."

I paused. Was that a joke? Was she being serious?

Silence.

Not a joke. Actual suggestion.

"Sorry, I meant, would you like it bleu, rare, medium rare..." I slowed down so Sharon could answer. I was waiting for her to pop in at any moment, but she stared at me dumbly. No response.

"Ah, medium, medium well, well done, or simply burnt to a crisp?" I finished, giving a bit of a chuckle at my last suggestion, because I'm super witty like that.

"Medium rare," she replied. Sharon never needed a please or thank you when speaking to service staff. You know how I mentioned there are no stereotypes in customers?

I blinked and the time had whizzed by.

I saw one of my tables had begun eating their mains. The one with the hibiscus jewelled phone and matching nails woman, Sharon. The guests were tucking into their delicious mains, except, of course, Sharon, who was looking about as frustrated as an interrupted masterbation session.

I casually strolled around the table, not wanting to interrupt any conversations. As there was a lull, I quietly asked to no one, "How are you finding everything?"

A unified murmur acknowledged me, as all but one diner nodded to affirm their pleasure.

"Excuse me," Sharon snapped, "I ordered my steak medium rare, and this," she grimaced, "this is just... vile."

I looked at her and asked her to elaborate, for she had been served a beautifully seared medium rare eye fillet – just as she had ordered.

"It's underdone. This is disgusting," she huffed.

"Sorry about that, madam," I began to reach out and take her plate.

"No!" Sharon tore the plate from my fingers, sliding the food to the edge threateningly. "Bring me the manager!"

"Actually, I'm the manager on tonight, and I'm happy to help if we can discuss this," I replied.

"Oh," Sharon looked at me disdainfully, "*You're* the manager?" she asked, knowing full well, I was the manager. There was a clue on my name tag that said *Management* right under my name.

"Yes," I replied, "I understand you're not entirely satisfied with your meal this evening," I paused, waiting for her to take over.

"Yes. I ordered my steak medium rare – I don't know *who* took my order - and what I got was… *this*," she said, grimacing around the table to ensure her company had all stopped eating and were listening. She lifted the plate for everyone to see. Some nodded in agreeance while others rolled their eyes discreetly, warning me that this had happened in the past.

One man muttered, "Here we go," silently wishing me luck with this bitch via a slither of eye contact.

I was perplexed. This woman had ordered a medium rare eye fillet, and presented a plate holding a medium rare eye fillet. It was still steaming, and I caught the scent of the grilled seasoned meat. It looked and smelt glorious. This woman was delusional if she were to complain of this chef-d'oeuvre.

"I'm sorry, madam, would you care to elaborate on where we went wrong?"

"Well, *clearly*, it's underdone!" she huffed, "I mean, *look* at it. There's *blood* all over my plate," she shuddered dramatically.

I delicately asked to see the plate more closely. There was a beautifully cooked medium rare eye fillet, melting with juices, producing a mouth-watering scent of seasoned perfection.

"I'm sorry. We must have misunderstood. We have taken your order as medium rare, which is how this steak is cooked. How did you actually request it done tonight?"

Sharon was not impressed. How could they have possibly gotten this wrong? It seemed that every time she ate out, the chefs could never seem to get her steak cooked properly. Tonight was no exception. She didn't understand. She thought chefs had to do training. Especially in an establishment as fine as this. How could they put someone so incompetent on in charge of something as important as the steaks?

She mightn't look it, but she was a seasoned steak connoisseur. She knew the best butcher in town, and at home, she produced the most delightful barbecues, impressing all her guests. Her steaks were cooked perfectly medium rare – crispy and dark out the surface, but firmly warm pinkish brown in the centre. Not a drop of that disgusting blood in sight. The way a steak should be cooked. Tonight she was being embarrassed by this stupid waitress who clearly had no idea about meat. She hoped her friends forgave her for this ridiculous stunt by these poorly trained staff.

"I *did* order my steak medium rare, like I always do. Instead of getting medium rare, I got this."

"What are you expecting in your steak tonight, madam?" I asked. She was delusional if she didn't think this is bang on.

Sharon and her bob haircut exploded! "I want my steak medium rare! Medium rare! Don't you get it?"

I barely flinched and stood idly, letting her continue. I wiped a fleck of her spit away from my cheek.

"Medium rare is cooked through so there is no-" she gagged dramatically, "-blood in it, but it's not quite cooked through! *I* know all the best chefs in town, so *I know*," she boasted.

Of course. This woman knew all the best chefs in town. Funny that – so did I; I worked with some, drank with others, and was shagging the head chef from the Wood and Spoon, and during all this work, drinking and shagging, I had never seen, nor heard of, this bitch before.

"I'm sorry madam, I will get you another cooked 'medium rare' for you right away," I replied, taking her perfect steak. As I reached the kitchen bin, I was saddened by wasting a perfectly good steak when my dinner would consist of cold chips the chefs gave me - too old to serve to the guests.

I know that some staff will eat leftovers off plates, but I for one will not. I have no idea what happens when the plate leaves the kitchen, but as far as I am concerned, it's contaminated. They could have sneezed on it, chewed it and spat it back out, laced it with something - who knows. Everything that goes on a table must be treated as filthy, and removed and cleaned thoroughly at the end of each sitting. There's no such thing as returning food to the kitchen for 're-use' (although a lot of places do it), and even if that cutlery hasn't been touched, it must be taken away. No one wants to find a 'unused' napkin with lipstick hidden on the underside.

"One eye fillet, Chef! Medium *well* please!" I shouted across the kitchen.

"Eye fillet, medium well!" Chef called back to confirm - the professional chef, who I worked with, who knew how to cook a mean steak.

After almost all the other guests in Sharon's party were done eating, the medium well steak was finally served.

She took a bite and chewed slowly, eyes closed in orgasmic euphoria as she savoured that first bite of delicious, perfectly overcooked steak. She 'mmmm-ed' and lovingly groaned loudly, arching her neck back, causing several men to stare at her with 'come-to-bed' eyes.

"How are you finding everything now?" I asked her brightly, deliberately timing it so she was interrupted mid-mouthful.

Two eyes snapped open and glared. If she could murder me right now, she probably would.

I beamed sunshine at the sight of her stifling her meat, forcing a swallow in order to answer.

"Fine," she gasped, grasping for the water glass.

"Excellent," I smiled.

Exactly five minutes and over an hour later, she was back, and now she refused to pay her bill - but we all knew that would happen.

"That first steak was disgusting. I really don't understand how incompetent your chefs are to cook a steak that's practically still *alive* and give it to me, trying to tell me it's medium rare!" she cried.

"Yes, madam, and we happily replaced your meal with one that was cooked more to your liking," I tried to protest.

"It was just as bad."

"But you ate *all* of it? I'm sorry, I must have misunderstood when I saw you devouring it. You told me it was fine," I continued.

"I could barely concentrate on my food over the noise that was coming from the next table." Sharon must love her complaining.

"The other guests nearby were unruly?" I questioned, "None of our staff, or any other table, seemed to notice…"

"That's because they were too busy walking around,"

"The staff? Busy serving people? Sorry about that," I replied tartly.

"I'm very disappointed with the service I've received tonight. Just you wait for the review I'll write. Needless to say, I'm *never* coming back," she threatened.

"Well then, madam, please pay your bill – in full – and then leave, and don't come back," I ordered.

"No!" she roared, "I'm not paying for it!" she insisted, stomping her foot. She leaned toward me threateningly.

The other diners in the restaurant stopped eating to watch the performance.

"If you refuse to pay, I will call the police," I told her calmly.

"You can't do that," she insisted. "I deserve a complimentary meal for what I've been through tonight!"

I have a few management standards I live by. I guess they'd be similar to the rules of working in hospitality, but every manager has their own style and approach. One of my things is that if someone tells me they're never coming back, I won't try to get them to stay. No discounts, no negotiations. I'll just tell them to pay and leave. Why should I offer a discount? If that's what it takes to entice them, I'd rather they went somewhere else. If they're 'never coming back' their minds have been made up. Why fight it when you can focus your service on loyalty?

"I deserve a complimentary meal for what I've been through tonight!" she argued.

"No madam, you don't, and if you leave without paying, you will be stealing. Please settle your bill," I told her matter-of-factly.

Sharon begrudgingly obliged, but not without muttering rude things under her breath, and dropping the dreaded, "Don't you know who I am?" to me "I influence a lot of people."

"Thank you. I'm sure you do. We look forward to your review," I casually replied.

| 21 |

Late at Night

We had finally finished stacking all the chairs onto the tables, ready to mop the floors. Lights were blaring inside, but outside they were off. Music was cranking and the door was locked. Suddenly, there was an impatient tap on the window.

We looked up to find a woman peering in, squinting, searching for any sense of life. In unison, the staff dropped their eyes to the floor, desperate to avoid contact with hers.

I, unaware, wandered out from the back of the house. The woman caught my eye. Busted!

I shook my head at her apologetically, but she ignored my gesture – if there were people in there, then surely it was not too late?

She started waving frantically, calling out over the blare of the loud unwelcoming music.

I shook my head again, but it only encouraged her to wave more. I stopped and stared at her, arms crossed, as the woman began flapping her whole arms, dramatically beckoning me toward her.

The other staff forgot their cleaning duties, and were mesmerised watching me. What will I do? What will I say?

She clearly needed attention right now.

I bravely approached the door.

The woman smiled encouragingly, nodding, drawing me nearer.

I unlatched the lock.

Woman moved nearer.

I pulled down the handle and pulled the door inward.

The woman leapt forward and burst in front of me. With a broad smile and wild eyes, she asked the dreaded question, "Are you still open?"

With a roar, I shut her down, "No!" I snapped as I stumbled back.

She did not – will not – accept my response. "So can I still grab a burger then?"

"No, sorry, the kitchen is closed, and so are we," I firmly said.

"Are you sure; I won't be long…" she began.

I turned to her, taking a deep breath to suppress the urge to smack the stupidity out of her. "Look, everything is turned off. The kitchen is clean. The chefs have gone home. The outside lights are off. We're cleaning the dining room. The till has been finalised and the door was locked. It's too late! We are closed!" I insisted.

"Well, you don't need to be so rude. I just asked a simple question," the woman snapped back aggressively. She looked around at the rest of the staff, staring at her. None of them had said a word.

"All of you are *so* rude!" she cried, "I'm *never* coming back!" she spat at the staff. She stormed away, muttering things like, "Unbelievable!" and "How hard can it be to make one little burger?"

I locked the door behind me, and the staff resumed their cleaning duties once more.

The woman went home and wrote it on the internet.

| 22 |

Every Transaction Ever

I looked around the restaurant. There was always something to do next. It was just a matter of prioritising what needed doing.

The first task presented itself, as a table made their way up to me, still observing the restaurant from the cashier's desk. I smiled, and several of the guests in the group smiled back. I often think my days are all about sunshine, happiness and smiling at people. It's the perfect lie. Most tables are as forgettable as the next. I do, however, enjoy my job.

"Hello. We're ready to pay the bill," a woman in a navy swing dress declared.

"Excellent," I responded, getting it ready. "How was everything tonight?" I asked her.

"Good thanks," no one replied.

The navy swing dress woman fished through her handbag and eventually dug out her purse, pulling out various cards and shaking her head until the correct one appeared.

I held out my hand to collect the card. "Thank you," I smiled courteously.

"I can never find anything in here!" the woman laughed. She looked down at my hand, and placed the card on the counter, next to my open palm.

Thanks for that.

I laughed with her, "Oh, my handbag's exactly the same!" I chuckled in a big, bouncy, fake Customer Laugh.

No response. Well, that was awkward.

I processed the payment. "Ok, that's all settled then."

The woman outstretched her hand to collect the card.

I hovered above it, and then placed the card on top of the bill folder. "Would you like a copy of your receipt?" I asked innocently.

"No, thank you," she never replied. She was already chatting to her friends as they slowly laughed and moved on.

"Well thank you very much, have a wonderful night," I smiled as they filtered past. "Thank you. See you next time," I half waved and Customer-ised. "Thank you. Thank you. See you soon," I nodded in general to the crowd.

They all ignored me.

I opened up the bill folder, and found five dollars in it. I hadn't noticed anyone slip it in. I was surprised.

You might be the best server the world has ever seen. You might go above and beyond and kiss-arse to no end. After all this awesomeness and arse kissing you might have someone slip you a twenty. Or... nothing!

You might be useless. It might be your first day. You might be in a bad mood, hungover, tired, or just plain stupid. After all the forgetting items, slow service, bored demeanour and total cock-ups, you might have someone slip you a twenty. Or... nothing!

That table who you've been chatting to for ages, who've invited you to drinks after work, given you their business card and laughed at your lame jokes? They might slip you a twenty. Or... nothing!

That table you've accidentally ignored, forgotten who they were and barely scraped a greeting? They might leave you a twenty. Or... nothing!

Whoever said servers earn a lot of tips obviously has never served tables before. Some days you get lots and some days you get none. They're not reliable, or expected, but very much appreciated. Given our terrible wages and hours, they don't go to waste (Ok, some/most will go to alcohol, who am I kidding?).

The point is, no one can't guess who will leave a tip – or how much it will be. So stop trying to. Just keep giving everyone the best service you can provide, and hopefully some will show their appreciation in cash.

One of the things I learnt whilst working in hospitality, is that you can never ever predict who will tip, or how much.

| 23 |

How to Not Apply for a Job

Friday lunch was always hectic. Businesses across Lonsdale treated their workers to celebrate the end of the working week, by taking them out for some group bonding. The bonding was so effective, that frequently little work would be completed after lunch and Friday night drinks would begin bang on five o'clock.

This Friday was typical, with no one in the restaurant at eleven forty-five. By midday, it was full. By twelve-fifteen, the wait list was full too.

In the midst of the door host highlighting off names, escorting guests to their tables, answering the phone, and apologising to several groups, that no, we couldn't seat them before two o'clock, but they were welcome to make a reservation for next week, a spritely young man barged to the front of the queue.

"Excuse me!" he barked, demanding my attention right away. "Who do I talk to about getting a job?"

"Just a second," I told him, as I shuffled some tables around to fit the next group in. The customers surrounded me, all vying for attention.

"Look, can I just drop this off?" the backpacker asked, not wanting to wait his turn; after all, he was only going to be a minute.

I looked up and observed the young candidate. He was wearing one of those fashionable floral printed button-up shirts in grey, with clashing board shorts, sandals and knee-high socks.

I was wearing a neat black dress, an apron, tidy hair and pride.

The backpacker had unkempt hair, uneven stubble and dirt under his nails.

The patrons surrounding him wore black, charcoal and navy, all neat and conservative.

The backpacker smelt of salt, sweat and yesterday's beer.

As the suits walked past, I got a whiff of expensive cologne, freshly washed hair and clean linen.

I glanced at my watch. "Come back at three-thirty," I instructed, then returned to my duties looking after the guests who were patiently waiting for a seat.

At three-thirty the young man returned, and with a "Hey, I'm back about the job," as his hello.

I was waiting for this. I was looking forward to wasting his time, as he had wasted mine during service. I could have just as easily said no on the spot, but knew it would be more effective to lead him on, and then shut him down. I'm a bit of a bitch sometimes.

"Yes, what did you say your name was?" I asked.

"Um, I didn't. David."

"Well, David," I told him, "we are indeed hiring at the moment."

He looked at me with hope. There was a brief sense of optimism in him that he had a chance.

"Not you, however." See - I told you I was a bitch.

David's face fell, and before he could ask why, I told him.

"We're hiring hospitality *professionals.* You barge in here in the middle of service, demanding attention before our guests, wearing board shorts, sandals and looking unkempt. You have demonstrated that you have no understanding of the hospitality industry, and are not a professional."

David stood gobsmacked while the rest of the staff snickered. I hoped he'd at least learnt something from this. I doubted it though.

I mentioned this scenario in the Lonsdale Bartenders Network, and someone commented, "I hope he spat in your face."

I take it to you then - what would you do? Would you have given him a trial, or told him to leave? Would you have made him come back to reject him? Or let him know on the spot that he wasn't suitable? Would you have accepted his resume, then chucked it out the second he left? Or would you actually read it?

What would you do?

| 24 |

A Bit of a Pickle

Friday night was bustling. The upbeat live soloist was drowned out by happy guests as they chatted boisterously and cackled with laughter in between mouthfuls of rich homely food.

The staff bounced in unison, bopping along as meals flew out. Productivity was gleaming, and customers were happy.

A man barged his way to the front cashier desk and slammed his plate on the counter, "Excuse me! I want to speak to a manager!" he barked, causing me to jump, hoping I didn't look too sweaty or flustered.

I wiped some stray hairs away from my face, and rubbed my upper lip on my sleeve. This was going to be the best I could look right now on a busy night.

I was greeted with a squat, balding man, nostrils flaring and eyes wildly piercing. I knew the type – a middle-aged, suit-wearing control freak, and I knew from his stance, he wasn't going to be an easy one.

I pasted on my Customer Smile, drew in a breath, and sweetly asked, "Yes, Sir, how can I help you?"

He was slightly taken aback, and shook his head, looking down at me, "No, I want to speak to the manager."

"Yes, Sir, I'm the manager on duty, how can I help you?"

He studied my innocent face, and his expression turned angry again. He tore the crown off his burger, squishing his stumpy fingers into the saucy bread, yelling, "I ordered my Colossal Burger without pickles, *and I got pickles!*"

I stammered, "Sorry about that…" and tried to apologise, remembering my training regarding how to deal with complaints.

He screamed over me, "Sorry? You're not sorry! This is ridiculous!"

"Well-"

"No! *Every time* I come here…"

I tried to interject but was cut off. I let him go, partially listening, and partially zoning out. I looked at his forehead. There was a small mole with hair growing out of it.

Don't look at the mole! Don't look at the mole!

I focussed on the crease between his eyebrows while he ranted.

"This is ridiculous! *Every time* I come here you guys just can't seem to get my order right!"

Well why do you bother coming back then? You won't be missed.

"Ok, let me just-" I tried.

"No! I'm not finished yet!" he barked, snatching the greasy burger and waving it frantically in my face, causing limp pieces of browning shredded lettuce to fly around.

I knew it was fruitless trying to help him at this point – he was being irrational. He was simply looking for someone to scream at. I had to just let him go.

He was building momentum now, and his tone became more threatening as he spat words at my face. "What kind of idiots do you have working here? How stupid are you? Or better yet – how stupid do you think I am? Do you think I'll just drop it? Well I'm won't, I'm sick of your staff not getting it right! You need to train your staff better! You shouldn't work here if you're that stupid you can't even get a burger right!"

He continued as I stood there blankly, hearing him occasionally say things like, "You'll never amount to anything!" and "They'll certainly hear about this!"

I struggled to understand his argument. I knew he was upset about having the incorrect meal, but his reaction? He was losing the plot.

He continued to rip me apart, not allowing a second for me to defend myself, or my team.

I tried to move my mind to another place, but I could not leave the restaurant. I vowed I wouldn't let him get to me. I wouldn't cry. Don't cry. Do not cry! I pleaded with the lump in my throat to disappear and the tears welling up to dissipate. The buzzing of the restaurant slowed down as onlookers vied to watch me get destroyed by this vulture, pecking at anything he could to enhance his argument.

We stuffed up. We put pickles on his burger. I blinked and tuned into what he was bellowing on about now.

"...and I'm *allergic* to pickles! I could have died..."

I finally plucked up the courage to confront him. "Sir... Sir?" he continued to rant as I tried to get a word in.

"No! You listen to me! Standards here are disgusting! You ought to be ashamed of yourself!"

I tried again, "Sorry - if can just-"

"Utterly useless staff here..." he ranted on.

Well, I tried. Being polite just wasn't working. So I tried the next tactic. "EXCUSE ME! DO YOU WANT ME TO HELP YOU? BECAUSE I'M SICK OF BEING SCREAMED AT RIGHT NOW!" I bellowed, forcing the man to suddenly stop and contort his face into a murderous glare.

They say that dynamite comes in small packages, and I proved it as I exploded. This little girl blew up with such force, and my volume demanded such an impact, it shocked the bastard into flattened silence.

I had had enough. The look I gave him tore down every ounce of superiority he was exuding over me. I went rigid and reminded myself that his height did not make him more important than me as a person. As youthful and petite as I was, I was not going to let some older man get away with abusing girls, simply because I worked in customer service and it was my 'job'. I knew that if *I* were another man in a suit, he would have been more respectful. I knew if I were closer to his age, he mightn't have thought I was thick. However, I suffered through the image I projected to him. I was young, female and wearing a nametag. This gave him all the ammunition he needed to ensure I was thoroughly attacked. I may have been the one in the uniform, and he may have been wearing the suit, but by treating me the way he did, he proved that no matter how much wealth he might have, he was still a poor person inside. I stopped caring if I was going to get a complaint via the internet. What gave him the right to treat me like this? Was the customer always right? If he complained, it would reinforce his entitled attitude by supporting that he could behave so foul and was allowed – was expected - to do so. So I decided to teach him a lesson.

"Have you eaten the Colossal Burger before?" I asked, daring him to say the wrong thing.

"Why yes I have, actually. I'm a very loyal customer, and I deserve to have good food and good service. This is not up to the standard which I expect from Silverman's!" he insisted.

For a 'very loyal customer' I worked full time and didn't recognise him. I smiled meanly and nodded in agreeance, looking him up and down, "You *obviously do* eat a *lot* of Colossal Burgers..." I paused so I could see him question my intentions.

Then, as he opened his mouth to speak, I cut him off again, "and so I can see what a huge error we've made. You *must* have meant no pickles, *and* no sauce, and there's a heap of sauce on this burger too..."

He stopped to process what I was saying.

I could see the confusion on his face, as he stammered, then tried to get angry again.

"No the sauce is fine, it's just the pickles that..."

"But, Sir?" I accused with aggressive eyes and a gritted smile, "There are pickles *in* the sauce. *Lots* of pickles. In fact, the chefs nickname it 'pickle sauce' due to the concentration of pickles in the sauce"

"Oh no, the sauce is fine, it's just the pickles I can't have..." He knew I had him.

"But, Sir," I persisted, "You just told me you're 'allergic' to pickles"

"Yes, but..."

"Well I certainly wouldn't want to put you in a position where you could die from anaphylactic shock."

"No, but..."

"So I'm going to rectify this right now for you. I'm going to get you to wait here – I can see you're a very busy man, so I'll only be just a few minutes" I caught Nicki's eye, and she stifled a smirk. "I'm going to go out the back and follow the proper procedures for making food when someone has an allergy. I really wouldn't want to put you at risk from falling ill. So here's what I'm going to do for you: Chef and I are going to wash and sterilise *all* of our equipment which may come into contact with your burger, as well as any surfaces we use to make the burger..."

"Oh, I really don't think that's necessary..."

"But you told me you're allergic to pickles, so I need to take all allergies seriously for the health and welfare of our valuable customers. We're more than happy to make you a new burger, and you can see Chef make it from here," I pointed to a space at the pass, "To make sure that our procedures are completely satisfactory to you. Oh – and what sauce would you like on your burger now?"

"As I said! The sauce is fine!" He dared to raise his voice at me again.

I forced a threatening smile, flames wildly flaring in my eyes as I reminded him, *"But you told me you were allergic to pickles! Remember?"*

He knew I'd won. By keeping composure, he had nothing on me. What could he possibly complain about? That he lost the plot over a pickle? That I tried to help him – went out of my way to help him? That he abused a small young girl (yeah – I'll milk it now) to near breaking point? Over a pickle. A pickle! He couldn't simply *pick* off the pickle and instead, he decided to go out of his way to take his awful mood out on me. Well I wasn't buying it today. I didn't care how bad his day had been. I didn't care how bad his life had been. I didn't care that he's in a career where he wore a suit to an office and probably had embossed business cards. Just because I was in a job where I was on my feet, I wore a uniform that featured a logo and shoes that had non-slip soles and I was on the other side of the counter; it did not make me a lesser person.

Customers varied greatly. Most were normal and forgettable. They were polite and pleasant. Some went out of their way to be nice. Some asked some really stupid questions which I had to front a serious response to. But then there were others, like this man, who for some or any reason, decided to barge into a Silverman's and abuse a staff member. I was there to help him, but I wasn't The Help. I could not do this, however, whilst I was being vehemently reprimanded about a pickle.

I got that man a new burger.

Chef took the time to clean and sterilise all equipment. He opened a new packet of disposable gloves, and made that burger from scratch, not daring to risk pickle contamination. He smiled as he splotched on the man's reluctant choice of sweet chilli sauce on the bun - knowing it would taste disgusting - every so often glancing up and pointedly making eye contact with him, so he knew what a special effort he was going to, to rectify the tragic course of events that resulted in pickle being where it mustn't be.

Eventually I presented a plate carrying a steaming hot sweet-chilli infused Colossal Burger.

"Is there anything else I can do for you now?" I politely asked as I went to put down the plate.

He gruffly snatched it and began to stuff his face.

I smiled to the audience of other tables, gave a curt nod and wave, before excusing myself to hide in the cool room and cry. I had done it. I managed to beat him, and still set an example to my team, teaching them an invaluable lesson.

I had won this battle, but the shift wasn't over, the week wasn't over, and my time with Silverman's wasn't over yet. There would others. He wasn't the first, and certainly wouldn't be the last. There are some people in this world who try to act like a big-shot. He was one of them, power tripping and taking advantage of a young girl just trying to do her best. Through his hostility, aiming to live up to his big-shot entitlement, he also taught my staff a lesson: That by acting so big, he proved himself to only be very small.

| 25 |

Petit Four: A Fine Example

I walked toward the exit, just as a small girl was approaching from the other side to come in. As she drew nearer, both the young girl and I hesitated and went to move out of each other's ways.

The young girl looked up, and automatically said, "Sorry."

Her father reached down to stop her, and with one hand firmly on her shoulder, he taught her, "We don't move for them, they move for us. And you *never* say sorry to them; they're not worth it."

| 26 |

Mother's Day

Ask any hospitality worker what the worst day of the year is for them, and no doubt, they will tell you it's Mother's Day.

There are big days in every calendar. These are days where it's expected people will book ahead, we'll get a lot of walk-ins too, but it is manageable, mostly smooth and at the end of the day, we can all sit down and share our stories of the day over a pint.

Mother's Day isn't just busy. It's insane.

It starts weeks earlier, just after Easter, when suddenly one or two families phone to book or enquire what we have on (really? We *just* had Easter). They will ask a bunch of questions pertaining to a non-existent menu (we *just* had Easter) which they will hold against you at a later date.

Will there be oysters? What will the weather be like then? Will my gran like it?

Some managers will see people as instant dollar signs, and try to shove as many guests in at the same time as possible. Actually, never mind possible – there are times where the venue literally does not have enough tables, and some idiot will continue to keep taking bookings.

The restaurant manager will keep track of bookings daily, blocking out times which are full (usually starting at midday) and try to spread out guests to less popular dining times (four o'clock dinner, anyone?).

The day before, when it's fully booked (if not the week before), the manager will phone and confirm all the bookings, only to be greeted with numerous changes, questions and enquiries.

Can we add another six people?

If my fourteen year old comes, do they have to pay full price or can they order off the kid's menu?

I know it says children are under twelve, but can I please order a kid's meal?

Actually, no, we're not coming anymore, we've decided to have it at home.

Can we let you know in the morning the exact numbers or do you really need to know now?

I know you said you're full at twelve, so we've booked for one o'clock. If we rock up at twelve, can we be seated then though?

I've actually got a severe allergy to garlic but the menu has garlic bruschetta. Can you ask the chef to make me something else?

Do we have to order off the set menu or can we get anything?

Can I change my booking? We'll be there between twelve and two o'clock.

Eventually, the manager confirms all numbers, and will spend the rest of the afternoon answering the phone, then telling people they are fully booked.

Yes, I'm sure.

No, we can't, sorry.

Yes, you can wait but we're unable to tell you for how long.

No, I don't know any places that may have a spare table.

After the phone quietens down, seating arrangements are done. It's kind of like juggling with furniture, begging how to fit the most tables in the smallest space and still be able to walk past without dropping any food or drinks on people's heads.

Sweat time! Time to actually move all the tables. Spend time scribbling reservations over the top of crossed out maps of table plans, slash big X's over pages, drag tables across and hope the customer who sits in the tight corner is skinny enough to squeeze in.

Double check the reservations actually match the floor plan – several times. Groan when you see someone has requested to sit near the window and you can only possibly physically fit their table near the toilet. Hope they won't mind when you offer them a complimentary bottle of wine for their compliance.

Groan when you've realised the only way to make a table fit is by sitting three groups at the same time in the same section. Roster your superstar server there. Hope she won't mind when you offer her a complimentary vodka for her compliance.

Set the tables to suit the set menu and make the day run smoother. If it's usually counter service, do *not* let guests collect their own cutlery, or you will run out. Allocate it. Allocate napkins. Allocate glassware. If it can be allocated, allocate it.

Write your staff shift plan and hope no one minds that they're unlikely to get a break when they need, but you may (or may not) be able to send them to the toilet if needed (and they're lucky).

Get home and realise you're about to get only four hours sleep before the busiest day of the year.

Shut your eyes for ten seconds and you're already back at work. The phone is ringing off the hook with people wanting to book, and people wanting to change their numbers. Then it begins.

Doors open and the first bookings are sat. Despite pre-telling them a week ago on the phone they'll need to order within fifteen minutes, they want to take their time ordering. Despite a table of eight booking for eleven, it's eleven thirty and only two people have shown up. They assure you the others will be here "soon" and are "on their way" with a chuckle, but you're wondering where you're going to sit your next table who is booked in that seat at one o'clock. You hope someone else will leave early, but know you'll have to pull a magical table out of thin air.

Need to pee. Shouldn't have had that coffee.

The line of walk-ins is overwhelming! You try to get the bookings sat so you can confirm which (if any) tables are available for walk-in guests and get sworn at for letting the bookings 'cut ahead of the line'.

Need to pee.

Sit a walk-in (somehow) then have them complain after only fifteen minutes they have now been waiting two hours for their meals.

No, buddy. You've waited fifteen minutes, not two hours. You arrived two hours ago, but you only ordered fifteen minutes ago.

Smile and apologise, explaining it's "busier than usual" and "we're doing our best" only to have one of the guests complain you've ruined Mother's Day for them. Think for a second about your poor mother who you've had to ditch (again) for work, to look after someone else's family. Feel the betrayal from the customer and wish you'd ever, ever, ever be able to have lunch at home with your own mother on Mother's Day.

Need to pee.

Chef calls you over to ask if the seating can slow down because the kitchen is struggling to keep up.

As the next booking arrives, ask them if they'd mind waiting in the lounge for fifteen minutes. Have the thirty-year-old daughter abuse you, because, "What is the point in making a booking if you can't sit us on time?"

Apologise and sit them right away, but take your time getting to them to order. Send order to the kitchen after delaying it as long as possible, and brace ones-self for the fiery inferno as the head chef explodes.

Need to pee.

By this stage, the restaurant is what staff would describe as an absolute shit-fight. People are waiting to be sat on tables that don't exist. Some specials are sold out and people complain we should have planned better. We're running low on forks and there's no one available to wash or polish them. Table four needs clearing. Table twelve needs ketchup. Table twenty wants water. Table thirty wants to order dessert but isn't ready, but wants you to hang around while they take their time deciding what they're having.

Can you take a photo of us?

Excuse me, where are the toilets?

How do we pay?

I'm not paying for that; we had to wait forty minutes for our food!

Can we get some more colouring-in sheets?

Can I get more sauce?

All reasonable requests, and on any other day, would be addressed happily. Not on Mother's Day. The questions, statements and requests keep going, faster and faster and faster. All staff move as fast as they can, prioritising tasks to save time, and answering as sunnily as they can, hoping the feelings of sheer terror and panic do not communicate back to the guests.

Most guests are happy, as they are in good company, spending time with their families and celebrating. Others are not.

The others are not your ordinary cranky, demanding, entitled customer either. On Mother's Day, they become an elite breed of soul-crushing demons – forceful, abusive and even violent, spitting their demands on a pressured team, threatening with poor reviews on social media and radiating an air of 'don't you know who I am?'.

At four o'clock, the stampede has left, and all that remains are dead remnants of a once lush inviting oasis, and the occasional twitch of a guest, who looks around astonished at what's left, and innocently asks if you're still open and if they're ok to stay. Of course they're ok to stay. You are still open after all. Amazingly, during the least popular seating time, they would be receiving the best service of the day, as the staff now actually have the opportunity to dedicate time to this table, and treat them like royalty in between cleaning tasks.

The staff spill into frantic scrubbing and tidying, with only an hour until dinner service is to begin. Go pee!

There's only one hour and there are twenty staff, so each are sent on breaks, carefully spread out two minutes apart, so the others can clean in between the staggering. They know what their job is – polishing cutlery, clearing tables, sweeping the floor, tending to the toilets, restocking – and who to hand over to when it's that exact two-minutes that they are due for a break. They fall from the floor like dominos, taking turns at using the bathroom, then the microwave, then the back passage for a smoke or two. If they're lucky, the chef may have left them a pasta bake to attack, but more likely, they will nourish themselves on cold chips, congealed gravy and energy drinks. As quickly as they leave, they all seem to reappear, chewing on complimentary mints they stole and smelling of teenage eau de toilette mixed with old ashtray.

Chairs are still being straightened and tables are still being allocated as the first group arrives, bearing a large cake and a bouquet of pink and purple pastel balloons. *It has to be a cake for Mother's Day, right?* The host and the manager look at each other, confirming what they both know: there are no birthdays booked for this evening.

The group approaches, confident in their stride, and the man of the house requests, "Table for eight, please."

We tell them that's not possible, at least until nine at night, as the group shuffles uncomfortably sharing their sob story about how, "We didn't realise it was Mother's Day" and "had no idea you'd have to book on a Sunday," and after all, "it's Nannie's eightieth."

You apologise profusely, wanting to help, but knowing you can't. Not tonight. Not on Mother's Day.

The other tables arrive and leave. It's not quite as hellish as the lunch session, but it's still enough to raise blood pressure and friction. At least the number of screamers has reduced significantly, and the staff might actually be able to attempt to serve without falling behind and drastically running after themselves to keep up.

The immaculately kept beautiful young waitresses who began the shift this morning, clean, fresh and athletic, had now transformed into dishevelled, sweaty lurches from the crypt. Black smudges stain under their eyes, as sauces and oils smear their uniforms.

At eleven at night, the floor is still a little shabby. The tables have been moved back to their spots, but the floors beneath them remain sticky. The staff finally sign off, and collapse into a pile of sore feet and unbelievable stories of what they survived that day.

They share jugs of beer and fits of laughter, as they check the reviews on social media. Only one has come though so far, and that was from that lady who... never mind. We tried. She was a mole. We'll write back in the morning.

It's our time now. Our reward. Our celebration. We deserve these beers as we paid tribute to the slaughter, sacrificing our families to look after yours (once again) on this day, the busiest day of the year, and the most hated: Mother's Day.

| 27 |

Not Another Walk Out

A line of guests gathered at the door, hoping to be seated. The full bar area indicated that they probably wouldn't.

There were children running happy rampages between tables, men trying to outdo each other with wine snobbery, and women teetering around in tiny heels and micro dresses laughing and singing along with the blaring music.

Servers bustled past each other, juggling hot plates against eyes vying for attention, and snapping fingers demanding it.

Then there was a table of youthly adults in Nicki's section not talking, but looking around the dining room, with the occasional whisper to each other.

Tables whose guests were not chatting were the ones to be weary of, so I had intended on checking up on them, and intended on checking in with Nicki - but I got stuck at the front desk helping the host.

I should have expected that table - given their enthusiasm practising their resting bitch faces - as freeloaders, and unable to please, but I was young and not greatly experienced. In other words, I was a bit dumb back then.

I was so dumb that as I was assisting hosting, I nearly missed them. I looked up, to watch fifteen people casually stroll past the front desk. Two of the girls glanced back guiltily, and shuffled forward faster. Sure enough, they'd just tried to walk out!

OH NO YOU DON'T.

There was NO WAY I was going to let this happen again. I would not pay for a group of fifteen. I had to stop them!

I dashed out the front door as they picked up their pace outside. They must have thought they were free, but they really shouldn't have underestimated the screamy running power of a sexually frustrated, hungry and poor restaurant manager. Plus I told you - I was dumb too.

"OI!" I bellowed, "*YOU HAVE TO PAY FOR THAT!*"

They scrambled and I ran like crazy after them, screaming at the top of my voice, "Shoplifters!"

Do you remember how I said I was dumb? I left a restaurant that I was running, alone, on a Saturday night. Oh - and I forgot to mention it to anyone else either. I left a busy restaurant to chase down some kids who skipped out on paying. I didn't think, I just ran, hoping to crash tackle at least one of them and bring them to justice.

A crowd of on-lookers froze, compelled to watch the action, curious as to who the alleged shoplifters were.

The kids (and when I say kids, they were easily in their twenties, but they were low twenties and I was mid-twenties, so therefore they were kids) split up and started running in different directions, with random members of the public heroically chasing after them.

I whirred around... *Who to follow? What do I do?* I focussed on two of the weaker looking ones and the chase was on! Pounding down the maze of corridors at the back of the shops, through fire escapes, belting along concrete floors while door after door whizzed past. I flung around a corner, desperately scanning for them.

Which way did they go?

I heard stifled laughter, and whirred to the left, flying toward them. I reached the end of the fluorescent tunnel and shoved open a heavy steel door. I was ready for my triumphant sting... but there was nothing there.

The crisp night air greeted me.

I looked around, desperate to find the perpetrators. Shuffle to the left, move back to the right. Nothing. Nothing! All I met was a deserted street.

I lost them. My heart sank.

I retreated back to work, anxious to succumb to my punishment. I really should not have left a restaurant mid-service on a Saturday. Perhaps chasing them was too far? What did I expect to do if I had caught them? Tackle them? Citizen's arrest? I really didn't think this one through, and now I had to face the consequences. Why was I feeling so guilty anyway? It wasn't even my table. I wasn't really responsible for it – was I?

As the manager on duty, I was always responsible. Blamed when things went wrong and ignored when everything went right.

If I had stood still, my butt wouldn't be on the line as much. I may have even talked my way out of it, or hidden it.

Instead, I'd reacted instinctively from classical conditioning, terrified of paying for my debts. Mavis frightened me so much that I'd become hesitant in ever making a mistake again, knowing that it wasn't a learning curve, it was a punishment.

I suspected freeloaders. I'd gotten freeloaders with a dine and dash.

Freeloaders were people who deliberately looked for something to whinge about, hoping to receive discounts, complimentary drinks or vouchers.

Most managers could see right through them.

They were the type of people who used social media as a weapon, never taking the time to complement, but jumping at the chance to criticise.

I was more than happy to compensate people who legitimately had a complaint. In fact, people who had actual complaints were usually people who never expected a discount. These were the types of people who I was more than happy to go out of my way to try and rectify the situation.

Freeloaders, however, would receive little or nothing off me. If they threatened to never return, I bid them farewell. I would rather work hard to look after people who wanted to come back. It was not worth the efforts grovelling at someone who was full of empty threats.

These kids were the worst kind of freeloaders. They had left before we even had a chance to do something – if anything – for them. They did a runner. They no longer were customers, they were thieves, and needed to be dealt with accordingly.

On my way back to the restaurant, I noticed a girl in a yellow dress. I wasn't really paying too much attention; just a girl in a yellow dress as I was making my way back, shaking my head and muttering a review of the events.

The yellow dress girl must have noticed me though, in my uniform, talking to myself, because she suddenly startled and walked faster, away from me into the loos, as quickly as she could.

I've often heard hospos say that all customers look the same, and it's true. Unless I've served them every week for a month, I'll forget a face the second I've finished serving them. I remember their drink, no dramas, but their face? Nope.

Based on this fact, she would have been off the hook, but she gave herself up when she saw me, and tried to hide away. Guilty much?

Right on queue, I saw a shopping centre security guard. These guys were always looking for a bit of wild action to spice up their important roles protecting the community.

He waited outside the ladies room for the cunning thief, then as he was sure the coast was clear of other women, he headed in. He was in there a while, so maybe he was waiting for her to do a poo. She might have been doing a line too, or simply hiding, but it was a while that the guard was in there.

He eventually escorted out the yellow dress wearing girl. She looked like a Carla, so from here, I'll call her Carla.

I'd like to tell you I was brave and assertive, but I was actually chicken and in way above my head. I really should have just let her go, but I was consumed with the power of bringing walk-outs to justice. Making her pay would be a major milestone for the hospitality industry. It'd be equal to screaming back at someone and getting away with it.

I was fidgeting with my apron, and chewed on my bottom lip nervously. I braced and told myself to look angry. If there's one thing I could pull off well, it was the subtle art of the Resting Bitch Face. I crossed my arms and glared, hoping I looked intimidating enough. I didn't need to pretend to be angry; this girl was the difference between Nicki and I having a job or not. This girl would determine whether Mavis would force us to pay out of our own pockets. I was furious.

I knew I had the right person as soon as I saw her. She really would have gotten away with it, if she didn't try to hide from me, but her face was plastered with a grudgey look that said, 'I can't believe you're still wasting my time.'

Before Carla could say a word, I smirked and said like an absolute boss, "Hello. You need to come pay your bill."

Without delay, she began to protest.

"No, I don't. Service was shizz; I'm not paying for that," she insisted with a superior air of entitlement. The fact that she argued back, instead of questioning my accusation, confirmed her guilty conscience. "I *know* what good food is, and that was rubbish. I've eaten out before, you know," she continued superiorly.

I stifle a laugh. *Did she just say that?* She literally said she's eaten out before. Who hasn't? I couldn't resist, and retorted in the same stuck up hipster-wannabe tone "Oh-em-gee, you've like actually eaten out before? Like at an actual restaurant that sells actual food? Wow it must be great being you! Bet ya'll hash-tagging the shit outta your awesome steal tonight. Hash-tag I'm awesome. Hash-tag bitches be like food stealers!"

Naturally, I was way not cool enough to be in on the lingo of the youth, so I winged it, hoping to sound like a boss, but probably sounded a bit like an idiot.

"WHAT did you just say?" Carla in the canary yellow dress demanded.

"You heard me. Come pay for your food!" I snapped.

"I am *not* paying. I am a customer! You can't speak to me like that!"

I laughed evilly, power tripping way harder than what it was worth. "You're not a customer! Customers pay! *You're a criminal!*"

She began to shout at me, arms flailing and nostrils flared.

I wondered if I'd overstepped the line. Ok, I knew I'd probably overstepped the line. It was a bit much yelling back, but these opportunities only presented themselves so rarely, and I relished in the fact that I had just done what every server secretly wanted to do: Fight back and stand up for myself.

The seccy interjected the screaming, commanding control of the situation. "So you admit to taking goods from a business without paying earlier this evening?"

I liked this guy. He knew what to do.

"But I- ah. No, I didn't 'take goods'! I just-"

"You just admitted to leaving a restaurant without paying. That's classified as stealing goods. What you need to think about now, is that out of such a large group, we only have one of you here. So unless you pay for all the meals now, you will be charged and take the fall for your mates!"

"Charged? No! I only just-" Carla stammered.

"You stole goods from a business. So either you pay for them now, or we can take you down to the station and you can pay then, and Silverman's can press charges against you!"

"What? No! I'm not paying for all of that! That's bullshizz!" Carla screamed. A little bit of bogan fringe hinted in her accent.

"I'll give you one last chance to do the right thing before I'll have to call the police," he told her matter-of-factly.

I could have hugged this burly seccy!

"Fine!" Carla snapped.

WHAT? I did it! I actually did it! This yellow dress wearing turd was being forced to pay the bill!

Struggling to fight back euphoric laughter, I skipped back to the restaurant, followed by the giant seccy escorting the dangerous criminal.

The restaurant erupted in applause!

Patrons and staff alike formed a standing ovation of cheers as this girl grudgingly paid, muttering abuse under her breath, "Unbelievable! I just can't believe she chased me! Like a *criminal!*" and, "The owner is going to hear about this!"

"Make sure you tell them the part about how you stole food and effed off!" a chef yelled at her.

I shot him a 'be appropriate!' look. There were still other paying customers to impress.

Carla exaggeratedly leaned forward and read my name tag aloud, "*Alexandra!* I won't forget that name!" she threatened.

I knew I was already going to be in a heap of trouble. The level of trouble I was sitting at was between written warning, and termination of employment. Well, if I was going to do something wrong, I may as well do it right.

"I look forward to your email," I replied in an over-the-top customer service voice. "Thank you for dining at Silverman's. I hope you have a pleasant evening."

"Eff you!" Carla screamed.

"Eff you, too," I smiled, waving at her, then flipping the bird.

All night guests were commending me on not letting her get away. Sure, it would have been easier to write it off, but I wanted to set an example: stealing is not ok. Abusing service staff is not ok. I wasn't entirely proud of causing a scene, knowing the potential social media repercussions, and dreading to think what my boss Mavis would say. It was a bittersweet moment of triumph and regret.

I decided I was darned if I did and darned if I didn't. Had I let the customers simply leave without paying, Nicki and I would have been the ones to suffer the consequences. I knew Mavis would force Nicki to pay somehow. If we didn't hand in cash then and there, Nicki would be issued a warning for neglecting tables, and her roster would be limited to the minimal two hours a week. I would probably be ok, but this would not be forgotten. I would be rostered out slowly as soon as they found a suitable replacement for me.

Having chased the kids around the restaurant complex, I had recovered the funds, but had risked reputation. The guests dining that evening enjoyed the show, so at least that was a positive. But the kids who were chased – officially customers or not – now had fuel to damage me. It was their words against mine, and the customer is always right. I knew that their complaint to Mavis would not be tolerated lightly – regardless of whether they were thieves or not. Carla the yellow dress wearing criminal could take on social media and the news. It didn't matter that she was in the wrong: as a staff member, I was wrong by default.

I filled in an incident report, outlining what happened. There was no point hiding it; Mavis would find out anyway, if not via the police, than by the others. I may as well have owned up to chasing them.

I filled out a factual incident report on what happened. Well, mostly what happened, you know, without the angry sweary bits and chase scenes. My finger hovered over the mouse, as I reconsidered clicking send. I closed my eyes and held my breath. *Click!* It was sent.

What have I done? I panicked.

It was done. Best not to dwell on it any longer.

A week later I was summoned to a meeting with the owner of the restaurant (who had never worked in hospitality before but bought a place because it would be 'fun' and 'easy'), and my favourite manager, Mavis.

I had been there for several years and was still intimidated by both of them.

It was exactly as I predicted. I sat there in silence while boss man dictated behavioural standards, with no sign of warmth or empathy. If I could remember his name, I'd tell you, but I honestly can't remember nor could I be bothered trying to figure it out.

"You should have behaved in a manner more in keeping with the reputation of Silverman's," he said tartly. "I am disgusted with you, and I'm disappointed in myself for trusting you as a manager. The customer is always right," he told me. "If they said the service was not up to scratch, they're probably right."

Wrong! The customer isn't always right, sometimes they're not even actual customers; they're arseholey thieves. Service actually was up to scratch, because Nicki is fantastic consistently, and if you ever bothered to work on the floor, you would know that!

I decided silence was the best response. My big mouth had already gotten me in enough trouble.

'The owner is always right' was my own private slogan – I knew he was *not* always right, but just like most customers, I made him *feel* like he was. Therefore, I let him say those dreaded clichéd words to me.

"So we have no choice but to issue you with a written warning for poor conduct and serious lack of judgement."

Whatever. You weren't even there that night.

I sat there in silence, glaring at them, concentrating on not tearing up. Silence had been more effective than defending my actions in the past, as a young lady who displayed any sign of defiance was a threat. I knew that they were somewhat threatened by me and wouldn't hesitate in looking for things to berate me with.

At the conclusion of the meeting, I left feeling high strung. I made a beeline to the Wood and Spoon's ladies' room to cry it out. I needn't dare use our own facilities for fear of being caught not having it all together.

While I was in there, my tears mixed with pride, relief and mascara. I peered into the scratched mirror and blotted my eyes, angry about the warning, but experiencing a soaring wave of achievement.

It was a rare and wonderful thing as a hospitality worker, being given the opportunity to actually stand our ground. All too often we're forced to stand and smile whilst unfairly being screamed at and abused, simply for the crime of working in customer service.

The night of the incident, I stood up for not only myself, but all hospitality workers. I felt as if I had lost one battle but won another.

| 28 |

PART 3: Clarkson, The Largest Supermarket in all the Land.

I love my job. I love the people, the free meals and the free drinks. The freebies aren't always frequent, and the awesome people aren't always there, but the freebies and awesomeness are worth it when they happen.

I love the fact that we can be ourselves. It's an industry where people are hired more for their personalities and big smiles than for their qualifications and experience. There are tattoos, there are piercings, bright hair colours and sexual innuendos.

If you're more of an introvert, the industry will love you for who you are too, in the form of fine dining and bars for the upper crust. No matter if you're loud or more of the quiet type, you can be yourself as long as you work hard and don't slack off.

Most of all, I love the pressure. There's pressure to keep smiling although you're flustered and pressure to keep it smooth when the world seems to crumble. It's a balancing act, keeping everyone happy while delivering the goods.

Hospitality is not too different from the month of December. It's busy. It's rushed. It's frantic. Everyone is celebrating the end of another year, their successes and their plans. In the crazy, there's pressure to get organised, the pressure to go here, there and everywhere all at once and pressure to keep it together because you love it. It's rewarding, there's lots of food, and often the boss shouts everyone drinks.

The true lifelong hospos are magnificent creatures who dedicate their lives to the cause. There is a particular romance with coming into work and doing all that you can to make the business succeed. We genuinely want everyone to be happy: the customers, the staff, the owners and the figures.

They say that if you love what you do, you never work a day in your life. I've never encountered an industry as full of love as ours. Hospitality is worth it. Being 'hospo-for-life' is not a job. It's not a career. It's a lifestyle. It didn't start like that for me though.

I accidentally made a lifestyle in hospitality whilst studying a much more respectable sounding bachelor of science. Like many people I worked with at the time, serving was a way to pay the bills (pay for alcohol) in between studying. I was the 'in the meantime' worker – in hospitality as a means to an end. As if I'd ever lower myself to becoming full time.

My unintentional career began with my first job at the local supermarket. I don't want to be sued, so we'll call this place "Clarkson" and leave it at that.

Clarkson is one of the big national chains. If you live around here, you've probably been there. Like so many corporations, it promoted itself with images of 'care' and 'quality'. The annoying jingles, the fluorescent lights, the branding and the standardised shop-fronts hinted at the fraudulent reality.

Television was enough to fool me though. I aspired to channel the ladies depicted in the ads with the bright name tags and beaming smiles, laughing as they swiped items through the checkout, thoroughly enjoying their lives there.

As much as my parents supported me as a child, as I got older it was expected I'd do things like, 'take some responsibility' and 'stop treating this house like a hotel'.

I had to get a job to help pay for my upwardly-mobile social activities - and for some reason, I thought Clarkson would be just great.

I looked forward to donning my own mustard yellow neck scarf and swiping items whilst making small talk with charming members of the community.

"So because you're sixteen, you're old enough to use knives, so we're going to put you in the deli..." mumbled Susan.

Susan was a pimply looking, twenty-something-year-old manager who left her personality at home and smelt like ham. Her hairnet failed to disguise her brittle mousey head mess, which she had shoved into a careless bun. Her eyebrows crept under her fringe, like caterpillars braving sunlight for the first time. Her oily complexion was hidden under compacted orange foundation powder. Given the warmth of the afternoon, she now appeared as if she were a hairy, frosted, sweat-glittering teacake.

I was horrified! This was not part of the plan! The deli wenches were never on TV!

"The deli?" I asked Susan apprehensively.

"Yeah... we need staff in the deli."

"The deli? Over there? With the ham?" I pointed apprehensively.

"Yes, the deli, over there, with the ham," Susan replied, wondering how difficult this concept was for the new girl to understand.

"But... but when I applied, I thought it was for the checkout job... you know, 'Service with a Smile'," I quoted the slogan hoping to prompt Susan.

"You applied to work at *Clarkson,* so you will work wherever we need you."

No.

"There are plenty of others waiting if you don't want this job," she continued. "We all have to do what is best for the business as a team. One team for one dream."

One team for one dream?

Did Susan really aspire for the best interests of Clarkson? Come on, it was *Clarkson!* Fine for a checkout job after class, but, let's be honest, people got *real* jobs eventually, didn't they? Nobody really worked in service for a career. *I* certainly wouldn't.

Susan had already started walking, expecting me to join her.

It seemed I had no choice in the matter. It was decided. I was escorted to the deli: the elusive land of frightening smells, sharp equipment and questionable meats.

I shot one last desperate look toward my fantasy checkouts.

A frumpish bored woman monotonously pulled a box of tampons across the red-lit scanner.

Beep!

Staring at nothing and ignoring the equally bored bogan she was serving, her hand slowly dragged some condoms through the checkout.

Beep!

It wasn't like the TV at all. No friendly faces, no bright smiles, no upbeat music and lots and lots of fluro lights.

"Wait!" I called Susan. "I'm coming!" I jogged after her. Surely the deli would be more interesting than this?

Interesting, yes, but there, the enigma of it all made me a little uneasy. I didn't want to be there, but I sure wasn't going back to those checkouts.

"Don't worry, we'll train you up," Susan reassured at the look of apprehension on my face.

I wasn't worried about not being trained; I just didn't want to put my hands in meat juice.

I explored the rest of the deli, finding items I was expecting. One end of the case was, I'll admit, slightly pleasant, offering cheeses, olives, and salads.

"If anyone ever asks," Susan explained, "You need to tell them we got them in pre-made, we don't make them fresh."

No one ever asked. No one would have cared. This part was ok. It was just salad. Salad couldn't hurt.

"Over here is the ham," Susan continued, pointing at the ham.

It was pretty obvious – there wasn't just a bit of ham – there were piles of it! Piles and piles of ham!

"And here," Susan pointed to the other sandwich meats, "are the other sandwich meats."

I recognised some of them: pastrami, salami and mortadella. The rest were sandwich fillings I referred to as the 'unknowns'. Who knew what devon was made from? It was cheap, it was pink, and it sold well. Berlina was the premium devon, looking slightly less pink and slightly more beige. It was still freaky mystery meat, despite the extra three dollars a kilo.

My chest was getting tight as a feeling of anxiety swept over me. What have I gotten myself into?

My eyes ran over the unknowns. A neat square of protein glared at me. It looked like gelatine with red bits in it. It reminded me of the end of a big night after I drank too many of those raspberry flavoured vodka thingys. I was grossed out by a lump of furtive jellied mystery meat, whose actual chunks of *other* mystery meats could be seen encased in the diaphanous skin within each slice.

"That's brawn," Susan proudly explained.

What?

"What's brawn?" I asked, hesitant if I really wanted to know the answer.

"Back in the day, people didn't have much money, so they made sandwich fillings with leftovers."

Devon was made with leftovers. Berlina was made with leftovers. Therefore brawn was made with the leftovers of leftovers. That's a lot of leftovers.

"So... you mean to tell me... this is *jellied leftover scrap meatloaf?*" I was disgusted! Who would eat this shit? Really?

Susan seemed a little offended. "...Some people... um... can't afford anything else." Her face burnt red as she winced. "Mostly pensioners get it, because, you know... well, they like it." Susan forced defiance but I saw what she was hiding.

Oh.

"Oh, ok. Sorry," I tried to sound genuine but felt flat. It's easy to forget that some people have nothing after one grows up with everything.

"Moving on," Susan stated.

I still felt a bit bad that I'd caused offence but Susan seemed to be over it and continued showing me the rest of the deli case.

I remained a bit overwhelmed and continued to zone out on the things Susan was saying. Thoughts whirred through my mind as I actively practised my breathing. *What am I doing here? This isn't me! This is gross! I can leave now, can't I? It was a stupid idea anyway! I just need to come here, not get fired and go home. That's it. Get enough money to fund my social life, then reap the benefits later.*

My eyes moved in horror to where Susan was going next.

Think of the money. Think of the money!

"Over here," Susan pointed to the far side of the ham. "Here's the uncooked section. You need to use blue gloves for these products."

The uncooked section was the depths of hell where cold meat went to die. This was the part I was afraid of.

Raw chicken breasts swam in bloody meat juice. Behind them were piles of bony necks, some with the heads still attached, the beady eyes forever staring into nothingness and the featherless scalps shrivelled from the cold death.

Squid tubes no one wanted to buy withered out but were still drenched in congealed soapy ocean goo and smelt like a sour salty toilet.

A small tub of maroon jellied offal, gorily flubbered together, daring someone to buy it. Nope. That's just all kinds of nope. Not touching that.

"So..." Susan began to teach me, but I was focussed on the raw meat.

I wasn't expected to touch that, right? What if some blood splattered on me? What if a fleck hit me in the mouth as I breathed? I clamped my lips tightly and vowed to become a nose breather.

"...Then wrap it," Susan droned on. She certainly knew how to keep my attention.

I pretended to listen, but I was actually focussing on the chicken giblets. I guessed they were called 'chicken giblets' because the label said, 'chicken giblets'. I stared intently at the tub of jiggly offal. They were some sort of body organ – an intestine perhaps? Maybe some ruptured spleens? Who would want to buy those? Who would consider eating them? Perhaps sometimes it's best to not ask.

"Then you give it to the customer and farewell them..." Susan continued.

"Yep," I replied automatically. "Farewell. Got it." I promised myself that I would only do this until I could get something better. 'Something better' was not in the foreseeable future, so this would have to do. At least my resume would have something on it now.

"Ok, well, have fun. I'll be in the office if you need me," Susan farewelled me mundanely.

That's it? Excellent training. I guessed I'd have to wing it. I was the boss of winging it. Time to have a crack at this 'serving people' thing. Wish me luck.

"Who was next? Yes, can I help you?" I asked politely to a line of people.

They all looked at each other, not knowing who was next.

So I smiled at them all, waiting for an indication of who to serve. My frozen smile made eye contact with each of the customers.

They all stared at me blankly.

My broad smile went through the queue again, stopping to make eye contact at every person. Maybe I wasn't doing it right.

"Can I help you? Anyone? Anyone..?" I sang out, trying to mimic the fictional shopkeepers of yesteryear, slightly waving to draw attention to myself.

The confused customers shuffled slightly, sort of half glancing at each other, but still, no one stepped forward.

Right. Well, I tried it their way, now I was going to do it my way.

I frowned, and tried again, this time *slightly* louder. "SORRY, WHO WAS NEXT PLEASE?!" I screeched to the queue, causing them to jump in unison.

The queue had come to life. They shuffled, glancing at each other, questioning who was first. Two women with designer leggings and lattes glared in deathly silence, clearly offended by my proactive chant.

A man raised his hand hesitantly, not wanting to be rude, but surely it was his turn by now? "Ah- yes? Over here?" he called to me.

I looked toward him and marched over, ready to go. It was decided. He was next.

The rest of the customers groaned, disappointed they failed to speak up. *They* were next. The designer leggings-wearing women grabbed their phones to report this travesty to the world.

"How can I help you?" I asked the brave man who raised his hand.

"What's the difference between a Kransky and a chorizo?" the man asked, pointing toward the sausage section.

I had absolutely no idea. I peered over to where he was looking and spotted a label. Confidence is key. Fake it until you make it.

"A Kransky is an eastern-European style sausage made of mostly pork, and a chorizo is a Spanish style sausage which is spiced with paprika and a bit of red chilli," I read off the back of the labels, pretending I knew it all along. "What did you need it for?" I asked confidently as if I'd done this a thousand times.

"We're making homemade pizzas," he told me nodding, impressed.

"Try the chorizo. It'll give it a bit of a kick." Winging with confidence. I really hoped his pizza wasn't ruined.

The man got the chorizo, as recommended by me!

I beamed. I'd pulled it off. I had no clue if I was right, and had never heard of those sausages before. That's all that selling food was about – being confident and convincing everyone that I was a pro – even on my first day. My ability to wing things had just paid off. Maybe this job wasn't so bad.

I glanced at the raw meat section and was reminded that food was not an industry with longevity. There'd be a *real* job after finishing studying in only a few years. Ok. It'll do just for now.

| 29 |

Yanking the Bird

The meats in the deli case were gross. The raw meats were the grossest. It was not uncommon to get flecked in the mouth with meat juice, and I saluted anyone brave enough to handle the expired seafood.

There was one thing we all fought over doing though, and that was the barbecue chickens. I say 'barbecue' like they're barbecued, but I think that's more of an interpretation. Much like instant 'mashed potato' or pasta 'sauce' in a jar.

The ovened chickens were the best! Not too icky to put into the oven, and the smell was unbelievably mouth-watering when they came out.

Although it was fine to sample the hams and salamis of the main deli case (and when I say fine, it was absolutely not fine, but it happened and the bosses turned a blind eye), one couldn't taste a whole chicken in between serving customers, because, well, it was a *whole* chicken!

We all craved that chicken. Every shift, the scent of caramelised herbs, crispy skin and flavoursome stuffing tempted us, but it was forbidden fruit, or should I say forbidden feast.

This was until Nicki devised a brilliant plan. She told me to be a bit rough when pulling the chickens off the rack. Instead of delicately prying them free, like Susan trained us, she told me that if we just gave them a big ol' yank, there'd be heaps of bits broken off the main bird and left behind on the rack, ready for us to pick off and eat bit by bit!

Reading that last paragraph back, I'm now realising why Susan wanted us to delicately pluck the chickens off. It's like she wanted the best produce for the customers. Crazy woman.

A new batch of chickens were cooked and it was my time to shine. I decided to try Nicki's new method of feeding the poor (us) and yanked the chooks off the racks, leaving behind a trail of delicious destruction.

I smashed through the remainder of the job on auto-pilot, giddy for my feast, feeling a bit naughty but mostly keen on my end of cook reward.

I bagged the chickens and presented them nicely to sell, and the oven racks were almost finished with their pre-scrub cleaning cycle. It was almost time. I couldn't wait!

The timer beeped, and I pulled the racks out again, greedily ripping off as much leftover chicken as I could and shoving the bits into a little tub I could hide under the counter.

I did a bit of a happy dance, looking forward to my deceptive dinner as I wrapped up my task.

I served two people with a bouncy little euphoria about me, beaming sunshine their way. I couldn't wait for the food! It was almost time.

Once my customers left, I crouched down and shoved a handful of bird in my mouth.

Before I continue, let's quickly revise my actions: Take chickens out of the oven; yank chickens off racks; bag up and present chickens and send oven racks through the pre-wash cycle. Once the racks were cleaned, I was free to pick off the bits I wanted to eat.

Well, karma got me. I should have delicately removed the chicken from the racks. I thought I could be smart and feed myself by deliberately ruining the produce and breaking the birds.

It only took half a bite to realise my mistake. Half a bite and I swore I wouldn't be cheeky and get a free feed again. I was an idiot, and my actions came back to bite me: I just ate some chicken that had been washed with commercial-grade detergent in an industrial oven!

I spat it out but kept the flavours and chemicals and sterility. Never again!

Served me right.

| 30 |

Initiation into the Industry

Saturday nights were slow and dreary at Clarkson. Most (civilian) people did their groceries in the morning, and by night, were out socialising – just like I wanted to, but I had to work.

I often found it funny that the more I worked, the more money I had, but I couldn't go out, because I was working. Then if I didn't get any shifts, I had plenty of time to go out, but no money to do so. In hindsight, I should have just worked and saved my money, but I was too proud to, plus I loved getting trashed with my friends.

After twelve months, I was still in the temporary job I was never really trained in but had figured it out over time. I was the absolute boss of bullshitting people, and by then had mastered the company slogan, Service with a Smile, automatically gleaming with syrupy happiness at the sight of any paying customer.

I'd become used to declining dinner invitations, and joined my already intoxicated friends after midnight at the local bars after the deli closed and I was free to leave. It helped me save money by going out later, plus Saturday nights were cruisy shifts, so I never minded. Better than being rushed off my feet.

Many people might have been in bed at that stage, like the elderly. The only people who visited a supermarket that late on a Saturday evening were either new parents who ran out of nappies or bored teens who wanted a break from smoking bongs in the park.

They say that one always remembered their first time, and I'll never forget the first night I was privy to the real industry standards of the supermarket service plebs.

Late at night, as the customers dwindled and the contemporary smooth store soundtrack crooned down the barren aisles, I removed the handle and the guard off the meat slicer.

From time to time, there are duties other than serving food that staff need to attend to. It's called side work and it's just as important as the service execution.

Chefs need to cut up vegetables for the next service. They also need to order stock, do rosters and wash dishes - yep even wash dishes. Not many places have a budget for a full time dishy.

Managers need to count tills, train staff and cover breaks. When they're not actively supporting the crew, they're doing administrative duties, like promotional strategies, chatting to reps and continually doing the roster.

Front of house staff need to polish cutlery, fill salt and pepper shakers and reset tables.

In the Clarkson deli, I needed to clean the meat slicer and close the section.

It was after eleven and the few customers were waning. Why any store would have a deli open until midnight was beyond me. Most of the late shift, I spent sampling the food and flirting with everyone. It really was a waste of labour, but that's what the bosses in their ivory towers wanted.

I looked around. It had now been maybe thirty minutes since the last customer, and enough time to try and get the place closed enough so I could play snake on my phone until midnight.

There was always the same predicament – one needed to clean the deli to make it look nice and appealing for the customers, but serving said customers would mess it up again. You know what they say: This job would be so much better if it weren't for those darn customers.

Should I start? Or would someone come to be served, making me backtrack and take longer? If I smashed through it (while still looking behind me, checking for customers), it would be done. It would be all finished and I could go home.

Then again, what if someone *did* come to be served? They had every right to – I mean, we were still open, right?

I continued to debate with myself. It was quite the predicament. The deli needed to look clean and presentable at all times. The case looked perfect, with all the tubs washed. The windows were clean and all stock had been rotated. The only thing left was the meat slicer and the floors.

There was the fear that someone might ask to have meat freshly cut. A lot of people didn't realise they could request freshly cut meats in supermarket delis. Those who did, requested it every time. Every single effing time. I'd heard horror stories of girls cleaning the slicer, then having someone ask for freshly cut meat at five minutes to close. Of course, we were obliged to, and of course, we served with a smile, but we sure hated you for it.

The slicer was the trickiest thing to clean and took the longest. I decided that no one would be doing a full grocery shop that late on a weekend night, and absolutely no one would be coming to the deli.

So I started to clean it.

Just quietly, I actually loved to deep clean things.

I pulled that meat slicer apart and scrubbed the individual pieces deeply, round and round, up and down, slowly with the scratchy distorted echo of the music, then frantically intensely to remove a small stain that wouldn't budge.

They were washed, then blasted with scorching water that steamed fiercely, then left to dry so every part of fatty residue evaporated, leaving a shiny metallic spotless surface. So fresh!

My fingers resembled prunes and there was a distinct whiff of bleach about the air: two things that determined achievement.

I glanced behind me – still no customers.

Celebrating that it would be an early close that night, I did a little happy dance, excited about the upcoming vodkas at the Wood and Spoon with my trashy mates.

All that was remaining to finish the meat slicer was the most delicate part – a razor-thin circular blade sheathed by a clunky medieval cutting mechanism. I began gently, sopping blotches of green soapy water onto the deli-meat flecked surface. I scrubbed at the ham residue with a toothbrush, viciously rubbing the disc until it ran smooth. Around the back were the scraps that fell and squished in a meaty pile – they would have to be removed, or they would rot, potentially risking health.

I'll be honest when I say they *did* train me to wear meshed gloves whilst doing this. I *did not* wear the communal meshed gloves because they were disgustingly moist and littered with meat and I felt icky knowing other people's hands had been in there. So I chucked them out, then lied later when they questioned me about it.

I glovelessly reached over the blade and carefully began flicking bits of meat out from underneath. I always loved it when they smacked the wall, dripping slowly onto the floor, even though it provided more work for me at the end. It's a twisted game, hurling bits of food at hard surfaces and watching them slither down and die.

There was just one lumpy chunk that the toothbrush couldn't quite flick out. I gave it several good stabs but it remained trapped. No matter how I jiggled it, it stayed put. Right. How do we get this one out?

I gingerly reached around and found it with my fingers; a mangled piece of fatty pork trapped around a screw. I delicately tugged at the pork to try to release it. It wouldn't budge. Tug... tug... tug... almost there...

THUNK!

"CAN I GET SOME SERVICE?!" bellowed a man as his broad hand slammed against the counter demanding me be at his full attention immediately!

I leapt in the air, ripping my hand out from under the slicer, heart racing. "WHAT?!" I spluttered. In my shock, I hastily turned, doe-eyed, frantically grasping to comprehend what kind of a person *did* that? A simple, 'Excuse me' would have sufficed. Even, as much as I resented it, I would have preferred the quiet little 'ah-hem' throat clear old ladies often did.

This man felt he needed to slam his hand down to frighten me! *What kind of a person did that?*

His angry why-aren't-you-serving-me expression quickly jolted to a concerned surprise.

I must have really pulled one heck of a how-dare-you glare.

We eyed each other off.

I murderously scowled at him.

Instead of retorting, the man cowered, looking more worried, and turning ghostly white, unable to speak. He must have realised what a douche he was.

I triumphantly sneered, knowing I'd taught that bastard a lesson on etiquette. He'd never spring on a service worker again.

He swallowed and clenched his jaw, sweating, pointedly looking at my hand, as if to tell me, "Go on, look!"

Something, I guessed, was very, very wrong. I wondered why my arm was wet. Until I saw it, I hadn't felt it. A crimson river pulsated down my hand and the warm gushing fluid, spilt down my arm, dripping onto the floor.

"My finger!" I screamed.

The man was dumbfounded by the repercussions of his impatient palm slam.

Without thinking, I wrapped my other hand around it, squeezing pressure. I could feel my pulse in my fingers, pounding down my arm.

I pushed past the horrified man, stumbling through the canned food aisle to the front service desk where I knew help would be available.

As I clamber along, my pulse grows more pronounced in my arm. The creaky music loudened to a blaring ringing - the only thing I could focus on through a foggy cloud. I could see the white lights in the tunnel, and forced myself to dig through it to the sanctuary of confectionery and smokes.

I managed to get all the way from the rear of the store to the service desk before I hazily collapsed into Susan's arms.

Susan was clearly concerned there was a bloody mess all over her staff member, and, more importantly, all over her pale laminate floors.

Susan proved to be as tough as nails and had no trouble carrying me back out to the staff area and into the butchery to find a first aid kit.

Susan had graduated into a straight forward anti-bullshit-taking store manager. I admired her bravery, resilience and dedication. I admired her majestic mullet even more.

Anti-bullshit Susan and her majestic mullet propped bleeding me onto the stainless steel bench in the butchery. At least the mess would be contained in the curved edges – a butchery is designed for handling lots of blood.

I was a bit of a woose and whimpered stupidly at the pain throbbing from my mangled finger.

Susan located the first aid kit, opened it and found nothing but a pair of scissors and some duct tape. That was all. Failing to find a bandage, she grabbed a questionable cloth and strapped it to my hand. It was clumsy and bulky, held together with workman's tape, but it was helping stem the bleeding.

I looked gravely at the lumpy dressing. Surely a big chain like Clarkson would have better procedures than this?

* * *

A nurse examined my hand, carefully peeling off the cloth, which was now stuck with clotted blood. The cab ride to the hospital had cost me my entire wage for that shift. No, I never got reimbursed for it. Hours later, as the night sky lightened to a pale grey and the birds began to chirp, I was finally being seen.

Lightning shot down my arm. I flinched as my muscles contracted instinctively. I looked at my finger in disgust. My index finger was gashed violently. Thick crimson blood oozed its way down my hand. I winced as I was sure I could see my pulse through the ripped muscle. I could certainly feel every heartbeat. A flaky crust covered my hand where the blood had dried.

I looked down at my shirt. It looked as if a massacre had occurred. I had instinctively held my hand against my chest, and it was evident in deep red slash marks. I chuckled thinking about how long it would take to clean the stains, knowing Susan would prefer that, to losing money by issuing an extra uniform.

The nurse carefully cleaned and stitched the gaping wound. Despite a local anaesthetic, I still flinched at the pulling of the threads, feeling like a doll being sewed back together.

An embarrassingly pop-tastic song blasted from my phone.

The nurse suppressed a snort, disapproving of my poor taste.

My secret shame had been revealed: I was into pop music, and not the cool kind. I snatched my phone, attempting to answer before any more of the song could play. 'Clarkson' flashed across the screen. I felt a little rude to answer my phone whilst being stitched, but it was Clarkson calling; they probably had some instructions or procedures for me to follow since I was injured. I didn't want to answer, but I didn't not want to, so I did. I shouldn't have.

"Hello?"

"Hey mate, it's Susan."

"Hi." For some reason, I felt like maybe I'd done something wrong.

"Hey, I wanted to ask... ummm... how's the hand?"

"It's..." I winced uncomfortably. "It's a bit sore. I've got stitches and they have to tape it to my shoulder to keep it up... so I guess I've only got one hand for now."

"But you're ok?"

I was surprised. It was really lovely of Susan to call first thing in the morning to check up on me. "Yeah, I'm ok," I smiled. So, so innocent.

"Ok, great," Susan seemed relieved. "So, ah, mate, the reason I was calling was to see if maybe you can come into work today?"

"Ah- really?"

She couldn't be serious – could she? I was such an idiot! Of course she wasn't calling to check up on me!

"I'm still at the hospital! I've pulled an all-nighter and I'm literally getting my stitches put in right now!"

"So you'll be done soon?" Susan pressed.

"Um, I... I guess? Hang on a minute." I covered the phone and turned to the nurse. "Sorry, but do you think it'd be cool if I worked today?" I whispered.

"You've just got stitches! Didn't you say you work at a supermarket?" The nurse was shocked.

"So is that a no?" I asked. I was worried. If I were to turn down this shift, I mightn't be rostered again. I'd seen it happen before. They only did favours for us when we did favours for them. My hand hurt - it really hurt! Surely I deserved a day off? I wasn't rostered on to begin with - she was asking me a favour. That meant that I *could* say no. It's ok to say no - right?

"Hi, Susan? You there?"

"Yeah, mate."

"Is... is there anyone else who can do it? I'm really not feeling good."

Susan paused. "Mate. You know I wouldn't call you in unless I needed to."

Shit.

My hand will be fine. It'll be fine. It's a good hospital and she's a good nurse. If it's taped up, it wouldn't be much different to chilling at home – right?

"So there's no one else... that's it?" I asked meekly one more time.

"Mate, you'd really be helping us out."

I wondered why the other staff could say no and I could not. Where was everyone else? Who called in sick? I was in the hospital with stitches! Perhaps everyone else had completely severed limbs. Mine was merely a deep gash. A wave of pain seared and I felt nauseated. Pinpricks tingled my side as a hazy blanket washed over my face. How would I possibly stand and work all day if I couldn't keep well whilst sitting?

"Look, Susan, I can't. I'm too sore," I said defiantly.

Susan sighed. "I asked you because I thought you were a team player," she said quietly. "I was going to get you to train the new girl this week too. I guess you'll be too sick to do that too though," she said sadly. "So I guess I'll have to take you off the roster then until you're better then."

Shit. So I had to work or I wouldn't have any more shifts. Work with an injury and prolong the healing process, or stay home and risk losing my job.

"Your call mate, but I'll need to know now. Can you work or will you be too sick for the rest of the week?"

"Ok. Ok fine, I'll do it," I'll mumbled.

"Thanks, mate! That's great! See you soon!" Susan beamed, then hung up before I could change my mind.

| 31 |

The Thing I Learnt Whilst Working in a Supermarket

I had learnt to take this job with a grain of salt. It wasn't glamorous, but it helped pay for things (alcohol) while I studied. That beacon of graduation became the reason for coming to work each day: a real job was just around the corner. It had been fun sometimes, and not so great at other times.

I'd learnt how to work the system. I used to eat all shift. They never gave me enough breaks, so why not? My pay was ridiculous, Susan and the other managers thought they're gods and, well, you really have to know the products before you sell them, so I did it! Sneak a mouthful of ham here and there. Hide an arms-length of a cabanossi to sneak a bite every time I'd walk into the dish room. Swallow the salad which I knew wouldn't sell by Friday. Accidentally drop a fresh 'barbecue' chicken on a clean floor, shouting, "Whoopsie!" so it had to be wasted. I earned it.

The silver scar on my finger stood as a badge of honour, but also as a constant reminder to get out while I could. Two years was enough and the end was nigh. Only a year left. Then one day, a man ordering some chicken breast became a catalyst for a sudden departure.

"I want to see the breasts better," he insisted, and who was I to deny this request.

"Ah... sure." I reached into the chilly case and selected a breast of chicken. I held it up for size, awaiting the customer's seal of approval.

He leaned forward and looked me in the eye. He pointedly looked down a bit, then back at my face again. "No. I want other breasts," he said quietly.

The hair on my neck pricked up. Was he asking me about meat still? I decided to give him the benefit of the doubt. In my brightest Customer Voice, I said, "We're actually getting our delivery tomorrow, so these are the only chicken breasts we have left. Did you want to get them, or..?" my voice trailed off as I waited for him to respond.

He was intently staring at my almost flat chest – or was it the chicken just below it? He wasn't talking about chicken – was he? He had to be talking about chicken, surely.

He blew a kiss and winked creepily, a slight chuckle under his breath.

My heart sank as I guessed what was going on. I looked around, but there were no other staff to save me. I thought about reaching for the intercom but was frozen on the spot. All I could think about was how to get rid of this disturbing man.

What was I to do? Should I say no? Should I just say yes and lift up my top to get it over with? Should I reach over and punch him, then run around and kick him in the balls? Should I just run? Or should I just pretend I misunderstood, play dumb and act innocent?

It's so easy to be in a safe environment and consider what one would, or should do. It's not easy to actually be there and react the planned or proper way. Girls can be trained in self-defence and assertive behaviour, but when under threat, instinct takes over. Fight or flight.

What do I do? Am I imagining this? What do I do?!

So I did what instinct told me to do - I froze. I nervously repeated myself, "Are you getting this chicken?" I looked at my feet, hiding my vulnerability from him, ashamed I wasn't braver. He was probably only talking about chicken. It must have been my imagination; customers don't say things like that – do they? Men don't say things like that – do they?

He leaned over the counter and came so close I recoiled from the smell of his odour.

My eyes welled, as I was paralysed, forced to make eye contact with him.

"I want the *other* breasts," he specified, pointing to my chest again – or was it the chicken just beneath it?

I *knew*, but, despite my pounding chest and shaky hands, I was a customer service assistant and not a young woman. The customer service assistant asked, "Which chicken would you like?" while the girl inside silently screamed, terrified of the implications, unsure of what to do.

Do I just keep serving him? Do I walk away, ignoring him? Do I yell and tell him he was being inappropriate? What was I supposed to do? *Is* there a 'right' thing to do? Really, he was only asking about chicken. He was only asking about chicken. He was doing nothing wrong. Just asking about chicken. Chicken!

He laughed quietly to himself, revealing feral teeth and confirming a true intention.

I froze, focussing on his decaying teeth while he intimidated me. "Which breast would you like to buy today?" I whispered defiantly, as a final effort for redemption.

"No. You silly girl! Can't you get it?" he smirked at her, smacking his hand on his forehead, as if he couldn't believe how stupid this girl was. "I want the other breasts! Show me your other breasts!" he taunted, "Show me your breasts you stupid girl!"

I backed away shakily. "N-" I croaked, unable to get a word out.

Deep breath. Compose. Try again.

"No," I said firmly, putting on a brave face but fighting back the tears. "No!" I screamed. I tried not to stumble as I moved towards the manager's office, leaving the deli unattended – an expressly forbidden action - and the man standing there alone.

I found Susan, re-drafting a roster.

"Hey," Susan greeted.

I stared, terrified of what to say. Should I say something? Or just go back to work?

"Hello?" Susan demanded, turning toward me and glaring.

I had better say something, for I was wasting time now. "He wanted to look at my chicken!" I blurted.

"He... what?" Susan asked.

"Well, I don't know exactly. He was talking about chicken, then breasts, then he wanted more, but I'm sure it was chicken, but I got scared for some reason. I think he wanted to see my boobs but it was just chicken he asked for. I don't know," I rambled.

As much as Susan took advantage of me as a manager, she was still a woman, and secret girls code meant that she understood, believed me, and had my back. In fact, in all my career, every woman has supported each other when it came to harassment, because chances are it's happened to them too.

She asked me to describe him. I couldn't. The only thing I could remember was him asking about chicken. Just chicken. Nothing else. He asked about chicken and I flipped out because...? It didn't matter; Susan was going to clear this all up and things would be back to normal in no time.

We flicked through the security footage and found him in the dog food aisle. Two teenage daughters jogged toward him happily, carrying packets of chips.

I was disgusted. He had been alone at the deli. He took an opportunity to act when they were in another aisle. He was a dad! His daughters were *my* age. That scummy bastard was a *dad!* Surely a parent would know better? I felt sick.

Susan and her majestic mullet went to deal with him.

I sat and had a cup of tea. It was the perfect temperature. Tea is a fastidious drink: too hot and it was too hot. Too cold, and it was ruined. It needed to be just right to have the desired calming effect I craved. I took a sip, then drew in a larger mouthful, and succumbed to its relaxing warmth, hugging my fingers around the ceramic mug. This cup of tea was my safe place. I was protected as long as I held my cup.

Susan barged back into the staff room, telling me he was gone, and acting like I should be grateful for her support.

"'Our Staff Come First'," she quoted, nodding to the Clarkson Core Values emblazoned on the wall.

Really? 'Our Staff Come First'? I was glad Susan had my back, but the damage was already done.

Our staff come first. Those words resonated within me. Here was a manager telling me what I needed to hear. 'Our staff come first'. It was textbook corporation lies – a line fed during training to demonstrate trust in the management team. A 'value' blaring across every staff area wall, to remind the team they looked like they cared when in actual fact it was a mere suggestion. It had no real meaning.

I looked down at the jagged white scar across my finger. Clarkson's staff never came first. There was no first aid kit when I slashed myself on a meat slicer. That customer who caused the injury just left without reprimand. I was 'forced' to work the next day. They didn't give a shit about me. Susan didn't give a shit about anyone except herself. Asking the man to leave would make her look good, like a hero. Susan was only helping me to cover her own butt.

She was trying to be nice but I saw straight through her. One sentence was all it took for me to realise what a sham the whole company was. The TV ads with the happy checkout ladies didn't represent the lurches who slumped across the counter, grunting at customers and counting down the hours until they were free. The slogan, 'Service With a Smile' was merely a rough guide, for all the staff operated with the consensus that the only customers who deserved a smile would be the ones who smiled first, while all the others should go eff themselves. Now fake Susan and her mullet were feeding me lines in an attempt to show 'Clarkson Cares'. Clarkson did care – about profits. They did not care about the wellbeing of their team.

I felt violated. I'd put trust in my job at Clarkson. It wasn't glamorous, nor did it have longevity, but I'd learnt to like it and wanted to stay there at least until I'd finished studying. Now I'd been hurt and they failed to take care of me properly. They'd let me down. Again.

I looked at Susan and the life she led. Susan had nothing except for Clarkson. Her whole life was an obsession with a supermarket. A supermarket which always came first, despite it destroying her soul.

One sentence from Susan was all it took for me to learn an important lesson about working in a supermarket: Get out while you can, or you'll end up just like them.

I still had ethics and values. I vowed to never end up like her.

The next day I resigned.

| 32 |

PART 4: The Wood & Spoon, Your Local Pub

The Wood and Spoon is your local. Whether it be owned by a supermarket monopoly, or by a guy who thought it would be fun to buy a pub, you've been there. It is the heart of every small town. It is the place to go watch the footy. The place where you catch up for trivia every Wednesday. The place you take the family, because there's Kids Eat Free and a playground.

The supermarket pubs are easy to spot if you look for the associated bottleshop next door. If you can't find the bottleshop (depending on which state you're in depends on the location), then simply look at the branding of the artwork and promotions. A sign saying, 'Guaranteed Opening Hours' (definitely *not* directed at pokie players, because, you know, that would be predatory), a menu that is *way* too big with a confusing fusion of cuisines, and a lack of soul are the obvious cues.

If you had any kind of ethics, you'd support your local independent. It's family owned, *not* run like discount bottled jar sauce, and the food's actually good.

Every pub has the same uniform: ugly leather non-slip soled shoes which cover the entire foot. Lace-less because they are frequently a trip hazard, and, let's face it, who could be bothered with laces? Comfortable and safe. Some girls will opt for ballet flats - which infuriates me when I see them behind a bar. Their feet are only a broken glass, a stampede, or a hot oil spill away from ruin.

If you're a new employee, err on the side of conservative, donning black jeans, a black shirt and hair pulled into a pony. Clean and fresh, yet unfamiliar. Just right.

Once you get to know them, they'll either enforce strict regulations, or they'll let you be in whatever outfit you want, as long as you work hard. The funnest places to work welcome staff with tattoos, coloured hair, piercings, loud voices and infectious laughter.

If you're a customer and the full timers know your name and your drink, you're in the right place. If the casuals know your name and your drink too, it's even better.

The supermarket pubs avoid creativity in their teams, preferring a streamlined approach across hundreds of venues, embracing words like 'compliance' while denying micro-management.

The independents prefer fresh ideas, and allow autonomy and trust in their team. After starting in the supermarket pubs (and I've worked for them all) and moving to independents, I can assure you that independents win hands down, and I will *never* work for a supermarket pub again.

My last job in a supermarket pub lasted four days. Four days of poisonous people, constrictive policies and straightjacket freedom. If it came between walking in there again, or gauging out my eyes with a screwdriver, I'd probably roll with the screwdriver.

The venues I've worked in have varied from greatness to terrible, and from trendy to dated and downright creepy. Let's start with the latter.

The Wood and Spoon was run by a man named Dean who bore an inflated ego and weak handshake. The pub was clean, with charming old furniture and strategically draped with throw cushions, intending on looking as if they were tossed there. There was a fireplace with a grand wooden mantelpiece surrounded by patchy maroon leather chesterfields and square ottomans. A glittering chandelier sparkled in the afternoon sun, rays beaming through the high windows.

The pub boasted a large restaurant, a sports bar, ten disturbingly dodgy ("boutique") hotel rooms, a place to bet on the horses, a gaming room and a large function centre - all of them almost empty.

I looked closer and saw the pub for what it was. Despite its image of being 'iconic', The Wood and Spoon was in shambles.

The decrepit carpet and mouldy ceilings were remnants of the once bustling locals bar. In its heyday, it was so full, they couldn't get any more people in. Now it was so quiet, they couldn't get any more people in. Either you can't get them in, or you can't get them in. At all. It was no longer packed, but eerily empty.

The same five men (who I nicknamed all 'old mate') sat in the quiet sports bar, occasionally getting up to order a beer. The bar staff polished spirit bottles for the umpteenth time, and pretended to look busy at the hint of a manager. A dozen large wooden picnic tables sat idly in the beer garden, waiting patiently for occupation that never came. Chef sat reading a paper, not daring to prep food that would go to waste. Upbeat music played to deaf ears, for the only people left were punters and gambling addicts, neither of whom were listening.

Upstairs, however, held promise. The function rooms had been recently renovated, creating an oasis of modern glamour in the otherwise dated dungeon.

Dean challenged me to improve the sales in the food area, seemingly the department that held the entire pub together – a very important trait. I looked at the empty restaurant, and decided to start in functions until eleven - restaurants were easier to view procedures while they're open and in action. I headed upstairs.

A dainty young girl with Resting Bitch Face looked up from behind the office desk. Her greeting was more of a scowl as she asked me which party I was booked for. I really hoped she didn't speak to customers like that.

I had to force a warm smile, for I too suffered from Resting Bitch Face. I bared my teeth, trying to look friendly, but I think it came across looking more like a circus clown on pills, both terrified and ecstatic .

Michelle was shoved into her role when there was no one else to fill it. She used to be a promo model, and then a bartender. She became the pub's shitkicker, doing everything from waiting tables to washing dishes, gaming, betting and maintenance. I was amazed she'd never worked at Clarkson. When the last functions manager left, Michelle picked up the slack, and clearly resented the fact that I may be cutting her grass.

I asked to see the functions package.

Michelle rolled her eyes and grabbed a stapled bundle of paper, and shoved it in my face.

I examined the 'package' with disdain. I cringed at the use of computer generic type fonts highlighted by cartoon-esque headings which made my eyes burn. No one should use that font. No one. The document attempted sophistication in its language, but it was let down by spelling mistakes and sketchy outdated grey photos. It had pushy instructions, demanding certain obligations from customers. It was trashy and cheap, just like Michelle.

I walked around the desk and picked up the phone and called the Lonsdale Tavern. "Hi! I was wondering if you do parties?" I jabbered down the phone. "That's great. Yes. Maybe about ninety people? It's for my thirtieth… Katie. Katie Jones. Thanks!" I hung up smiling.

Idiotic Michelle stared, fascinated with what I did. "Why did you tell her your name was Katie?" Clearly, brains were not her forte.

"I wanted her to think I was a guest." I grabbed my phone and found what I was looking for. "See – I just got her to email me their functions package."

"But we already have one," Michelle said with ennui.

"I want theirs to compare to ours and fix it," I replied.

"It's fine," Michelle insisted, growing threatened by my motivation. "We've always used this one and it works fine."

I asked her what was booked that week.

She looked at the diary in the computer to check, and told me there was nothing booked.

I asked her what was booked next weekend.

Michelle looked at the screen again. She couldn't remember the empty diary slots she'd just seen. There was nothing then either.

"That's why we need a new one," I told her. "So we can portray to our guests that *we* are the place they need to have their function at."

Michelle raised an eyebrow and snickered.

I was fully aware of the challenges I faced. Time to get to work.

| 33 |

The Wrong Booking

Everywhere I've worked, I've enforced the rule of receiving a non-refundable deposit before an event is actually booked. Most guests don't question it, but some managers have. History has taught me that the general public are just excellent at letting everyone down. Unless they're locked in with cash, there'll be those wanting to stuff everyone around.

When I say 'non-refundable', we would, of course, have incidents when we would refund and deposit. Say for example, we have a wedding booked and the bride is abducted by a motorcycle driving ninja. Refund granted. The pub burns down? Refund granted. Coronavirus causes society to shut down? There's a refund on that too.

Reasons for not refunding (that people have actually tried!) include:

- My friend has her party booked there the week prior.
- We didn't realise there'd be so few vegan items on the menu (*We're happy to create some, but, no, you can't just cancel*).
- We booked our engagement party, but... we broke up.

Call me tough, but these have all happened really close to the booked date. With more notice, I could have worked things out. Within two weeks, we have ordered their food and rostered staff. I can't just send food back. I can't just remove staff from the roster and tell them they may not be able to afford rent that week.

The phone rangs in the office and I leant over to answer it.

A man started to explain his predicament, asking for a refund on a function deposit, and cancellation of a booking.

I felt a pit in my stomach. I'd never had a cancellation before. I wondered what I'd done wrong. I tried to ask the man why - quite delicately – there may have been a death in the family for all I knew.

It turned out it wasn't a family emergency at all.

The man who called and asked for a refund, had paid a deposit to us (the dingy pub down the road) when he 'meant' to book in at Rutherford (a five star hotel with a snot covered buffet). Not kidding.

I had to clarify on the phone a few times just to be clear on what the man had done. I looked through confirmation emails, all with our letterhead and signature lines; I found the booking form, again with our letterhead, and I had also given him a tour of our venue! There was no way that anyone could have gotten it wrong - he'd booked his party at the Wood and Spoon and it was confirmed!

He would not budge and kept repeating himself, "I booked it in with you, but I thought you were Rutherford!"

I figured out what he did. It was usually a trick people played for dinner bookings – this was the first time some scumbag decided to do it with a private function.

What normally happens, is a party host books a table at a dozen different restaurants, just to secure their place. On the night, the group decides where to eat and rocks up to one place, leaving the other places as a 'no show'. No need to worry about getting a table if you've booked everywhere. Too bad for the other restaurants that miss out!

What this knob-jockey did was the same thing, but on a private party scale. He booked a function room in every venue in town, then decided on which one - three weeks before - then cancelled the rest. What a spectacular waste of time!

Too bad, he got me on the phone. I'd make him pay. I sat on my high horse and gave him what for.

"Look, you have confirmed the booking with us, and acknowledged the terms and conditions. Plus, there's a big email signature saying WOOD & SPOON! Therefore I cannot offer you a refund at this time."

He went ballistic. He demanded his money back - his accent becoming more pronounced as he grew angry.

"I'm sorry, Sir, you have signed our terms and conditions, stating that the deposits are non-refundable, so I will *not* refund it for you," I told him loudly. "We cannot rebook that room with such short notice."

"You will refund the deposit this instant!" he shouted.

"I'm sorry, but that's not going to happen," I firmly stood my ground.

"You taking advantage! You ripping me off!"

No, I didn't misspell there. He said it wrong.

"How am I taking advantage of you? You thought the pub was a hotel! Please, Sir, stop screaming at me, so we can discuss this like adults," I replied.

He ignored me and kept firing away at me. He rambled on and on about not being able to afford it, and "You should do the right thing!" persisting that I refund him his money. There was no way I could do that – we were now several thousand dollars behind target because of his sneaky trick. A cancelled booking does not purchase a food and beverage package. Plus – he was being pretty rude!

After a few minutes of holding the phone out from my ear (it was that loud), I had lost my patience. I didn't feel like being screamed at. I drew several breaths, trying to determine the correct starting point. He was on a roll, going so quickly. I was fed up and decided it was easier to just go, so I screamed down the phone at him, "You will stop yelling at me, or I will hang up the phone! You will be courteous or this conversation is over!"

He started again and was quickly greeted with a dial tone as I slammed the receiver down.

I was shaking. How dare he!

The phone rang again. I took a deep breath to try to sound professional – it could be anyone calling. Deep breath, and smile, "Wood and Spoon, this is Al-"

"How dare you hang up on me!"

Dammit.

I hung up again.

The phone rang again.

I could ignore it. *It could be a client,* I worried. "Wood and Spoon, this is Ale-"

"You stupid bitch! You not listening! You rude! You rude!"

Again, no misspelling. That's what he said. I hung up.

The phone rang again.

It could be a client. It kept ringing as I looked at it, debating whether to answer again.

It went silent – Tim downstairs answered.

I jumped as the connection tone sang out from my line.

I hung up.

It rang again.

I stared at it.

It kept ringing.

I stared at it.

Ring... Ring... Ring... Ring... Ring...

I stared at it. I gave up. I sang out a greeting, unable to help myself at using my Customer Voice.

A quieter tone responded threateningly. "I want to speak with the manager."

I decided to respond, for he finally ceased his abuse and was conversing at a more humane level. "Yes, I am the manager. How can I help you?"

"Not you!" he retorted.

"Careful or I'll hang up again," I threatened.

He paused, likely to compose himself. "I want to speak to the senior manager, who is in charge."

I knew what he was asking. I put on my smarmiest Customer Voice and replied, "Why yes, of course, Sir, hold on one minute," then reverted back to my own sound, "It's me! I'm the manager."

"No, you don't understand. I don't want to talk to you. I want the big boss man."

Yep, that's what I guessed he wanted. "Well, unfortunately you're going to have to settle for a woman. I am the only manager here, and the only one willing to listen to you. So, I'll ask again, how may I help you?"

"I want to speak to the boss man, not you, little girl!" he spat down the phone. Enough was enough.

"I am the boss! *I'm* in charge! And I'm the only one who might help you! So you'd better be nice!" I bellowed over his ranting. I slammed down the phone. I was shaking with fury.

The phone rang again.

I picked up the receiver and dropped it back down without so much as a listen. I winced as I remembered the possibility that that may have been another client trying to call. I picked the phone up again and paged the main bar, telling Tim to ignore the phone, and that I'd handle it.

I paced around my office, replaying my attack in my head. I could feel my face burning hot, and noticed the sweat dripping under my clothes. Should I remove my cardigan to cool down? I would be risking wet patches, potentially offending the afternoon clients. Keeping it on would surely overheat me though. I continued to pace, shaking my head and whispering profanities under my breath. This guy was obviously not going to leave me alone. What to do?

Ring... Ring... Ring...

It was difficult to think with the shrill blare of the ringer piercing my mind. What to do? What to do? How would I get him off my back?

Ring... ring... ring...

I picked up the phone and slammed it again. Then...

Ring... Ring... Ring... It started again.

Was there a way to turn that noise off? Could I call the phone company and get them to block the caller? If only there were a way to make him spend his money another way. What to do?

Ring... Ring... Ring...

There was! An idea popped into my head. If he didn't want to spend money at a function here, I'd make him spend it on something else!

Ring... Ring... Ring...

I couldn't take it anymore. "Wood and Spoon!" I sang. "This-"

I heard the bar staff downstairs cheer at the peaceful silence.

"You don't hang up! You listen to me!" a wicked voice demanded.

"No, *you* listen to *me!*" I bellowed.

"No, you don't hang up! I am paying customer! I have rights!" he cried. He still couldn't get the sentence correct, and before you say anything about anything - English was definitely his first language. I usually wouldn't mind, but he was being so rude. Luckily he didn't say 'youse' or I would have really lost it.

"No, you don't hang up! I am paying customer! I have rights!" he cried.

"Yes!" I screamed.

"I'm paying customer-" he ranted.

"YES, YOU ARE!" I thundered.

He finally stopped yelling at me.

"You *are* a paying customer, because I will *not* refund you. Do you hear that? You're *not* getting a refund – so stop asking!" I screamed violently, causing my throat to catch.

I heard a protesting breath begin to argue, so I cut him off and continued. "I have a proposal which you will need to either accept – in writing – or decline and you will lose your deposit."

Silence.

"My offer is to invite your family to dinner in the bistro on Monday night, to spend your money then. As you well understand, we are *not* issuing you a refund, but under these extenuating circumstances, we feel that it's plausible to *transfer* your deposit. Do you accept?"

There was silence for a while, before he questioned the offer fishily. "So you want us to come to a $500 dinner?"

"That is my final offer, and this offer expires in five minutes, or I will disconnect the phone and you will lose your money," I dictated.

"What if we spend less than $500 at dinner?" He was trying to find loopholes.

I wasn't having a bar of it.

"You lose the rest. You will not receive any change."

"Ok, ok, so what if we spend more?" he was still searching for ambiguities.

"You will pay the difference!" I stopped caring if she sounded nice. "It's quite simple, I will give you $500 credit toward a dinner on Monday - *this* Monday – and if you go over that amount you will pay and if you go under, that's your loss! Let's not forget, this is a huge favour! *You're the person stupid enough to book the wrong venue!*' I snapped. "I will email you a confirmation and book you a table. You will write back and confirm, or the deal is off!"

"So I need to confirm on the phone or in writing?" He was trying to trip me up.

"In writing, and the deal is for Monday this week at 6pm only, do you understand?" I shrieked.

"Ok," he said, and hung up.

I smashed out an email to him with very explicit instructions. I read it. I re-read it again, searching for loopholes – this was just the kind of guy who would try taking me to the cleaners.

I closed my eyes and clicked 'send'.

After it was sent, I slumped into my chair and stared into space. My head pounded and I shook with fury. Definitely time for a scotch and ciggie soon.

Ring... Ring... Ring... That bloody phone again!

I was dreading that phone by now. I rolled my eyes and restrained myself from simply screaming, '*What?!*'

"Wood and Spoon," I grunted.

"Oh thank you! Thank you so much!" he praised loudly. His entire tone had changed from vehement to joyous.

"Heh?" I meekly asked. Was this the same man?

"Oh you've saved me! God bless you! You angel! You so kind!" he praised.

I was disgusted. "You're welcome!" I snapped and hung up.

I get quite perturbed that customers often believe that nasty behaviour is the only way of getting what they want. It isn't. That's what bullies do. This man represented the many who refused to ask nicely. Instead he expected a poor response from me, so abused me first. It wasn't right. It wasn't fair. I would much rather help those who are nice and don't expect it. Nice people really *do* finish last. Bullies are winners, and by me succumbing to his needs, I inadvertently supported his cause. I hate myself for it, but what other choice did I have? How long before he would have given up?

I hoped that awful man didn't use this as encouragement for next time he dined out. I was thankful I stuck by my decision not to refund him completely.

The next afternoon, Michelle was looking at the diary computer. "What happened to the booking on the fifteenth?"

"Don't even ask," I sighed, "It's all sorted now; he's coming for dinner on Monday instead."

"He's what?" Michelle shot me a disapproving look.

"He's coming in for dinner on Monday," I replied casually. "Long story, but I sorted it."

Michelle's eyes narrowed as she blew up at me, "*What* do you mean he's coming for dinner?" she roared.

Who was this? Where was lazy Michelle? I was so shocked by her stance, I was forced down in her chair while she huffed in between rapid screeching.

"This is ridiculous! You've been changing everything and putting in all these rules and you won't even follow them yourself! You think you're so good, but -"

"I *am* so good!" I interjected, "We actually have bookings for once!"

"Not if you keep cancelling them and letting people get away with keeping their deposit!"

"It's not like that!" I yelled back, "This is an extenuating circumstance-"

"It's like you want to run this whole department yourself when we're meant to be a team!" Michelle grabbed her things and stormed out.

It was true. I would have much preferred to run things myself. Michelle was a deadweight, doing the bare minimum and lazing about whatever chance she could get. I tried to get her involved but I was met with condescending glares.

I returned to my computer screen, which displayed next week's roster, yet to be posted. I confirmed the Monday, which the man had rebooked his dinner, and smirked as I rostered Michelle on to serve him. Those two deserved each other.

| 34 |

Old Mate

The punters gripped their tickets, eyeballing the screens, egging on their horses. At the conclusion of each race, they either cheered or swore, quickly forgetting their celebration or demise as the next race began.

I regarded the wagering punters as the most arseholey as a population, as Old Mate became more aggressive with every second he left it too late to place a bet. It was always my fault if a horse was scratched, and I could never move fast enough to replace Old Mate's number selection before the race jumped.

He smacked his hand down on the bar, demanding service. He always ordered the same drink, and although I knew what it was, I patronisingly asked for his order every time. It was the only sense of power I held over him, as he continued to call me 'dahl' and 'sweetheart'.

"Hey dahl? Grab me another beer?" he called out to me.

"Just a second," I replied as I processed three terminals of bets.

I pulled the ticket out of the first, flicking it onto the counter, grinding the drawer open, dropping in the cash, and slamming it closed.

Flick. Grind. Drop. Slam. Flick. Grind. Drop. Slam.

"Dahl? Dahl?" he called me more persistently.

"Yes, what would you like?" I curtly replied, appearing out of nowhere, surprising him.

"A nice house, a million dollars..." he creepily checked me out, "a young blonde girl."

I forced an over the top fake laugh, "No, really. What now?"

"Just a beer, love."

"What kind do you want?"

"Oh, the usual," he announced loudly, eyeing off the other patrons, as if to inform them that it was *his* local.

"I'm sorry, which one would you like?" I snapped. I stood motionlessly and frowned as he pointed to all of the taps. "Which one? This one?" I tapped on the decal, "You need to specify which one you'd like."

"Oi, sweetheart, hurry up will you!" another old mate called from the terminals.

"On my way," I called back as I abandoned Old Mate and zoomed over. "You've entered the wrong location. What's the code for the one you want?"

The terminal flashed red over the location.

He quickly scanned through the newspaper and pointed, shrieking at me, "*That one!*"

"Number four has been scratched. Which horse would you like instead?"

"Ah... ah... two!"

I punched in the number two, replacing all the horses that were no longer racing. As I submitted the bet, the ticket spat into the rejection slot. "Sorry mate, the race already jumped."

He blew up at me. "It's your fault! You were busy stuffing around at the bar! You've made me miss my race!" he aggressively yelled at me, shocking me into fury.

I wasn't having it. "The bet is placed as soon as you put it in the terminal! You do *not* have to wait for me to process it! If *you* filled it out correctly the first time, then *you* would have successfully placed your bet! Do it right next time, it's not my fault!" I walked away before he had the chance to retort.

He slumped back down on the couch, muttering to another old mate, throwing filthy looks at me.

I silently returned to the bar when Old Mate started on me about taking my time. I ignored him as he continued to dig at me. If I were at the bar, I'd be needed at the terminals. If I were at the terminals, sure enough, he'd want a drink. I couldn't win, and the cost of labour wouldn't be justified by how little he spent.

I held out my hand to collect his money.

He dropped it on the counter next to me.

"Thank you," I breathed coolly. I dropped in his payment then grabbed his change out of the drawer, in ten cent pieces, spending time to double check it was the correct figure.

"Don't you have anything bigger?" he asked.

I looked down at the till, full of notes and all kinds of change. "Nope," I said, pursing my lips.

As long as he tormented me, I would do small things to make his visit uncomfortable.

He never realised the few times he said please or thank you, I smiled and served him more quickly next time.

I never worried about being rude to him. He deserved poor service. He deserved a good smack too, but I couldn't deliver that.

Every day he screamed at me for something I'd done wrong. The air conditioner was too cold. The music was too loud. The commentary was too soft. The sound quality wasn't clear. The race was delayed. His horse got scratched. Someone scribbled in the newspaper.

Every day I took it, acting cool and slowly was my only revenge.

Every day he threatened to never return. Every day he was back. On Saturdays, he was nicer, for there were other punters to monitor him, and extra staff to serve. On Mondays, he was gruelling. I never held a grudge from a previous day and gave him the benefit of a doubt. I hoped that maybe once he'd be in a pleasant mood.

Every time he let me down.

I still served him, however, my face revealing no feeling, as it was my job.

| 35 |

A Free Drink

It was late on Saturday afternoon, and a woman no one had ever seen before slinked toward the bar.

I opened my mouth to greet her, but was interrupted by a rather rude, "Can I have a lemonade?" then a lean over the bar.

"Sure," I smiled, and proceeded to make the drink. "How's your day been? Good?" I asked, only to be ignored. "Had a good day?" I asked more forcefully, as the woman looked away and pretended not to hear me.

The woman didn't need to waste time on niceties, and held no interest in boring herself making small talk with service staff.

"Three-fifty," I told her, placing a straw in the glass.

"Wha-? No. Don't pokie players get free drinks?" the woman demanded, suddenly commanding my full attention.

Now, legally, bar staff may not 'service' a gambling area, however, this is more of a blind eye rule. In reality, pokie players are usually treated like royalty.

In every venue I have ever worked in, gambling addicts (sorry, 'players') are treated to canapes and unlimited tea and coffee. Every venue has an espresso machine. Some have snack jars, and others even reserve parking for their 'VIP' guests. Venues that offer memberships advertise competitions and perks for *all* members, however, only those who stick their card in the little pokie slot are able to really reap the benefits. How could one entry with a meal purchase to win a new car possibly compete with the hundreds of entries automatically printed with every five dollars that spin through the machine?

The laws are simple: no special privileges for pokie players. In some states, venues can't even advertise the machines there, which is why they hold signs for 'VIP Lounges'. The people who feed their salaries into the machines are very much treated as VIP guests, and anyone who comes for the food, live music or pretty much anything else mightn't bother.

So when this woman approached the bar, and so rudely demanded her drink, with full expectation it was free because she played pokies, I shut her down.

"Complimentary drinks are at the manager's discretion," I advised. If I were caught randomly giving out free drinks, I'd get a warning. If it were Old Mate or any of the others who I saw day in and day out, I'd make their drink and comp it off – no questions asked. This surly hag demanded a free drink and she wasn't even playing.

Why should I give her a free drink? What if everyone came in asking for free drinks? That's not how to run a business! Free drinks are a privilege, not a right.

"Fine!" she snapped, throwing some coins at me, which fell through the glass racks to the bottom of the fridge.

I ducked down to fish out the coins (and still missing a dollar) and I saw the woman shooting a filthy look at me, then bitching to her boyfriend. *He* was playing a pokie. She was 'supervising'. She was complaining about me.

A pit sunk in my stomach. Service staff would never win and would always be blamed. The customer isn't always right, and when they are wrong, they are ropable.

The boyfriend stomped over to the bar and barked, "I want a refund on this drink! This is bullshit!"

"Fine," I snapped as I tipped it down the drain and refunded the drink.

He stomped back over to Michelle lurching in the crypt.

She looked horrified!

He kept looking over at the bar and pointing, then pointing to the machines, then glaring at me.

Because Michelle had been there for so long, she'd become a territorial veteran and actively pushed away new team members, because she knew better. A lifelong career as a pep talker to addicts was lesser than working at Clarkson. At least Clarkson staff had a bit of dignity and pride that they were doing a service to society. I would always be nice to service staff, whether they be checkout chicks, deli wenches like myself in a former life, or call centre operators. I, however, had very little respect for gaming cashiers.

Michelle, pub shitkicker, functions fill in, and gaming lurch, stormed over to the bar, and furiously poured a new lemonade, growling, "Pokie players get free drinks!" then leaving to go suck up to her new bestie.

She wasn't even playing, and Michelle thinks she's in charge of the manager. Brilliant.

It was an unfair standard and reality – pokie players would get pretty much anything they want. They were arseholes. Smarmy when it suited them and slimy when it didn't. Most were polite, but others held a distinct air of entitlement, knowing that their addiction was fuelling the business. One less player could cost a job. As the man and his lemonade-sipping mistress stormed out, I hoped it wouldn't be mine.

| 36 |

Petit Four: Vegetarian Salmon

The guests sat admiring their menus, discussing their choices between the five main meals offered to their private party.

I moved between each guest, taking their orders. I was travelling at a constant pace, merely smiling, as each guest anticipated my question, and offered their selection.

"I'll have the chicken please," one man articulated, glancing at his menu to confirm its presence

I smiled, and replied, "Of course," to each person, before tallying the meals on my notepad.

The next man was clearly still contemplating the menu, for he was holding it in front of him, peering over the top of his spectacles, brow furrowed. He looked like an Arthur, so I'm going to name him Arthur.

I smiled at Arthur, waiting for his order, then gently prompted him by asking, "And you, Sir, what would you like?"

"Actually I have a question," he told me.

"Go ahead," I encouraged him.

Arthur scanned the five descriptions one last time, then asked me, "Is the salmon the only vegetarian option you have on the set menu?"

I was confused, and asked, "I'm sorry?"

"The salmon... Is that the only vegetarian option this evening?"

I went to speak but stopped myself to process whether he was being serious. A stern face looked up at me, waiting for my response.

"I'm sorry, sir, but the salmon actually isn't vegetarian."

"Really? Why not?" Arthur was not impressed.

I paused to confirm he wasn't joking.

He wasn't.

"It's got fish in it," I quietly informed him.

His eyes flicked back to the description of the dish on the menu. "What kind of fish?" he demanded.

"Salmon."

"Oh!" Arthur raised his hand, chuckling.

I nervously forced a smile, confused as to why he thought this was funny.

"Of course! But vegetarians usually eat salmon!" he chortled.

"Ah – do they?" I asked, knowing full well, they don't.

"Yes, of course they do!" he cried, laughing at my silly lack of education.

"Oh, I didn't realise!" I lied, " Thanks for letting me know.

| 37 |

A Great Misunderstanding

A group of hip young thirty-somethings came in, with a hot pink frosted giggler who would tell anyone that listened, "It's my birthday!"

They all approached the bar to order stereotypical party drinks – shots of wet pussies chased by basic spirits with insistence that the birthday girl didn't need to pay (but secretly thanking her for doing so).

One guy came up to the bar and asked for his favourite shitty beer.

"Would you like lemon or lime with that?" I asked.

"Yes."

"Sorry, would you like lemon? Or lime?" I asked again.

"Yes."

"Lime it is then," I said, sticking a lime in the beer.

"Oh! Sorry, I didn't get what you meant!" the guy laughed.

"No problem," I smiled.

An older (not by much) suave fellow rocking the latest fashion spectacles moseys up to the bar to order for his temporary date. In a polite, softly spoken tone, he requests, "Fancy yacht club vermouth. With fresh mint, cucumber, lemonade and..."

"I'm sorry, I'll just stop you right there," I interjected, not wanting to waste the gentleman's time. "We don't have mint, or cucumber, or fancy yacht club vermouth. I have shitty vermouth – somewhat similar although not the same. I can do it with lemonade and fresh lime. Would you like to try a dash first?"

"Oh no, shitty vermouth, lemonade and lime would be good" the man responded, keen to accept this drink and return to his date.

I filed through the shelves to find the dusty bottle of shitty vermouth, and placed it on the bar. I flipped a glass out of the rack, impressively tossing it over to my left hand and shot a wedge of lime into it. Flipped the muddling stick over, and dramatically smushed the citrus into a juicy pulp. Flicked up the scoop to fill it with glittering ice cubes. The metal utensil crunched as it was dumped back in the well. Poured a shot over the iced highball, and topped it off with lemonade... and don't forget the straw! Voila!

The man took the refreshment to his date, and returned while I was still making the rest of the round (from memory too!).

He caught my eye, head shaking. "No. She won't drink shitty vermouth. I'll just get a vodka, fresh lime and soda."

"No problem," I replied. With a smile, I grabbed another glass, muddled some fresh lime in it, filled it with ice, took the first-pour vodka, tipped in a shot, and topped it with another fresh lime and soda. I placed the drink on the bar and looked up at him, ready for payment.

After witnessing the drink being made, he looked at me unapologetically and emotionlessly said, "No. Not that house stuff. I want Expensive AF."

Unfortunately, we don't stock Expensive AF. We have a first pour, a mid-range, or a moderately premium Sorta Pricey. I hope he understands. I broke the bad news.

"Sorry we don't stock Expensive AF. We have this first pour, or I can offer you these mid-range, or our moderately premium is Sorta Pricey," I pointed to the shelves. "What would you prefer?" I was curt yet polite. To be fair, I really should have asked which one he wanted before making it.

"You really should have asked me *before* making it," he huffed.

I really should have asked him before making it. Whoops.

"Would you like the Sorta Pricey with fresh lime and soda?" I offered him, ignoring his rude interjection.

"That's fine," he shrugged.

"This one you have is fine? Or would you like me to make a new one with Sorta Pricey?" *Seriously - just tell us what you want!*

"I said it's fine! Just... Just forget it," The hipster sauntered away, with a hand flip in my face, twice shooting a death stare, then joining the tart he was with, so they could both mutter things and shake their heads.

A wave of anger washed over me. I picked up a filthy cloth and chucked it at the bin, missing. Sports were just not my forte.

I cleaned my station, grumpily thinking about what went wrong. I had politely offered him and his tortoise-shell spectacles a beverage, made it, then made another, and then offered another. In his opinion, I just hadn't done enough. That's hospitality for you. I went to the back bench and grabbed the wastage sheet, scribbling in my disasters. *Vermouth by 30ml. House vodka by 30ml. Reason? Customer was a douche-canoe.*

| 38 |

Teeth

Please call someone to fix the smashed mirror in the men's room (sports bar).
Cheers.

I read the note left on the desk from Tim. I'd have to get back to fixing the mirror. It was 10am and time to open the doors.

Friday was a busy night usually, and the mess left by last night's staff indicated that they must have been *really* busy – too busy to leave the pub clean. It happens. Not a huge deal, just fix it.

Ha! That's a lie. It was a big deal, they shouldn't have left until it was done, and I'll remind them when I do the rosters next.

The glass bench (the bench for dirty glasses, not a bench made of glass - that'd be dangerously impractical) still had the final two racks of odd beer and wine glasses waiting patiently to be washed. A pile of grotty wet towels were dumped in the laundry sink. The fridges revealed gaps of missing stock, inviting the fluorescent lights to peak a furry glow in the dingy bar.

My feet gripped to the sticky floor as I meandered toward the espresso machine. At least this had been cleaned properly. I poured some fresh beans in the grinder and turned it on. I could smell the warm aroma as they dissolved into a thick deep brown powder.

Old Mate called out to me.

"Sorry?" I reply over the whirring of the bean grinder.

He pointed behind him and called me again.

I switched off the grinder. "Sorry, mate, what was that?"

"There any other bathrooms available, love? I'm not going in there – holy shit that's bad," he told me.

"Bad? We just opened, no one's been in there yet," I mused mildly, walking over to have a look myself. I was curious what Old Mate was complaining about. A smashed mirror wouldn't have prevented him from peeing. When I got to the bathroom entrance, I found out why.

"Whoa!" I exclaimed as I observed what Old Mate had seen in the men's room. The cleaners had clearly skipped this area. Even so, it was much worse than the usual wear and tear.

The mirror was indeed smashed. A glittering web of glass shattered in a spiral, creeping to the edges of the long frame. Near the centre, where the blow was concentrated, several hairs spiked out, gripping to the silvery glass with a bloody adhesive. I'd seen it before: someone's head had gone through it. Jagged fragments littered the sticky tiles below and crunched under my feet as I crept in further. Both the sinks were smeared deep ruby, as if someone had attempted to wipe up a mess. They must have given up, as crimson stained wads of wet toilet paper were dumped in the piss-stenched urinal. The white tiled walls were gashed with blood splatter, streaking in lines, spraying long arrows toward the stalls.

Three cubicle doors were closed over, and I stared at them, concerned about what may be behind them.

I kicked the first door, slamming it into the wall, anxious for what I might find. It didn't take too much effort to open, for it was only dangling by a single hinge. Someone had tried to rip it off completely. I blew a sigh of relief when I saw what was behind it: the usual Saturday morning culprits of blocked toilet and shit stains. Disgusting, but I'd been humbled by the number of times I've observed it.

The next stall had a shiraz coloured handprint smeared on the centre of the door. The stain held a light flaky crust, but at closer look, still seemed moist underneath. Whatever happened in there, happened recently, possibly only hours before I'd arrived.

I bent down slowly, careful with my balance, not daring to touch a thing. I was searching for feet. Although it is a rare occurrence, it isn't unheard of for patrons to pass out in the toilets unnoticed and spend the night.

Thank goodness, I thought, as I confirmed their absence. I gingerly pushed the contaminated door forward using my foot, swearing I'd douse my shoes in bleach and then burn them anyway. The laminated door creaked as it swung forward, revealing a vacant toilet.

The bloodstains were worse in there – deep rivers lined the chequered floor and almost a whole wall had been dyed deep scarlet - but at least the culprit had vanished. I'm not sure how I would have handled a vigilante – alone - first thing in the morning, before my beloved coffee.

I recoiled as the acidic stench of vomit reached my nostrils. I gagged as I saw the chunks resting on the seat and dripping into a puddle on the floor. I slammed the door closed, breathing through my mouth, but now tasting the tingling sour smell of someone else's fermented alcohol-infused stomach contents. I recoiled as I tried to collect myself. It was bad, but not the worst I'd seen, and certainly nothing to be afraid of.

The final cubicle loomed, with the door partially ajar. What would I find there? Again, I steadied myself lower to check under the door. There were no feet, but there was a curious mass to one side. Tiny, but curious. I couldn't quite tell what it was.

I pushed the final door forward, slowly, using the tip of my leather shoe. This toilet was the cleanest. It had only a bit of wee in the bowl, and no big bloodstains, just a single trickle of droplets leading toward... *what is that?*

I squinted and cocked my head to the side, attempting a better view of the little mass. *Is that a..?*

I removed my glasses and rubbed them on my shirt. *Surely not?*

I crept above it, and saw it wasn't just an it, it was in fact a pair. There on the floor in front of me, lay two mangled human teeth, each torn out from the root, with bloodied flesh attached.

"*Oh shit!*" I screamed, as I realised I was observing human body parts.

"What?!" Old Mate shouted as he scrambled to my rescue, bursting into the bathroom.

"There's teeth! Effing teeth! Effing teeth on the effing floor for effs sake!" I screamed and shuddered, pointing to the third stall.

Old Mate felt compelled to have a look. Who knows why people felt compelled to look at gory anatomy? Tell someone there's something gross over there, and they'll need to affirm it.

"Urgh!" Old Mate dry wretched and bent over, hand on his knees. His etched face depicted that he'd seen a lot in his time, but this was pushing it.

"Oh my goodness I'm sorry!" I cried.

Old Mate looked at me, shaking his head in sympathy. He was at a loss for words. Big guy, who normally looked as if he'd slit your throat, was in shock.

I escorted him back to the bar and shouted him his beer, promising I'd be back out there soon. I said he'd watch the bar for me. Let's see how that one goes.

I was shaking as I fumbled in my pocket, retrieving my phone. I took photos of everything – the smashed mirror, the blood, the vomit, the shit, the rubbish, the teeth and the hanging door.

Snap, snap, snap, photos were taken from every angle, depicting every scene.

A thought occurred – why? Why was I taking photos? As evidence? Was it a police matter? Should I call the police? Was this a crime scene? Or was it the frantic remains of a drunk lynch mob? Should I call Dean?

Don't be stupid, I told myself, *You can handle this. Just make sure you write an incident report just in case.*

I decided against calling the police. I did not need to add any more conditions to our licence. The Wood and Spoon was already 'dangerous' and held restrictions and rules to reflect that. Plus, the closing managers would have handled a fight last night. It was not my responsibility. I just needed to get it cleaned.

I constructed a barricade made of a rope balustrade, two wet floor signs and three mop buckets with taped a note directing the patrons to the restaurant restrooms at the other end of the venue. It was not an ideal solution, but the best I could achieve.

If I knew how head office wanted this pub run, the priority would be the gambling addicts. This was their nearest bathroom, and if they had to walk around to the restaurant part, it'd be less time at the machine. Time was money. Five minutes less playtime per toilet trip over the whole day could rack up to thousands in lost revenue. Fixing this mess was top priority.

I called the cleaning company to ask why they didn't clean it up. The cleaning guy told me his staff didn't deal with bodily fluids.

They don't do heavy duty cleaning? It's a commercial cleaning company! There was no note from them, nothing at all to say they weren't going to clean the bathrooms. They just left it for me to deal with.

One of the regular punters, walked past and huffed at the bloody mess. I'd better get a move on before he complained. I demanded the cleaning guy send out a team immediately!

He told me it'd be a higher fee, as if to make me hesitate; I called him out for being a douche-canoe.

By the time the bodily fluid cleaning crew arrived, it was already late afternoon, and time for changeover with the night manager - Tim, who did close last night.

He asked me how my day was.

"Ha! Started off a bit hectic but we managed," I chortled.

"Did you see my note about the mirror?"

"Yeah, thanks for the heads up!" I snorted sarcastically. "A little warning would have been nice!"

He looked at me confused. "Warning? What for?"

"About the men's room... Yeah the mirror was smashed, but what about the rest?" I asked.

"What are you talking about? A guy came up at the end of the night saying the mirror had been smashed. I was going to look, but I forgot." Tim seemed lost as to what I was talking about. He only knew about a mirror.

"Well, was this guy injured at all? Did he seem ok?" I kept prying, certain he knew more than what he let on.

"He was fine. Why? What happened?"

"Really?" I couldn't believe it. "So you never heard a fight, or a scuffle? Did security go in there at all?"

"What are you talking about?" he demanded. "Nothing happened. It was busy, but everything ran smoothly, we were a bit cruisy, then right at the end a guy came and told us about the mirror. That's it! Why do you keep asking? What happened?"

I showed him the photos on my phone.

He swiped through the photos, his eyes widening. There were several that he zoomed in on. "Wait – are they..? Urgh! Gross! I can't look at anymore!" he shuddered and tossed my phone back on the desk. He was adamant he had no idea about what went on in the men's room.

Me too. I tried to justify how something like this was plausible.

I finally had time to write up an incident report, which I sent off to Dean then I also printed one to take home. One of the first rules to being a manager is Cover Your Own Butt. By writing it all down and sending it off, I was off the hook.

We never did find out what happened that night. No one knew why there were teeth on the floor. There was no explanation for the blood splatter, no injured patrons on camera and none of the staff saw a thing. No one ever wrote back to my email about the incident, and it wasn't even mentioned at the weekly manager's meeting. After that day, it was like it'd never happened.

Why would two teeth be ripped out and left on the bathroom floor? Where did all that blood come from? Whose head went through that mirror? And why? Why didn't anyone hear anything? And why didn't they say anything?

Dean's dignified silence kept him away. Out of mind, out of sight.

I couldn't remove the images and the putrid smells from my memories.

| 39 |

Petit Four: A Real Job

"Just a lemonade thanks," a man ordered from me. "Say, my daughter has always wanted to push one of those buttons..." he added hopefully.

"Sorry?" I asked. I looked down and saw a smiling eleven year old beaming up at me, fascinated by the soda gun. "You want to push the button?" I asked.

The little girl nodded excitedly.

I placed a glass on the bar, and extended the gun hose to full length, so it would reach her.

Lemonade spluttered out the end and into the glass, exciting the child to no end.

"There," the father bent down, rustling her head. "You've fulfilled your lifelong dream, and now you might focus on getting a real job one day."

I couldn't help my mouth. "There's nothing wrong with working in hospitality!"

"Oh, there's nothing wrong with it for you," he said, "but we have high hopes for her. She'll be a surgeon or something one day. You know, something with prospects."

| 40 |

A Rude Awakening

It was seven thirty in the morning.

I woke up to the sound of my phone ringing. *What time is it?* I foggily thought, attempting to focus on the light blaring from the screen of my phone. It stopped ringing. *It's... seven thirty... Who calls me at this hour? Everyone knows I'm asleep in the mornings...*

I immediately slipped back into a deep sleep.

It started ringing again.

It took me until the end of the tone to realise it wasn't part of a dream – my phone was ringing. It needed to be answered. I rolled over toward it.

It stopped.

Who was that? I didn't have to look in the call log, or wonder any longer, for before I could comprehend what was happening, it rang again.

'Wood and Spoon' flashed across the screen. Great. It was work. They knew I only finished at four! That was less than four hours ago! What could they possibly be calling about now?

"Herrow?" I croaked. I cleared my throat. "He-hello?"

"You need to come in. The safe is missing money." It was Tim, the opening manager. He sounded worried.

"What? No, it's not; I counted it this morning. Check it again," I mumbled, and went to hang up.

"Wait!" Tim pleaded, "This is serious. I've counted it. Dean's counted it."

I sat bolt upright. *Dean thought I left the safe down?*

"We both checked your calculation sheet and it's down exactly one thousand dollars in ten dollar notes," Tim told me, expecting me to come up with an explanation.

I had only counted the contents of the safe a few hours earlier. I was *always* thorough with cash and knew that when I had left, it was spot on. Tim must have miscounted it. "There should be five bricks of tens all up. Five thousand dollars," I mumbled, still hazy from being woken after only a few hours.

"Well there's not," he told me finitely. "There's only four K and Dean wants you to come in right now and find the other thousand."

"Right now? No. I start back at eleven; I'm on mid-shift. I have to get some sleep. Just leave it down and I'll count it when I come in then. It's there. I'm certain it's just a miscount," I assured him.

"Look, Dean and I have both counted it, and if you don't come down right now with the cash, he's going to give you a written warning for theft," Tim cautioned me.

It seemed like I had no choice but to go in – after only two hours sleep! Two hours! "It's still peak hour so it'll probably be another hour before I get there, with the traffic."

"Just – just get here as soon as you can. This needs to be sorted before we open or you'll have to come up with the cash yourself," he threatened, before hanging up.

I'll have to come up with the cash myself? No way that's ever happening! I thought about whether they could get away with this. Two hours. *Two hours sleep!* Now they want me to come back in to balance the safe because they were too dumb to. This was ridiculous.

I scrambled through a ten-second shower, splashing my face several times with scorching hot water to try to help myself wake up. I smelt my pants to check they were still ok from last night. They stank like a stale brewery, but I realised I had no other option after seeing the filthy laundry pile. I pulled the stinky beer pants on, finding a fresh shirt in my closet, and doused myself in deodorant to mask the scent of yester-pants.

I'm not sure how I made it to work. My mind sunk into auto-pilot mode and I blinked and realised I was pulling into the driveway.

It was early but I knew on a Wednesday – uni night – the busiest day of the week – the idiots would be out tonight, so I parked in the far corner, away from potential scratching or vandalism.

I arrived before the pub opened, but was due to start at eleven. My shift was due to end at nine that night – but I knew I'd be staying until at least midnight. I was chilly and shaky from lack of sleep. A headache threatened. I pulled on some dark sunglasses, updated my lipstick and puckered my lips in the rear view mirror. I didn't bother with mascara for now – I'd try to make myself look decent later in the afternoon. For now, the best I could hope for was 'living ghost' with a hint of 'pretty zombie'.

Me and my thermos of steaming coffee fell through the door as Tim pulled it open at the same time I tried to turn my key. My pants now smelt of coffee mixed with yester-beer. The wet patch would dry, and at least the tingly burn shook me more alert. Thanks, Tim.

He didn't even greet me, concerned with potential repercussions. "Right, the safe is open. You count it and see if you get the same figures as I did," he commanded.

"Good morning," I grumbled. I was not in the mood for niceties. No sleep and spilt coffee made Alex a moody bitch. I *knew* that the safe was right and the boys had miscounted. I knew Dean had called me in to degrade me in front of Tim – to make me a fool, and to show me as a scapegoat in front of the team.

Humiliated and furious, I begin to count the safe. I call the bundles out, *exactly* the same as they were left last night – just as I expected. "Ten times one hundred equals one thousand in hundreds. You have... eight thousand in fifties..."

I was stewing in my anger, shaky from exhaustion. So far, the safe matched my calculations from last night, and Tim's from this morning. I imagined if the tables were turned, it would still somehow be my responsibility to balance the safe. Dean would never call Tim in early after close. He wouldn't have called in any of the other duty managers either. Actually, the spineless bastard hadn't even called me in; he got Tim to do his dirty work for him. He was the worst GM I'd ever worked for.

Tim wasn't a bad guy. I actually quite enjoyed working with him. Tim was knowledgeable and friendly. He seemed like pretty much an all-round nice guy. I resented him, however, for being the ideal manager for Dean. Tim was tall, broad and in his early thirties, meaning, because of his stance, his penis and his age, he deserved more respect than me.

I was far more experienced than Tim, and held proper qualifications in the field (which Tim lacked), yet Tim was given the better jobs, a better roster and more respect.

If any other manager had been left on close, and the safe was down, and they were due back at eleven, the safe would be left down until they came in at eleven. This was because there would obviously be an explanation for it. No one would leave a safe down if there weren't a valuable reason why.

Because *I* was on close the night before, I was called in. It was the vicious double standard I dealt with in this job. There was one expectation for the boys, and one for me.

I looked up and glared at the security camera, knowing Dean was watching my every move. Every bundle of cash, I placed in clear view of the camera. There's that silent management rule for working in hospitality again: always cover your own butt.

I exaggeratedly pointed to several bricks of fives and pointedly looked at the security camera. "Twenty five thousand in five dollar notes," I articulated, nodding.

I knew that if money was missing, that I would be blamed for theft.

As if I'd steal one thousand dollars from a safe! How foolish! There were better ways to rob a workplace. Not that I'd ever do it, but... if one *were* to rob a workplace, it wouldn't be for a measly thousand dollars. I knew how much cash they held there. I knew how to make money disappear without anyone noticing. It would be a hell of a lot more than just one grand! I was sure that every manager had shared the same thoughts – how to rob the joint and get away with it. It was possible, and people had done it in the past and gotten away with it.

I could never go through with it. The guilt would eat me alive. Others would and would never resent it, nor tell a soul.

They were everywhere in the industry. Petty thieves were rampant, pinching cigarettes and coins from other's lockers, or snatching an apron that had innocently been forgotten post-shift. Everyone stole food. Chips that left themselves unattended on the pass would be tasted by starving, hungover waitresses, while managers raided fruit from the walk-in long after the chefs went home.

Money was different, however. All staff were aware of the cash flying in and out of the venue. It was a strange sensation, looking at thousands of dollars at the time. One distanced themselves from reality. That five grand that just got deposited into the pokie's change box? It's not life changing to us. It's not a new (dodgy) car or a small renovation. To a worker, it's not a deposit on a large purchase, or a furnishing of an apartment. It's a fiddy-brick. It means nothing. We are numb to the reality of the cash we see. It's not money to us. It holds no true value; it's merely a professional tool we work with. No one would be stupid enough to get caught stealing twenty bucks from a till. That's an instant dismissal in most jobs. No manager would be dumb enough to take only a thousand dollars so obviously.

Wait! *Did Tim steal the money?*

It made sense. He was constantly moaning about being broke. Plus I would be the perfect person to pin it on.

Don't be silly! I scolded myself. Tim and I were allies. Best to keep it that way. It had to be a miscount. It *had* to be a miscount.

I thought of paperwork procedures and knew there was no way they could reprimand me for stealing. I was clean as a whistle, and my paper trail matched the calculations perfectly. They couldn't prove it was me, or Tim. I looked up at the cameras again, and continued with my count.

"In tens there's... *four?*" I was stunned. There were five this morning when I left. Five. Not four. This couldn't be right.

I looked up at Tim, who looked worried. "That's what I got too," he said sadly.

"Hang on, let me look," I told him. I believed that Tim wouldn't take the money. I trusted him. There had to be a feasible explanation. If twenty dollars was missing, it'd be missing. A thousand dollars didn't just disappear. Obviously, a mistake was made somewhere.

I stuck my whole head into the safe before stupidly realising there was no light in there. Two hours sleep, thank you. I then began to remove the rest of the contents of the safe.

"Ok, so fives are right. Coins are right. It's definitely tens missing," I confirmed with Tim. *There's always a logical explanation to cash missing*, I reminded myself as I tried not to panic. I ran my hand along the inner edge of the metallic wall, and immediately found what I was searching for: a brick of ten dollar notes!

I whipped out my hand triumphantly and showed it to Tim with a broad smile, "I found it! It must have fallen down the side when the safe door closed!"

"Aw, sweet! I knew it had to be there!" Tim beamed.

"So you're all good then? Just count it one more time to be sure," I requested.

We counted the money together and both signed for it. What a relief!

"Yep, all good."

"Great, I'm out of here!" I went to leave.

"What time are you back?"

"Eleven," I sigh. It was almost nine by then. Two hours until work starts again. "I'm going to have a nap in my car. I won't have time to make it home and back now."

As I made my way through the back passages of the pub, I spied Dean in the hotel reception. A pit boiled in my stomach.

The idiot was showing off the new staff aprons to Michelle, who he desperately wanted to eff. He posed and laughed flirtatiously, looking far too old to model a staff uniform.

I barged past him.

He was strutting around, humorously, imitating his young team. He looked up and saw me. "Hey, did you find the cash?" he asked lightly.

"Yes."

"Good. See you at eleven," he waved happily, completely unaware I was imagining him being punched in his smug face.

Just as I stomped out toward my car, I felt my skin prickle and my ears burn. I hid out of view of the cameras, realising from his tone, which echoed in my mind: he'd done this deliberately.

There was no apology. Nothing. He'd gotten me out of bed, to count a safe that could have waited. Tuesday night close then Wednesday mid-shift was always a tricky part of the roster, but five, maybe six hours sleep, was do-able. Two hours was unreasonable.

I was shaking and chilly despite the burn of the morning sun, and an overwhelming exhaustion caught up with me. My head began to pound and my mouth felt like cotton. My eyelids scratched and felt raw. I was freezing but sweating. My mind was scrambling, as I thought about what he did. I sobbed, heaving and moaning in between silent cries and gasps for breath. I felt cheated and betrayed.

Dean had really hurt me this morning. By forcing me to come in on no sleep, when I was due to start back just hours later, to throw me under a bus was just a cruel thing to do. This time, Dean hadn't just belittled me, he'd actually set me up for fail by ensuring I wouldn't be properly prepared for work. It wasn't the usual misogynist wankery stabs I usually endured; this time, Dean had hit a new low. He'd actually stabbed me so hard, that a part of my soul was ripped from me when he removed his knife.

"Hey, did you find the cash?" he had asked me so nicely. Behind his caring query, and his pleasant demeanour, I had seen his eyes. There was no warmth there. His mouth smiled, his cheeks lifted as they should, and his voice said the words which were expected of him – concern for his staff to demonstrate leadership. It was a front to hide his true intentions. Him, seeking concern, was a cover, a way for him to fit into the role of manager. He had no actual care for anyone else. He was a predator, whose only concern was benefiting himself.

I wasn't fooled. I saw him for what he truly was. Dean was a cold, heartless sociopath, and I didn't trust him one bit. I hated him, and to a point, I was scared of him. He may not physically hurt me, but he was capable of ruining me, by damaging my career, my reputation and my soul. I knew to tread very carefully around Dean – if he wanted something, he would stop at nothing to get it. Anyone who got in his way, he would remove. This morning's antics proved that I was next on the firing line. If he couldn't find a way to terminate my employment with the pub, he'd encourage me to quit by bullying me until I couldn't take it anymore.

I thought about every interaction I'd ever had with him – from the floppy handshake I'd first started, to this performance he'd orchestrated this morning. His entire demeanour was a lie.

I wiped the tears from my eyes, and set my alarm, hoping I'd wake in time for my sixteen hour shift. I did. I swore one day I'd get Dean for everything he was doing to me. I didn't.

| 41 |

Sleepless Nights and Days of Slumber

"How could you be drinking coffee now? It's 8pm!" exclaimed Kathleen, who was checking into the hotel.

"Ah, you caught me," I said, noting to conceal my vices better next time.

Kathleen didn't leave it at that though, and was intrigued by my bizarre behaviour. How could I possibly sleep well after drinking a coffee that late in the evening?

"Don't you need to sleep?" she asked, needing to know how I could do this.

"I thought you said you were a nurse... you don't do nights?" I queried.

"I work in pathology, just days at a clinic... I could never do shift work... I don't understand how you function the next day." She sounded a bit condescending.

"I don't," I reply.

"You don't?" Now Kathleen is floored! "Sorry, I don't mean to press... but *how* do you do it?"

"Oh that's ok," I assured her politely, "I don't mind," I took a breath and thought of the nicest – yet clearest – way to say this. Kathleen wouldn't understand, for she, unlike shift-working hospital nurses, fell under the 'civilian' umbrella: a term I used to describe people who led normal lives and worked normal, sociable hours.

"Ok, so I started at five tonight right?"

She nodded intently, clearly fascinated with my lifestyle.

"Well I won't be finished until about four in the morning. So take your day... and shift it to suit the hours. I woke up at three o'clock this afternoon, and-"

"Three o'clock!" Kathleen gasped, "But how do you sleep during the day?" she begged.

"I work at night and I sleep during the day," I answered simply enough, knowing my response wouldn't suffice. I was right.

"You sleep *all* day?" she questioned sceptically.

That was it. That line was there and she crossed it. This civilian no longer looked at me in awe, instead, she saw me as lazy. A person who slept all day and stayed up all night must be lazy.

I shut it down before it could escalate further, "I'll just need you to sign this, then you're good to head to your room," I said, passing her a reservation confirmation form.

She signed, and bid me farewell.

I waited for her to be out of view, and slumped in the swivel chair, hiding behind the high wooden reservation desk, returning to my steaming cup of coffee.

I'd heard it before, from family members who couldn't understand why I could rarely make it to Sunday roast dinner, to extended family who would sympathetically ask on Mother's Day, "They wouldn't let you have the day off?"

It was one on the downsides of working in hospitality: Society never understood the hours.

Overnight staff were not lazy, but they would never infiltrate society's regular business hours. It was a full lifestyle adjustment. There was no such thing as morning or brunch, but eggs benedict could be consumed at 5pm of course.

Night time was when life happened in my world. Even on my days off, I would sleep all day and wake all night to keep in a regular routine and cycle. It was strange to begin with adapting to the life, but after a while, hospo-hours seemed natural.

I would wake between two and three in the afternoon, and have breakfast while everyone else did the school run home. Groceries, banking, haircuts, doctor's appointments and anything else only open during business hours got crammed in before six. While society ate dinner, washed up and socialised or watched prime-time television, I was in career mode, either serving on busy nights, or writing plans and doing investment analyses during quiet ones. While customers partied to celebrate Sharon's disco-themed fortieth, I offered them satay skewers and prawn cocktails. At midnight, I'd scoff some gaming room deep-fried offerings and perhaps a piece of fruit in a weak interpretation of dinner. While people slept, I'd be counting tills, balancing the safe, replying to business emails and monitoring the alcohol consumption of the patrons. As the evening waned to the deep chill of the darkest part of the night, and most people rolled over in bed to curl up under their doona, I waited for the few lowly fellows to collect their 'winnings' from the pokies so I could close the pub. While the stars glittered across a navy velvet sky, I cruised down the dark streets toward home, sometimes passing a truck but more often in isolation. As the dedicated health nuts woke to hit the gym or go for an early run, I swigged beer and played on my phone.

Lastly, when breakfast radio began, and others woke with the rising of the sun, I showered, escaped from the light under an extra pillow and curled up to rest.

| 42 |

Petit Four: A Normal Beer

A woman approached the bar and confusedly looked at all of the taps. All twelve contained different varieties of beer – but these were not what the woman was after.

I greeted her, "Hello, how can I help you?" but instead of answering, the woman flicked up her index finger, as if to indicate she was still looking.

She peered over the bar toward the glass-doored refrigerators, displaying many more types and brands of beer, wines and pre-mixed spirits. There were craft beers and imported varieties, local lagers, dark ales and pilsners among them. There were white wines and rosés, sparkling brüts and piccolos. There were cans of cola and lemonade and glass bottles of mineral water. But what this woman was after, it seemed, this bar did not stock.

Once more, her eyes returned to the taps. One-by-one she read the labels, hoping the one she was after would jump out at her.

"Are you looking for anything in particular?" I asked.

A raised index finger and a look of determination answered. It had to be here somewhere. It wasn't.

She noticed the shelving behind the counter. There were bourbons and vodkas, gins and rums. There were strange bottles with labels that may as well have been written in another language. In the fridge below that, were juices.

Surely she'd missed them again. She better ask.

"Excuse me!" she called to me; I was messing about with glassware and not helping her.

"Yes, how can I help you?" I asked for the third time, curious as to what exactly this woman was after.

"Do you have any *normal* beers?" she asked.

"Excuse me?" I was perplexed.

"I want a normal beer. What do you have?"

"Well, it depends on what you're after. On tap we have these ones," I indicated, reading the labels.

"No, I don't want a pale ale, or a stout. I want just a normal beer," she stopped me.

"Ah… ok," I was a bit lost. "So when you say normal beer… do you mean a full strength rather than a light? Or a local rather than an imported? I'm just not quite sure what you're after," I said.

"Look, I just want a normal beer!" the woman shouted, "What would you give someone who just asked for a beer?"

"Whichever one they want," I said.

"Look, I've had enough of this!" the woman snapped, "Just get me a *normal* beer!"

I had had enough too. I picked up a glass, and poured a beer from the tap closest to me – one of the more popular varieties, a local mid-strength lager, moderately priced.

"Thanks," she scowled, snatching the glass, splashing froth over the bar mat. "Now that wasn't so hard, was it?"

| 43 |

A Scotch on the Rocks with a Twist

A man came up to the bar and ordered a scotch. This was no joke, although the punchline was probably more amusing.

"I'll have a Slightly Mid-Range Everywhere Scotch, thanks," the man said, before allowing Tim a chance to greet him. The man ordering the scotch had no need to greet a mere bartender. He simply wanted his scotch, and the bartender was being paid to serve. The bartender was obliged to fulfil any simple appeal by a customer. A rock glass filled with ice and amber liquid was dumped on the bar in front of him.

"Eight dollars thank you," Tim requested.

Slightly Mid-Range Everywhere Scotch handed over a tenner, took his change and headed to 'his' poker machine. The glass had barely reached his mouth, and only a sip of chilled alcohol reached his parched lips, when Mid-Range realised with shock that the bartender had clearly made a mistake! This was not the drink he ordered! Mid-Range stormed back to the bar, slamming his glass on the sticky mat.

"Excuse me!" he insisted on Tim's attention. There was no need for his demanding shout, for there were no other guests waiting to be served.

Tim smiled, and went to reply, but was cut off.

"I ordered a slightly mid-range scotch with a black label, and you've given me the wrong drink!" Mid-Range complains, clearly disgusted that his drink of choice was not the drink he was served.

"I'm sorry, I must have misheard you; that's one with a black label, is that not what you ordered?" Tim, the bartender, queried.

Mid goes from perplexed to furious. Not only did the bartender pour the wrong drink, now he was insisting it was the right one! *What happened to 'the customer is always right?'*

"No! It's not. I drink black labelled scotch all the time. I *know* black labelled scotch. And this-" he shudders, "*This* is not a scotch with a black label!"

"Sorry about that," Tim replied. Tim took the glass and poured it down the sink, grabbing a fresh glass, and flicking it theatrically to his other hand, then scooped a spadeful of ice into it. He filled the glass with exactly thirty mils of the scotch the man asked for and dumped the glass in front of him. Of course, he's only human. He *could* have made a mistake. If this man was sure it was the wrong drink, it was easier to pour a new one than to argue. Certain he had selected the correct drink this time, he again apologised and farewelled Mid. "There you are. Sorry about that."

Mid snatched the glass and left without a word.

"What a wanker," Tim muttered. "Oh- here we go again!" he whispered under his breath, seeing the reapproaching figure.

Mid returned to the bar again, only thirty seconds later. This time, he was ropable! He slammed down his glass, causing flecks of liquid to splat into the face of the confused Tim.

Tim innocently asked, "Can I help-" but was cut off.

Mid had turned a vivid shade of beetroot in his anger. As he began to scream, Tim's complexion competed with him, morphing into a bright shade of vermillion. He was getting furious but forcing himself to remain calm.

"Just what do you think you're playing at?" Mid demands. "First you pour me the wrong scotch, then you *deliberately* pour the wrong one again, then you lie about it!"

"I'm sorry, but I must have made a mistake the first time, but I'm *sure* I've poured the slightly mid-range one with the black label! I can-"

"Who do you think you are?! You think you can pour me cheaper shit and charge me the full price?"

"What? No!"

"*WHAT?* Did you just say, 'what' to me?" Mid exaggerates quotation marks dramatically with his fingers. "I'm a customer, you don't speak to me like that!"

"But-"

"Your manners are disgusting, mate! I *always* drink the same drink," he roars, "and you've lied to me, not once, but twice! *This*," he spat at the disgusting glistening poison, "This is not the one with the black label!" He took a breath, and allowed Tim to speak.

Tim took a deep breath too. He was counting to ten silently.

"I will pour you another one, please - just look at the bottle I'm pouring it from and you will see-"

"No! No!" Mid yet again barks on top of poor Tim, "No! You've refilled the bottle with a cheap scotch! Do you really think I'm that stupid? Do you?"

"Look, I can assure you, that has *never* happened here..." he started.

"Yes, you did, you refilled the bottle to make a better profit! Just wait – wait until I tell the media about this scandal!"

By this stage Tim was shaking, shocked by the absurdity of these claims. He was torn between serving a customer to save his job, or throwing the towel in, citing he's not worth it. Images flashed before Tim's eyes of glasses being hurled at Mid's face, soda water being sprayed in his eye and feet being belted into his fat stomach. He took a deep breath and thought of the money – was it worth staying? He was honestly suggesting that we refilled expensive bottles with cheaper products.

Then, Tim had an idea – could it work? Would the managers be on board with it?

Eff it. I'm a supervisor. I'm making the call, he thought.

Shaking, he took the cowardly, but safe route and made the man an offer.

"Ok. Ok!" he shouted aggressively. Then, he smiled, so the man would forget the shout. Big smile. Big, big wholesome smile. "Here's what I'm going to do. You clearly know your scotch."

Mid gruffly attempted an interjection but was cut off by Tim.

Tim's plan was building his confidence as he envisioned the repercussions from it. This guy was a douche-canoe. No one refilled that bottle. Seriously – who would do that?

Tim decided he would do just as the customer asked, for the 'customer was always right'. He would open a fresh bottle of scotch in front of the man, so he could see it really *was* what the label claimed.

This man will get what he deserves.

"So what I'm going to do," Tim continued, "is run down to the cellar and grab a fresh bottle that I will open *in front* of you, so you can be satisfied it's the right scotch."

"Well I should hope so!" Mid exclaimed, baffled at the stupidity of a bartender to dare double cross him with cheaper scotch.

That was it. The last nail in the coffin. Tim had tried to make peace, but he was shut down by this arsehole of a man. Now, Tim was going to teach this arsehole a lesson.

As Tim decided this, Mid, clearly still furious, shook his head, muttering rubbish to himself, and praying another customer would catch his eye so he could complain about the (lack of) service there.

Tim, also still furious, grabbed another glass from the rack and stormed down the back corridor, shouting random profanities at no one in particular.

He got to the cellar and immediately found what he was looking for – a brand new, unopened bottle of scotch. Looking behind him, he quickly checked there were no witnesses. He knew there was no camera there, but he still scanned the ceiling to confirm solidarity. Assured he was alone, he licked the rim of the glass. It left a residue, so he wiped it off again with his apron.

"You refilled the bottle with cheap scotch!" resounded in Tim's mind. Saliva was not good enough for this prick.

Tim unzipped his pants and whipped out his genitals. Discreetly, he found the scotch glass, and ran the rim of it around the tip of his privates. It was cold, and sent a tingly zap of electricity through his nerves.

Football! Think of football! Tim instructed himself, knowing that time was very limited. He dipped his balls in and jiggled them around inside the glass, giggling as they gently bounced against the edge. Almost satisfied, he pulled the glass out of his pants, checked there were no tell-tale hairs attached, and lifted it up admiring his handy work.

"I know Slightly Mid-Range Everywhere, and this is not Slightly Mid-Range Everywhere!"

He repeated the customer's abuse in his head and decided this just wasn't enough. He thought of one more thing. He unzipped his pants again and brought the glass to his behind. Spreading his cheeks, he forced a nutty fart into the vessel. *The arsehole meets the arsehole,* he chuckled to himself. Now, he was satisfied.

Very aware of time, Tim clambered up the stairs and sprinted down the corridor, appearing suddenly in the bar. Before the man noticed him, he shoveled some ice into the tainted glass.

Casually he conversed with the customer, as if he'd been there for ages. "So I managed to finally find a new bottle for you. Sorry it took a while; I couldn't see it at first," he blatantly lied.

Tim dumped the ice-filled contaminated glass in front of the man. Lifting up the bottle so the label could be clearly seen, he cracked the lid, shoved in a nip, and poured thirty mil into a shot, then into the glass.

Mid lifted the penis-vandalised glass to his now parched lips and took a deep swig, swirling the golden liquid around his mouth, before deeply swallowing. He took a moment to appreciate his favourite drink. He turned to Tim, and proudly proclaimed, "Now *this* is a drink. Thanks, mate."

Tim merely smiled and said, "You're welcome."

| 44 |

Petit Four: I Don't Want Ice

"I'll have a cosmopolitan please," a young girl told me.

"Sure," I said, pulling down a martini glass and placing it on the bar in front of her. I scooped some ice into the glass to help it chill, while I was making the rest of the cocktail.

The young girl snatched the glass off the bar, and tossed the contents into the ice well!

"I don't want ice!" she screamed. Ice was definitely going to ruin her drink. It was going to ruin her night. It was going to ruin her life! "I ordered that one because in the picture it *doesn't* have ice!" she shrieked. "I don't want ice in my cocktail! No ice!"

I stood calmly and looked at her. I was suppressing the urge to scream back at the stupidity of this girl. How dare she ruin my craft! "The drink doesn't have ice in it!" I snapped.

"Then *why-?*" the girl protested.

"I WAS CHILLING THE GLASS FOR YOU!" I bellowed, causing the young girl to flinch. Then I gave her a huge smile.

"Oh, oh," she stammered. "Sorry, I didn't realise…"

| 45 |

I Just Want Some Cash Out

"Excuse me, can I please get some cash out?" the woman asked.

I pointed to the left, at the ATM, positioned where they usually were, right next to the gaming room, but strategically not inside the room, because, you know, that would be an irresponsible gaming practice.

"There's an ATM just there," I motioned, not because I wanted this addict to spend more money, but because it was my job to, as a hospitality employee, to be hospitable.

"I want less than $20," she frowned at me.

"Sorry," I apologised. "The minimum it dispenses is $20." I started to frantically think of how I could help her. It was an automatic reaction of conditioning - I felt compelled to always try to say yes to customers. How could I help her?

"So can I get cash out over the bar?" she asked me hopefully.

I thought about it. In other bars, yes I *could* do cash out over the bar. Here at the Wood and Spoon however, the card terminals were integrated. There was no way to put through a sale, unless there was an actual sale.

"I'm so sorry, I don't have a way to offer you less cash out..." I started. Panic began to set in. An unhappy customer was bound to complain, even if circumstances were out of my control. She'd huff and puff and mutter and tell people that the staff at the Wood and Spoon were useless. I looked at her; she was already putting on the cranky face.

She stared back at me, disappointed with my lack of helpfulness.

How dare I not have the ability to offer cash out over the bar?

The woman's face sank.

"I've only got $3 in my bank account. That's why I just want to get $3 cash out, but you're saying you won't do it."

I never said I *wouldn't*; I had told her I *couldn't*. Big difference. A good employee would never say they won't; they would always negotiate a solution - which I did. Just because she's broke it's not my problem.

Hang on! It's *not* my problem!

"I'm really sorry, but as much as I'd love to help you, there's no way I can get you $3 cash out," I told her firmly, but with my gentle encouraging smile, perfected by years of customer service.

As she shuffled away, as disappointed as a disappointed customer could be, dramatically shaking her head, I reminded myself that some people cannot be helped if that do not want to help themselves: If she had poured all her money into a poker machine, and had only $3 left, and was unable to retrieve it, then maybe it was a sign that she should stop gambling. I knew that was the lesson to be learned. I doubted she did.

| 46 |

An Inconvenient Delivery

I was delighted that I'd finally saved enough money to buy a couch. The only problem was, how would it be delivered?

I phoned the delivery service, as instructed by Threadson, the upmarket department store from which it had been ordered.

"Hello delivery!" barked a man over a static line.

"Hi, how are you?"

There was silence, then a suspicious, "Yeah, good... How are you?"

Customer service representatives were always taken aback by my manners. It was a little sad to appreciate how rarely members of the public were pleasant. It did happen, just not as frequently as it should.

"Good thanks. I have a couch on order and I'm calling to arrange a delivery time. Are you the best person to speak to about that?" I asked.

"Yes, love. Let's see... Yeah, we've got you down for 7am 'cos you're right near the factory," he told me.

I winced. Seven is not a good time. "Ah, any chance that maybe I could get it delivered later in the day? Say mid to late afternoon?" I suggested.

"Nah, it's all good, love. We've got your address in Walnut Grove yeah?" he didn't wait for me to confirm. "Well our factory is just in the next suburb in West Leighton, so we can swing by yours first thing, first delivery of the day, then that way you can head to work straight after and you don't have to wait all day for us," he told me proudly, as if he were doing me a favour.

To most people, getting a delivery at seven in the morning would be enormously convenient. As the gentleman on the phone stated, it would enable them to leave for work straight after, and not have to wait the entire day. As most people can appreciate, delivery brackets can vary dramatically, and having an almost exact time promised should be held in great regard. Not, however, for me.

"Look," I said to the man, "I understand that normally it would be convenient to have it delivered at seven, but I was hoping that maybe I could be the last person of the day, rather than the first. Seven just really isn't a good time for me."

"It's all good, love. We'll drop it at seven then you can go. Don't worry, love, first thing we'll be on time; you won't have to wait," the man promised.

"I'm sorry I don't think you understand," I tried to explain, "I work overnight, and at seven I'll be sound asleep."

"You'll be asleep?" the man asked fishily.

"Yes, I'll get home at four-thirty then I'll be asleep by five. At seven I'll be dead to the world asleep. So is there any chance you can come last?" I was losing my patience now.

"But you're right near the factory, love. So we'll do you first then you can get on with your day or whatever, and-"

"No!" I snapped, "As I said, a 7am delivery is incredibly inconvenient. Any time before three is inconvenient! I will be asleep at seven, after having worked all night before, and god help your delivery driver if he dares knock on my door at seven!"

There was silence, then the driver told me quietly, "Look mam, I get that you need to sleep at seven, but that's the only time we can do. We have to do your house first because you're closest to the factory. I'm sorry."

"Fine," I said, wondering how I would even hear the door, mid-sleep cycle. A seven o'clock delivery to me was the equivalent to a midnight delivery to civilians. I would be in the deepest throes of slumber. I'd have to set an alarm and hope that it was enough to get me out of bed and decent to answer the door.

| 47 |

Amateur Gardener

I pounded through my travel path. Start at the kitchen and do a loop of the restaurant. Check in with the restaurant manager and the host then back to the kitchen. Check toilets. Loop around the restaurant again. Into the gaming room. Say hello to regular patrons, check everything is clean and everyone has drinks. See if Old Mate needs food. See the evil gaming cashier. Check toilets. Loop around the sports bar. Say hi to the locals. Check in with Tim at the bar. Meander through the floor picking up glasses, emptying ashtrays and monitoring alcohol consumption. Check toilets again. Zip outside and chat with security. Start heading down to the function room. Wait! *What is she doing in the garden?*

"Hey! Excuse me!" I called out, jogging closer. "Sorry, you can't be in the garden." There she was. Woman in the garden. As you do.

"I've... I... lost me..." the woman mumbled whilst pottering away. She was shifting the broad ferns apart and digging at the soil.

"What have you lost?" I asked politely. I always gave patrons the benefit of a doubt.

"Me... me diamond! Me earring!" the woman muttered as if it were so obvious to me.

Benefit of a doubt, doubted. She was a couple of bricks short of a barbecue.

The woman scooped up some dirt and held it up to her face, then scattered it away, shaking her head, upset that her prize was nowhere to be seen. She seemed gravely concerned that dirt was just dirt. She pawed away at the ground, clawing at chunks of soil, aggressively tugging at ferns for growing in the wrong spots.

Nope. Not happening.

"Look, I'm really sorry, but you need to get out of the garden now. We can take your details and look for it tomorrow," I directed professionally.

This wasn't the right thing to say.

The woman ceased searching the dirt, and staggered up to her full height, glaring at me. She was at least eight foot tall and twice as wide, wearing a scabby, thin muumuu. A slab of an arm jutted out to her side, questioning who dare challenge her. The ugly hag bore an etched face, indicating that she'd seen a lot and been very well used in her time. Her ebony irises pierce a fierce warning to me: Don't mess with her.

"Copy security? Security to functions entrance right away," I spoke quietly into the microphone attached to my collar. I crept a few silent steps backwards, with my hands visible, terrified to break eye contact.

It was enough.

The woman slunk back down and returned to attend the garden. A leafy lily grew in her way. She strangled it and ripped it up, shaking the stem to search for her 'diamond'. She hurled the bulb away, abusing it for holding only dirt.

"Hey," the security guard appeared.

"Wh-? You scared me!" I gasped.

"Oh... sorry," The seccy apologised. "You called?"

"Can you ask her to leave?" I pointed to a pile of rags topped with a scowl. "She's ripping up plants. Be careful though, she's not right in the head."

"You don't say," Seccy replied, his head cocked in fascination, watching Muumuu at work. I just really wanted to use the word 'cocked' again.

Paaaaaarp!

A loud fart erupted from her enormous bottom. She jumped in a small fright and whirled around, wondering where that noise came from. She cackled hysterically when she realised she'd let one rip. "Scare meself then!" she guffawed.

"Oh my..." I held my hand over my face recoiling.

"Well, that's ladylike," Seccy muttered. "Yeah, she's crazy alright... Argh!" he bent over in disgust as the stench reached him. He covered his nose and mouth, but he felt the putrid odour burning his eyes. "Alright, she's out of here," he decided, and marched toward her, on a mission. He mustn't have realised her size, for he just as quickly returned, saying, "On second thoughts, let's just leave her be and watch her. I mean, she's not hurting anyone. Maybe she'll get bored and leave of her own accord."

I considered the volume of patrons visiting that night. "Can you watch her?" I asked, "I have to go."

Seccy scanned around for another guard. Surely, someone else could watch her? Mohammed, the head of security, was checking IDs. Another guard scanned them. One patrolled the perimeter. The rest were allocated their areas. There was no one else. "Yeah. Yeah, I'll watch her," he agreed reluctantly.

I looked at my watch. It was one o'clock.

"Sports bar cleared," a guard barked down the radio.

I looked at my watch again and it's three in the morning. A crisp breeze swept past me and I shivered in my maroon blouse. It was certainly fresh out. I couldn't wear a singlet underneath, for I would have been too hot earlier running around. Now, my arms tingled with goose bumps and I could feel my nipples slicing into my bra. I'd need to get my hoody soon.

I paced around the venue with Mohammed, checking areas were clear, then locking up. We briskly strolled down the side car park, picking up the odd bottle that had been tossed in the bushes and chatting about events of the evening. We found the seccy where I'd left him, chilly and agitated.

"She's still here," he reported. "She's crazy. Been yelling at patrons as they left and throwing things. She's got to go. She's a hazard to stay."

Mohammed barged forward. "'Scuse me, Miss? Miss, the venue has now closed and I need to ask you to leave." He'd said that line a thousand times before. It was dignified and well-rehearsed.

The frumpy beast looked up and squinted. She eyed Mohammed, and then Seccy. "I'm not going anywhere until the police come," she huffed.

"Police? Why would the police come, Miss?" Mohammed asked her.

"I call 'em," Muumuu stated, staring into nothingness.

Mohammed looked around but could spy no obstacles. He asked her gently, "Why did you call the police?"

The woman looked blankly into space. Her focus moved to me and she scowled. "You!" she bellowed.

"Me?" I whispered.

"What you name?"

I didn't reply, but discreetly removed my nametag and slipped it into my pocket.

"Where you live? Where you car park? Answer me, dammit!" the woman demanded, growing frustrated at my silence.

I froze, wondering what I'd done and what this psycho would do with me. I didn't need to wonder long.

"You," Muumuu growled quietly, like a dog protecting his owner. "You effing bitch! Effing run, bitch! Cos I'm gonna get ya!" she screamed menacingly as she lunged forward. She raised her arm and howled, "You on my hit list, bitch! I'll kill ya!"

In slow motion, I (still frozen) witnessed Muumuu the land-whale fly toward me.

I braced myself for impact, cringing, terrified, arms up and eyes widened.

Muumuu hurled closer, snarling, determined to squash me, reaching out to attack me.

I squinted, ready for the fall; there was no time to get away.

Two beefy security guards leapt toward her, intercepting the attack, and slamming her to the ground with a loud smack.

I stumbled and time sped back up. As I retained my balance, Muumuu was shoved into a headlock.

One guard sat across her back, wrenching her arm awkwardly behind her while the other guard radioed for backup.

The beast was so heavy, she kept writhing, trying to flip over to get back up and get to me.

"Get inside and lock the door!" Mohammed commanded urgently.

I scrambled away, running for my life, but desperately wanting to see what happened next. I could hear the woman moaning, "Stop hitting me! You hit me!"

Mohammed yelled, "We never hit you, lady!"

I scrambled far enough to where I could pause for a breath. I gasped in shock, a fog forming against the chilled air.

Shit!

I could still hear Muumuu taunting the guards, "You all on drugs! The police come drug test you and take you away!"

She spied me down the path and screamed, "I'm gonna kill you, bitch!"

"*Go!*" Mohammed urged, waving me away.

But... But... I wanted to see the show! It's not every day that a crazy person dug up the garden and tried to fling herself at me. I had to know what happened next and there was only one way of finding out: via camera. I zapped inside, and sprinted past the staff who were cleaning the sports bar.

They looked up at me briefly, questioning why I was running, then recommenced scrubbing along to their heavy metal playlist. Meh. Nothing to see here. It would take some real action to get the staff excited. They'd seen managers run around frantically before.

I bolted down the back passages, darting past empty kegs and drums of chemicals before meeting an impenetrable steel door. I unlocked it, and then the next door soon behind it, falling into the office and gasping for breath.

Tim was surrounded by piles of cash, empty till drawers and elastic bands. "What the hell's going on?" he amused, as he whizzed another pile of notes into the note counter. His phone was creakily playing music beside him.

"Did you see the footage?" I blurted.

"It keeps popping in and out. They're right on the edge. I can't see them right now," Tim answered as he bundled a brick of hundreds. Managers often seemed so calm in the face of danger. Besides, nothing would reach him in the hidden depths of that office.

I squinted up at the screens. My eyes were still adjusting to the bright lights. I found the camera aimed at the function entrance. I could see Mohammed's shoulder popping in and out. Not close enough!

"I've been listening to the radio calls, what's been happening?" Tim asked absentmindedly.

I grabbed a bottle of water from my bag and skulled it. It was a perfect soother to my raspy voice. "This- this woman. She's crazy, right. Keeps ripping out the plants chatting to herself saying she's looking for diamonds or something. Anyone goes near her, she flips. Loses it. She just tried to attack me!" I exclaimed. "Mohammed is with her now but I don't know what they're doing. She's massive. It'll take a few guards to restrain her."

"Yeah, I might stay away from that one," Tim laughed.

I couldn't stop talking about this woman. "She scared herself farting and then laughed about it. She's so gross!"

Tim wasn't listening. He was weighing the money brick and adding the values to a spreadsheet. "I'm listening..." he vaguely stated.

The phone rang. I looked at my watch. It was three forty-five. Who would be calling the pub at that time?

It was the police.

The policeman on the phone asked me if we were requiring assistance. *How would he know?*

"Ah, well sort of. But there's no emergency here." Emergency to me means bleeding and life endangerment. Not crazy muumuu wearing diamond seeking farters.

"No emergency? We've had someone call the emergency hotline eight times in the last fifteen minutes," the policeman stated.

"You're kidding! Yeah. Of course she did. She's not in an emergency situation though," I replied. "Not actually a patron either. She hasn't been inside at all tonight. She's a crazy pain in the arse who's ripping up the plants and screaming at people and refusing to leave. She tried to attack me even. Security is with her now."

"Ah, so do you require police attendance?" he asked briskly.

"If it's quiet, that would be great; just to move her along. But if you guys are busy, don't worry. It'd be a lower priority," I decided.

"A car is on the way," he replied.

"Sorry – if you do send someone, you better make it two cars," I warned.

"Two? Sorry, is this an emergency or not?" he demanded.

"No one's life is at risk, but this patron is very large, very strong and will need multiple officers to restrain her."

"Very well. Please confirm your full name and address with the exact location."

I confirmed the details, and soon after I heard the sirens wailing down the hill. I tossed my nametag and phone into my bag, chucked on a hoodie, wrapped a scarf around me and joined my guards outside.

"How's she going?" I asked Mohammed.

"Well we've managed to get her out of the garden, but she won't leave. She's over there outside the bottle shop, so technically still on premise. Are those coppers coming for us?" he asked, hearing the sirens draw nearer.

"Yeah. Apparently she called emergency eight times," I replied.

"Good, they can take her away. She can be their problem, not ours. She's not right in the head," Mohammed grimaced.

Two policemen hopped out of the single car and asked us what was happening.

"Patron refusing to leave," Mohammed replied, pointing to Muumuu, who was sitting in the gutter shaking her head and muttering angrily to no one.

"*Not* a patron," I interjected. "She was never granted entry." It was simple descriptions like that that could get a venue a fine or not.

"Sorry," Mohammed agreed. "Trespasser refusing to leave," he corrected.

"Right. Let's go have a chat then," Constable Miller suggested.

I wondered how two weedy guys like this would take on a behemoth that, but, then again, not my problem.

Constable Miller and Constable Bright strolled over to Muumuu and spoke with her for what seemed ages.

We craned our necks, trying to listen, but they were just too far away.

Muumuu seemed quite calm and normal as she discussed her concerns, nodding, smiling and listening, then chatting away with them. From where I was standing, they could have been talking about their favourite recipes. It was like she was a different person.

Constable Bright outstretched his hand, presumably to help Muumuu stand. She had been in that gutter for some time now.

I wondered how her butt wasn't iced over.

Muumuu waved his offer away and shook her head. She didn't need him. She struggled to lift herself up and began rolling her eyes in frustration. As she finally staggered and rose, she stretched up, lifting her arms, and released an almighty belch which echoed through the quiet carpark.

"Was that a burp?" I blurted, disgusted that any human could project such a hefty bodily function.

"Yep. She's a real classy one," Mohammed nodded.

As professional as they had been, Constables Miller and Bright recoiled and bent over away in disgust.

Muumuu lifted her skirt, etching length after length of fabric up over her thighs.

"*What is she doing?*" Mohammed asked, horrified.

Miller and Bright attempted to restrain her, but with her sheer strength, she merely flicked them away, tossing them to the floor.

I could see Miller pull out his radio and speak into it.

Miller and Bright got up and reassessed, taking a side each, not quite touching her yet but more so gauging her weight to figure out how to restrain her.

Muumuu's skirt was now up around her waist. Of course, she wasn't wearing knickers. Her wobbly bottom cheeks glowed a bright sheen of pearl in the moonlight, like a pair of lumpy giant albino citruses, and she eased her legs apart, squatting on the tarmac, holding her skirt up.

I could see thick hairs dangling from the crevice. I wanted to look away, but was somehow compelled to keep watching, drawn to the hideous beast, mystified as to what would happen next.

Muumuu turned her head, and a crafty smile flashed to her audience. She steadied herself, then pissed a strong golden steaming conduit, splashing down her legs, over the footpath, and rebounding onto Constables Miller and Bright.

The policemen sprang apart as Muumuu cackled hysterically. They groaned and scampered away in disgust, damp and smelling of someone else's wee. Miller shook his hand forcefully, and droplets flicked off it, sizzling as they hit the icy ground.

"Ah- should we go help them?" I asked timidly.

Mohammed turned to me as if I were the crazy one, "What? Are you volunteering? I'm *not* touching that! Just let the police do their job; they know what they're doing," he almost convinced himself.

A paddy wagon arrived and two more coppers hopped out.

Muumuu must have been delighted to see them. She bent over, exposing her juicy lady-bits, and shook her lumpy booty and hairy clamburger at the police, flapping away in a rigorous performance, cackling hysterically.

This was enough for them. She hadn't just gone over the line – the line was so far gone it couldn't be seen anymore!

The four police huddled quickly, then breaked with their game faces on. Time to slay the dragon.

Three of them lunged at Muumuu, faces contorted with defiant aggression.

She swaggered and swayed, trying to fling them off her, but the police were determined to beat her.

They attached themselves rigidly to her slab arms, using their weight to rock her and shift her balance, bracing themselves for the eventual fall.

Muumuu shook and groaned, heaving around, desperately trying to be rid of them. One wrong foot and she slipped, howling as she plummeted to the concrete, with a smack and a thud.

I was certain her weight would crack the slab.

The coppers released their grip just in time, rolling out of harm's way, as Miller swooped in and handcuffed her. She thrashed about, trying to get away, but there were too many of them restraining her.

The rest of the coppers surrounded Muumuu, pulling her up and dragging her toward the wagon. She deliberately lay limp, as a dead weight to make their job harder. Her calloused feet dragged along the ground and that filthy muumuu she wore stretched and tore too.

Miller ran ahead, unlocked the back and returned to her the others. Slowly, they pushed the mammoth up into the wagon.

She swore and screamed, "I'll report you! You attack me! You attack me! Police brutality!"

Mohammed rolled his eyes.

With one final shove, she fell into the van, and the metal door slammed and locked.

The police whooped a cheer of relief. Bright and Miller high fived.

The paddy wagon sagged under Muumuu's weight and swayed as she rumbled around, howling and searching for an apparent escape.

The police knew they had to make a move quickly. She may even be strong enough to tip the whole truck over!

Miller jogged over to speak with the pub staff. There were two broad and tall guards in uniform, with ID tags and wires. Not them. They're security. There was a little blonde chick wearing a hoodie and fake lashes. Her?

"You in charge?" he delicately asked me, the tiniest person there.

I nodded, "Yep."

"Oh. Alright," he took a breath. "So we were going to charge her for refusing to leave a licenced premise, resisting arrest, attempting to assault an officer, urinating in public, indecent exposure and misuse of the emergency phone service," he listed. "Anything else?"

"Sounds good to me," I breathed. "You got a business card in case I need to contact you?"

"Here you go," Miller pulled one out of his shirt pocket. "She'll be spending the night at Swanston Watch House before she's formally changed. Do you need anything else from us?"

"No. Thank you," I said genuinely. I yawned. The sky had started to lighten to a pale grey and I could hear birds starting to chirp sweetly.

It was a pity my night wasn't over yet. I was rostered the next day off (today, really?) so I had to write the incident report right away, so I didn't miss the twenty-four hour compliance window. Dammit.

I stomped back inside to the computer, grabbing a bourbon on my way through.

Tim had gone. The staff had gone. Mohammed waited patiently as the other guards signed off.

I did my bit, and filed an incident report straight away. No one ever asked me about it.

| 48 |

He's Not Here

"Wood and Spoon, this is Alex!" I sang down the mouthpiece of the phone.

A woman began to speak. "Hello, I was wondering if Jeff Thorne was there?"

I froze and stared at Old Mate standing in the bar. "Jeff Thorne? Is that a customer here? There's nobody by that name who works here."

"Yes – a customer. He's not home or at work and I was wondering if he was there?"

I looked around the near empty bar, silently pleading to make eye contact with Old Mate. "Hold on, it's quite busy in here, I'll have to ask around because I'm not sure who he is... Just hold on," I popped the handset onto the receiver and made a beeline toward him. I approached and waited for a break in conversation. "Ah, excuse me. Can I have a word?"

Old Mate apprehensively looked around his group of friends and agreed.

"Excuse me, are you Jeff Thorne?" I whispered to him. I knew exactly who he was and exactly how much money he put into the poker machines, but still, I was required to ask.

Old Mate nodded in confirmation. He wasn't even surprised I mightn't for sure know his name.

"There's a woman on the phone for you. Shall I, ah, put you on?"

Old Mate uncomfortably shuffled and stared straight ahead.

"Or, maybe you're not here?" I suggested.

"Yes," Old Mate relaxed and made solid eye contact with me, "Tell her I'm not here."

I picked up the receiver, "Hello? Are you there?"

"Yes, I'm still here," the woman confirmed curtly.

"Sorry, I've had a look and asked around, I can't see him. I don't think he's here," I lied to the woman. Years of customer service meant I knew it was believable.

Old Mate meandered toward his usual seat in the gaming room. "Can I grab a drink?"

"Of course," I replied. I collected his usual and walked it, on a tray, to the dim gaming room.

Old Mate placed twenty dollars on the tray.

I knew the rules: never assume someone will tip. I smiled and said, "Oh, that's on the house."

Old Mate smiled straight ahead at the musical machine and the promising symbols lining up, and simply said, "I know."

| 49 |

The Gambling Addicts

At the far end of the bar, in a dark room, a handful of players plonked themselves in front of 'their' slot machines.

They all sat in the same manner, leaning forward, staring straight ahead at the glow of the bright colours hazily glaring, illuminating their prematurely aged faces. Tap. Tap. Tap.

A woman paused briefly and tore her eyes away from the spinning figures, desperately praying for eye contact, so someone – anyone – could join her in potentially celebrating her feature win.

I caught her eye as she practically burst with giddy excitement, her hands patting away on the side of the machine as if to encourage it. The music whirred dramatically longer as the last symbol spun through the wheel. It slowed down and the woman frantically pleaded with the machine to keep going... keep going! It stopped. A bell buzzed, and the woman cried out a small whoop of cheer as she won the feature, earning her back only a fraction of what she had donated in the first place.

Old Mate chuckled as he passed me, making his way to the ATM. His laugh was justification for his expenditure. He'd been past several times now, each time, making small comments. "Well, one more won't hurt... better luck this time," he said to me in passing.

I forced a Customer Laugh and replied, "Oh yes," knowing that I could have said literally anything and he would smile back.

I didn't know what was worse: watching people pile all their money into a machine, or the fact that it was my job to keep them there.

I looked around the room. Pokie players were treated far better than any other customer. They had reserved parking near the door, free coffee, complimentary canapes, and floor service for drinks.

It was a moral blur. They weren't doing anything illegal. I thought it should be though.

I watched the same people pile thousands of dollars a week into the machines. Old Mate lined up waiting for the venue to open at nine. Half an hour before closing at three in the morning, we'd warn him. With fifteen minutes to go, he'd be asked again, then reminded to cash out. At closing time, security would pry him from his machine. He would frantically plead with them for him to stay, desperate for just one more spin, one more win, that feature that kept promising to come soon, that small win which hinted at a bigger one, but no matter how big, it would never be enough. The next morning, he would be back. If it weren't for the free food the venue supplied to him, he wouldn't eat. It was an oxymoron naming it free food: he was ultimately paying for it.

The staff of the Wood and Spoon began bringing around platters of cocktail spring rolls, greasy dim sims and dry sausage rolls to the pokie addicts. It was fashionable to tempt players into staying longer by supplying food. When the staff realised that those snack platters were the only food Old Mate was consuming, they brought it upon themselves to improve the quality of his diet – with the amount he drank and smoked, paired with his sedentary and addictive lifestyle, his diet was the only thing they could contribute to an otherwise limited lifespan. It seemed a bit odd saving the life of someone who would spend his longevity wasting it on the pokies still.

The first time I dropped a plate with a ham and salad sandwich in front of Old Mate, he questioned why he was given it. I shrugged and said, "I thought you might be hungry."

After a few months, he moved to a cycle of stir-fries, steaks with vegetables, roast chicken, salads and fruit platters. He knew never to question it, and we knew never to say a word as we dropped it off. The plate would be ignored as a lengthy cigarette sat perfectly stationary between his lips. The occasional puff of smoke gushed out of his nose, but not blustery enough for the entire length of the ash to form one delicate branch attached to the soggy filter. Suddenly he'd blink, and the perfect ash stick would fall into his lap, where it would stay, staining the creases of his top and track pants. He'd glance down and notice the cold plate, and reach for the fork. He'd lift that fork to his lips, tasting just a small lick, probably to guess if it'd been poisoned. Each time, he'd realise it was real food, and that slither of a sample became ravenous shovels as he inhaled the dish. There was never a thank you as his plate was cleared, even when the empty crockery was replaced with his favourite beer.

Old Mate was important, as his contribution paid the salary of around half the management team. They needed him to stay playing as long as possible, for it was good for business, yet I seemed to be the only person concerned for his well being. It wouldn't have mattered – no one could stop him, but himself. The gambling helplines and government exemptions and counselling were useless to those who didn't want the help themselves.

In order to work in the gaming room, I had to undertake a course. The course was a joke. It was required by law that all staff did it. It was probably so the government workers felt better about making so much money on taxing pokies. If there was a course saying that it was done responsibly, then it must be ok to watch and encourage people to throw their lives away.

It wasn't entirely dire – there were a number of community services funded by gaming tax. I also liked to think it was a way for tax evaders to pay their fair share. Playing the pokies was the only way dole bludgers paid tax. But when it came to seeing exactly how much money people played, it was enough to make me feel sick.

I thought about my measly bank account. There was roughly fifty dollars in it, after the bills had been paid. Enough to get a bit of groceries, but I had to skimp, stealing toilet paper, coffee and cleaning products from the pub. The hand wash was quite versatile, and I found it made a great body wash/ shampoo/ face wash/ dish soap. Nobody noticed the distinct lime and bleach scent.

The patrons I served poured thousands of dollars into their machines. I dreamed that maybe one day, someone would tip me generously instead of donating it, but tips were rare and unreliable. No one would ever walk in offering me a grand; instead they wasted fifty dollar notes at a time, never comprehending the extent of the damage they were doing.

The same rule of working in hospitality applied here. I could never predict tipping. If a woman did it once, it did not make her a sure thing. If a man handed over a twenty after a huge payout, he mightn't be as generous when he was losing.

On my gaming course, I learnt that the only way to know if someone had a gambling problem, was if they told me. I was not permitted to ask. If someone approached me, I had a helpful protocol to follow. But I wasn't allowed to suggest help out of nowhere.

I was hopeful that my patrons were all just really rich. That's what Dean kept telling us. I knew in my heart they weren't.

The gaming room was the number one money-maker for the venue (if not all venues). It cost the least to run and made the most money by far. Food and entertainment brought customers into a venue, but pokies kept them there. While food cost was high, and the return on invest-ment was moderate, pokies held a low running cost. The return on in-vestment was phenomenal!

It was no wonder management meetings were dominated by pokies. Who was playing? How much? How do we get them to stay longer? How do we make them more comfortable?

Old Mate came up in conversation. I was disgusted to witness this man being profiled by the Wood and Spoon.

"Ask him about his grandchildren," Michelle suggested, "he loves to chat about them. It will make him feel more comfortable."

"But how do we get him to stay past lock-out? If he goes to get some-thing out of his car, and it's 1am, we legally can't let him re-enter the building. That's two hours of lost revenue," Tim commented.

"JEFF THORNE CAN ENTER ANY TIME HE LIKES!" Dean barked. "IF WE'RE OPEN, YOU DO ANYTHING YOU CAN TO GET THAT MAN IN!"

I sat seething.

"But what about fines?" Tim asked. "If the compliance team sees footage of him leaving and coming back, not only will the venue get a fine, but we get one too!"

Dean made her an offer he couldn't refuse. "If Compliance issues you a fine for letting him in after lockout, I will pay that fine for you."

Even the managers had to think about this. It would certainly help them reach their targets.

Dean saw him thinking, and he saw me stewing. "JEFF THORNE CAN ENTER ANY TIME AND THAT'S FINAL!" he snapped.

For the next week, all managers (except me who quietly revolted) nosily questioned Old Mate on his family. How are they? What are they up to?

As they saw him walk in, Dean ordered them to make a small plate of the fried crap for themselves, so it looked like they had the opportunity to say, "Would you like one too, Jeff?"

For the whole week, he was showered with niceties, extra small talk, and little favours. The law forbade advertising and promotions for the 'VIP Lounge' (as it was craftily known from the external building signage) so the staff had to be creative. Being nice to regulars, offering the platters of shittly food, and plonking an automatic 'espresso' maker in the room were standard practice. For high rollers like Jeff, they were offered steak dinners, multiple entries into competitions (so non-gamblers would never win) and as many free drinks - even expensive ones - as they liked. The managers were coached to never slow down on the drinks especially. There was no limit, and the liquor service laws never applied in this room. Get them wasted, be their best friend and get them to stay. Just stay in that room forever.

Well it backfired. Old Mate, a seemingly thick man, cottoned on fairly quickly that they were being overly nice. Instead of staying longer, he moved to the Lonsdale Tavern.

I smirked to myself. I knew it.

The week after, gaming figures were significantly lower and casual staff saw their hours being cut. A month later, when a duty manager moved to another venue, she wasn't replaced. All the other managers had to pick up the extra hours (in line with their 'salary package'). It's not like I wasn't already working a severe number of hours overtime, now my sixty hours had become sixty eight. As I liked to think about it – my hourly rate dropped down to seven dollars. Fast food workers earned more than me.

The true cost of one customer filtered down to threatening someone's job.

It was awful. I despised the reminder of how important the addicts were: if it weren't for them, I wouldn't be employed. Their contribution paid my salary. As much as I loved the restaurant part, it didn't nearly supplement the cost of running a business. No wonder most pubs had pokies now: they'd suffer to survive without them.

Pokie players weren't loyal. They played where it was convenient and they wouldn't be bothered by anyone. They would just as quickly go elsewhere if they felt uncomfortable.

If they weren't doing it here, they'd be doing it somewhere else. So they may as well be doing it here.

| 50 |

Just a Regular Friday Night

It was Friday night and I was rostered close – the late shift, named appropriately as I had to close the venue at the end of the night. Friday nights were demanding shifts. It was go-go-go from five o'clock, and didn't stop until the 4am finish (if I worked on time). Incidences, a requirement to help on the floor, a busy restaurant and missing cash all contributed to a later night, but the key was to be on the game from the beginning.

I loved being organised. I planned my evening and allocated my staff. I worked on the 'aces in their places' theory, and put myself and the strongest team members where it would be the busiest: restaurant until nine-ish, then sports bar, and try slot in breaks before all the food-only staff go home. It would be tight, but manageable.

I highlighted several names in yellow – these were the people who'd need to move to the sports bar. The remaining restaurant staff were highlighted orange. I decided purple was a lovely shade for the gaming attendants. The dedicated sports bar staff were blue. I put myself and my DMs in green. Almost finished. I wrote another section down the bottom, titled, 'Breaks' and allocated staff every ten minutes to go on break, so they'd overlap and all be back in time for the ten to eleven o'clock rush in the sports bar. There. I admired my beautifully coloured run sheet.

There were three staff yet to be allocated. I looked at the names of my weakest links. Two were easy – they'd do the floor, picking up glasses and clearing plates. The third was tricky, because she *thought* she was very good, deserving of management even. She was not.

I thought about the best way to allocate her without offending. *Make it seem like it's a compliment. Make it seem like you are relying on her.*

"What am I on tonight?" Zoe asked, interrupting my thoughts.

"Tonight, I've got you on…" I scanned the sheet, pretending to search for Zoe's name, "float in the restaurant."

"*Float?*" Zoe was not impressed.

Time to make it look like a compliment.

"Yes," I said, "I need someone I can really rely on to help put out spot fires. Help me be my eyes and ears when I can't be there. So keep doing loops from cashier, to host, through the tables and to the pass, and keep me up to date of where I need to be. Oh, and in between, help keep things tidy by clearing and resetting tables. The new floor staff need some good guidance and support."

It worked. Zoe was keen as a bean. She bounced around the floor enthusiastically.

"Excuse me, can you help me?" an elderly woman asked as she approached the bar. She looked gravely concerned.

"Of course, what did you need?" I asked her.

"We… I've had a bit of an accident. I've, ah, dropped my drink and it's… broken the glass." The woman appeared rather apprehensive about admitting this dire mistake to me.

"That's ok, where were you sitting? I'll just grab a cloth and come fix it up for you," I offered, smiling.

"Just over there," the woman pointed to a coffee table with a family around it. She was frowning. The rest of the family seemed oblivious to the treacherous breakage, laughing and chatting. A pile of wet napkins sat in the middle of the table.

I went over, wiped up the mess and cleared the shattered glass, making small talk with the family. I said, "You can't take her anywhere!" causing them to burst into fits of laughter. I'm hilarious like that.

The woman who broke the glass, however, was quite concerned and fished out her wallet. "How much are they?"

"Wh- the drink?" I asked, "Don't be silly, I'll grab you a new one of course!"

"No, the glass. I'll have to reimburse you," the woman offered.

Oh, bless her cotton socks. "No, of course not! That's not necessary!" I exclaimed to one of the sweetest elderly ladies ever. *Awww, she offered to pay for the damages,* I thought fondly.

The evening picked up pace and I found myself in supersonic mode, being needed everywhere, and speaking to everyone.

"I'll get another bottle for you now," I told Tim, who was low on vodka.

"No, no requests," I directed to the DJ about to play the latest fad song.

"If you're wondering if she's drunk, that answers your question. She's not coming in," I confirmed with the security guard.

"Do you need an increase?" I asked the new gaming attendant, whose name I didn't know yet, and couldn't be bothered to find out.

Muffled noises in between yelling via the radio in my ear made me drop everything and run.

Three bar staff dashed to meet me. They looked worried.

"Quick! There's a fight!" Tim yelled.

I burst into the sports bar to assess the situation. I ducked as a bar stool crashed down next to me. There was a brawl. Arms swung at anyone. Shirts ripped as young guys fell, then hurled themselves up, bloody, going back for more. People lashed at each other everywhere, screaming and shouting.

Bang! Thud! Crash!

A girl screamed as her boyfriend was smacked in the eye socket. *Priorities*, I thought.

"Security to sports bar immediately!" I barked into my radio. "Priority sports bar! Security to sports immediately!"

What next?

"Staff! Stay back! Lights on, music off!" I ordered.

The bar flooded with Ugly Lights, causing everyone to squint, but the brawl continued on. I barged to the DJ booth and shut off the power, ceasing the music.

The brawl was building and moving toward me. I pulled a woman, glued to the spot in fear aside, "Move away! Over there!" I pointed to the bar area and pushed her along forcefully. The woman stumbled, unable to process the situation.

Security circled in, pulling fists off each other and wrapping arms behind backs as feet swayed threateningly.

I moved other patrons away, who were paralysed with fear and compelled to watch the action. I just had to let security do their job, stay out of the way, and keep others safe. A wide enough space had been created around the brutes in the middle. A bar table fell to the floor, smashing the glasses that were on it and splattering beer and spirits all over me. An elbow smacked me between my shoulder blades. "Ow, shit!" I screamed, steadying myself and ducking out the way. A painful lump began to swell and throb.

A girl fell next to me, banging her head on that fallen table. I ripped her up. "You ok?" I yelled, pushing her to safety. The girl nodded tipsily, as she was pulled away by her friends.

Men swearing and yelling around me clawed at each other's faces. I stayed low, desperately searching for a way out. *There!* I saw an escape!

Teeth were bared. *Smack!* A body sunk to the ground with a thud. A chunk of my hair got ripped out as I scrambled away, around the bar. I dabbed the back of my head. Bleeding and sore.

I watched the guards rip people off each other and stand in between those who tried to pry their way back in.

The instigators were carried out the front and detained by the guards. They kept pulling away in a rage, wildly trying to shake off the guards who'd secured them. It was moments like this, I was thankful my security team are so threateningly huge. It was moments like this that reinforced why our license was so strict, and we were required by law to have security every night. It was moments like this I was grateful for that too. The brawl dissipated and people began collecting their things.

"Bar is closed!" I screamed at a girl holding money.

"Water and non-alcoholic drinks are still available!" I ordered to my bar staff. "In plastic cups!" I added. I took three staff onto the floor to help tidy while I moved between patrons asking if they were ok. Everyone was fine, and they chatted excitedly among themselves about what they saw.

The place was a mess. Tables lay on their side. There was glass and liquid everywhere. Sticky puddles of foamy beer pooled around the tables. Posters were ripped down. Betting tickets scattered. Contents of handbags lost.

"You better come here!" Tim called me over hurriedly. I looked over and spotted a slumped figure on the floor under a table. It was the guy who fell next to me. In all the commotion, I'd completely forgotten about him.

"Shit!" I gasped as I ran over to assess him. Without even thinking, I grabbed my mobile phone from my back pocket and called an ambulance, tossing the phone to Tim so I could do first aid. *How did that phone survive?*

"No, he's conscious, he's responding to our questions..." Tim told the operator while I asked him his name and where he was and who he was here with. I was trying to determine if he'd been knocked in the head.

He hesitated when I asked how many drinks he'd had, and as he answered, "Dunno, seven... or eight..." he dribbled thick dark ruby blood from his mouth. Tim waved over a staff member, requesting a first aid kit.

"Can I see inside your mouth please?" I asked, worried about what I might see.

He was swaying – while on the floor – with too much blood for me to be comfortable.

He opened his mouth and his eyes started bulging. He gaped like a goldfish, struggling to breathe. He started thrashing about desperately! He was choking!

Without even thinking, I shoved my bare hand in his mouth, guessing the problem. I felt around as he gagged, and right toward the back of his warm wet mouth, I found what I was looking for: two jagged teeth. I ripped my hand out and forced his head forward, as he finally took a breath, and promptly spat, then vomited the blood which had choked him.

I had no idea if the first aid I did was right, but he stopped choking and started breathing, so I think I did ok.

I offered him a sip of water, which had miraculously appeared next to me, along with some disposable gloves, a jug of ice and some towels

I regretted not seeing earlier. I felt the warmth of bloody vomit on my legs.

"Thanks," he whispered croakily. A scarlet river crept down his face.

"No problem," I whispered back, holding out my palm displaying his teeth.

He tried to smile, but winced in pain, revealing raw gums with black liquid oozing from them.

"Chew on this towel," I directed, shoving a moist towel in his mouth. "It's got ice in it. It'll help stem the bleeding." I have been looking for an excuse to use the word 'moist' for so long now. Moist. Moist. Moist.

The ambulance arrived and whisked off the poor guy, his teeth in his hand. He tried to offer the towel back to me as he left.

I grimaced, telling him, "No, you keep it."

"You better get cleaned up," the paramedic called over.

I looked down and realised why. Congealed blood was smudged over my shirt. There were wet, sticky patches on my pants, which thankfully, being hospo-black, couldn't be seen, but I knew they were there. I was reminded it was vomit, and the smell started to haunt me. I could feel a part of my neck starting to crust, and strands of my hair grew straw-like.

I carefully manoeuvred my way through to the office, tossing my shirt in the bin (dammit, I really liked that one!), and remembered the cameras only after tearing it off and exposing my ugly sports bra. I found a pile of skanky promotional tops lying around, and put on a black one. It was far too tight and revealed my midriff, but I decided no one would care. It was a pity there were no pants. I honestly considered running around in just my undies for the rest of the shift. If I were wearing my grannie panties it might have been ok, but of course I chose the hot pink g-banger today. As much of a skank I usually was, I didn't want to entice the creepy older men of the pub any more than they usually preyed upon us girls with smacks on our bottoms and kisses and cuddles hello and goodbye. If anything, vomit pants might be a good thing, except, you know, the vomit part.

I went to the bathroom and scrubbed my hands, arms and neck. The water ran a deep red then orange, and then clear. I had to lean over the sink to wash my hair, using good old lime scented hand soap as shampoo. The sopping mop of my hair washed off half my makeup, exposing my pasty skin. I patted myself dry with a paper towel, taking a deep breath to suppress the emotion.

Teeth. *What was it with me and teeth?* I pulled this guy's teeth from his mouth and now I was wearing his blood as a badge of honour. I shuddered, praying the guy was clean.

What if I get hepatitis from this? What if he has HIV?

None of it had gotten *into* me, so I should be right, but even so. I'd saved his life, but in doing so, I'd risked my own. There was a very harsh reality that I could become ill. I promised to book a doctor's appointment for my next day off.

I stared at myself for some time. I looked haggard. The youthful beautiful face I used to have, had been replaced with a prematurely aged pale mannequin. I was gaunt from the constant exercise of running, heavy lifting and lack of nutritious food, and was ashen from lack of sleep. When I spoke normally, my voice croaked from the years of yelling over loud music, sneaky backdoor cigarettes, loud patrons and loud kitchens.

Was I still happy doing what I did? Was working in hospitality worth the price I was paying? I had poor health, no social life and limited money. My friends weren't even real – I relied on patrons to befriend and other staff to eff. Everyone was shagging each other. Everyone shared secrets with each other. Hospo bonds were tight but temporary. I knew as soon as I'd leave this job, I'd leave them too.

A hospo's family is their staff, but as jobs move on, the family units move on. The people we see more than our own blood disappear as quickly as they came.

With every new job, there's be a new group of the same people, as there are in every venue – a territorial veteran, a few dumb casuals, a rockstar bartender, and a group of some of the coolest people ever – but these people aren't transient. They don't care about me – really – same as I don't care about them – really. They're fair-weather friends. Here for work, partying through all the best times, and watching each other's backs in the tough times - but with no longevity. Loyal as hell on the floor, but soon forgotten a year later.

To The Wood and Spoon, I was a manager – a number required to produce better numbers in the form of profit. To everyone – the staff, the corporate and the customers – I was dispensable. We all were. The only way to prove importance was by smashing results that made my resume look good. This was the only way I'd properly build a network, and the expertise for opening my own place one day.

I had to go back to work. I had to set an example. I had to show the bar staff I was a professional leader and not a whimpering mess. Game face on.

Just as I had dreaded, it was a late one. I was on the floor far too long, so counting tills fell behind.

The staff cleaned the bar, then needed direction on tidying the floor after it got destroyed in the brawl. Security needed my authority on handling the brawl instigators. The police needed me to report on the incident. I had to supervise the closing of the pub so it would open again in a few hours without a hint of last night remaining. It needed stocking, cleaning and setting up.

By the time I'd done the incident reports, I was well overtime. It was coming up to fifteen hours without a break, on salary. I knew there'd never be a cent of overtime paid and I'd never recover those hours. I was over it. I was tired and just wanted to go home. I promised I'd leave early next shift. I didn't.

Urgh; I'm so gross. Covered... just covered in... I need to have a shower...

I threw my shoes into the laundry, peeled off my filthy clothes and chucked them in a bucket of water to soak. I pulled on an old sundress and a hoodie for now.

I stomped into my kitchen and ripped a bottle out of the fridge, going outside, and was alone for the first time all night. The tears finally fell from being overwhelmed and exhausted. My head pounded as I inhaled a deep drag of a joint. I swigged my beer, watching the sun rise, and only headed inside after I was drunk, high and too sweaty.

While I swayed in the scolding heat of the shower, I finally felt the burn of the water, the first thing to break through the numbing resilience of a hospitality worker.

Those feelings that I'd suppressed to the far corner of my mind were rushed to the front, pounding heavily into raging aches. The thoughts and feelings became too much as my body convulsed, and my stomach wretched. One swift twist and pull and I vomited, and vomited and vomited. Expel the badness and expel the experiences. I came to terms with what happened. I pulled out some guy's teeth. His teeth! I had his bodily fluids all over me! He would have choked without me. I'd saved his life. He probably wouldn't remember me. There were no thank yous, and no procedures for that shizz. The only counselling would be the stories passed around at staffies, hospos supporting hospos. Alcohol, cigarettes, white lines and weed suppressing feelings, and staff shagging staff in the dry stores and fingering each other out the back to help them feel loved and needed.

Why am I doing this job again? I asked myself. *Because it's worth it sometimes.*

Was it?

| 51 |

Petit Four: A New Role

"Hey, it's Jacqui from the Lonsdale Tavern here," a deep female voice curtly greeted me.

I had had enough of the Wood and Spoon. I was sick of being ignored and sick of being talked down to for being a girl. It was too violent and Dean was a douche-canoe. I was searching for a similar role in Lonsdale – senior management at a busy venue. My resume was impeccable and I knew any venue would be lucky to have me. This was just the call I had been waiting for.

"Hi, how are you?" I asked professionally.

"Good. I understand you're currently at the Wood and Spoon but you were hoping for a new venue?"

"Yes. I'm looking for a similar role, if there's one available. I understand you're quite close to me, so that would be very handy," I answered formally.

There was a slight pause on the line as I heard a muffled sentence. Jacqui from the Lonsdale Tavern must have been speaking to someone nearby. Then, "Are you available to work tonight?"

"Tonight?" I questioned. This sounded a bit suspect. What kind of a venue offered a role to a manager they hadn't even interviewed – to start immediately? Should I take this as a compliment? I knew better than that and erred on the side of hesitation. "Ah... tonight... what would be involved?"

"We were thinking you'd be really good in gaming, so thought we'd put you on trial for a few hours... see how you go..." Jacqui's voice trailed off.

I was furious! I knew what they were doing! "So let me get this straight: You're short staffed and you want to put me on as free labour to fill in the roster?" I demanded.

"Ah- well..." Jacqui began.

"Didn't you read my resume? It says I'm an assistant hotel manager, and you honestly want to put me on a junior unpaid trial to 'see how I go'. Go waste someone else's time – you're not taking advantage of me!"

Jacqui was silent. Then she stupidly needed clarification. "Um, so... is that a no then?"

"It's a no!" I screamed, and slammed down the phone.

| 52 |

Link Chasers

It was five minutes to nine when the bus arrived. As I pushed the main door ajar to open the venue; thirty one people forced past me to ensure they were the first ones in.

They barged past me; I didn't even get the chance to say, "Good-" before I was shut down with lack of eye contact and closed body language.

The thirty one people – who no one had ever seen before – took their places in front of each pokie, and were eagerly perched, keen to get started on their business transactions as the machines auto-powered up. As soon as the bandits lit up and ticked over, thirty fifty-dollar notes were shoved in, and all was silent but the tapping of the spin button.

I stood in awe, for on a Tuesday, I had never seen so many people in that room at that time. In fact, no one before then had seen *every* machine played at once.

The players were different to Old Mate, and the scruffy locals who usually presented at that time. They were dressed neatly, and rather than speaking, they were working. They weren't there for enjoyment, but rather for a purpose.

Word had somehow gotten out that the link was due. One hundred thousand dollars would be awarded to any of the machines who happened to spin at the exact right moment. At ninety nine thousand and the rest, it was bound to happen today.

No one knew how they knew, but when they found out, no one else stood a chance. The ringleader watched on, clearly in charge of the investment, as he walked around importantly in his beige linen lounge suit, handing bills to those running low on credit. They knew the return would be worth it; they just had to be patient. It was going to be – *had* to be – one of them.

In the deepest corner, nature had other plans. A young man squirmed and flinched, rigid and panicking. How long would the link take?

After an hour, it became too much to bear. He slipped out unnoticed, knowing he had three minutes to reserve his machine, but less time before any one of the rest tore their eyes away from the machine and alerted the others.

In his desperation, however, he forgot a crucial piece of equipment: the reservation sign. He left a vulnerable pokie alone to be played.

The locals had left for there was nothing else for the venue to offer them. There was no one threatening the link at all, it seemed. No one, except a frail elderly woman, who had just been dropped off by her son, who needed something to distract her and someone to mind her while he went about other business.

The woman shuffled in at snail's pace. She would have been easy to beat, if anyone tried, but no one did. No one took focus off their machine. No one noticed as she slowly propped herself up, leaving her walker to the side. No one noticed as she fumbled around in her coin purse, and retrieved a single dollar, and slipped it in the slot.

The woman next to her did notice, just as a musical tone chimed, claiming the machine was ready to be played. As she noticed, the others snapped to attention too, all turning with horror realising what was happening: there was an outsider playing their machine.

With no reservation sign, no credit, and no player, legally that machine was free to play. Thirty sets of eyes were fixated on the one woman, who took her time deciding her bet.

The thirty-first pair of eyes emerged from the toilet, relieved from his pee-gasm, then shocked when he saw his place had been taken.

The other players rammed their hands against the spin buttons, tapping vigorously to encourage the link to go off.

The old woman ran her fingers across the options, deciding on a single bet of one dollar, thinking she had nothing to lose by trying.

Tap.

The others stopped tapping as they turned to see the woman's bet. She only had one dollar – were the odds really in her favour?

The dials spun in slow motion, and one by one, the columns settled on their matching positions, except for the last one, which seemed to roll and roll and roll before slowing... to... a... stop.

The lights above every machine darkened, as hers lit up, shimmered, then... POW! A shot of lightning zoomed across the room, splintering across the tops of every pokie, before returning to the old lady's. A ball of energy festered up, glittering silvery blue, before momentous music erupted and her screen exploded into a dazzling waterfall of electricity.

The little old lady had no idea what happened – staring in shock at her machine. She timidly looked at me and asked, "Does it always do that?"

Thirty one people stood up and marched out, furious.

The woman, who had, until then, an audience, found herself alone, unsure of what was happening.

The screen in front of her buzzed excitedly, and numbers flew past the bottom, ticking so quickly they could not be seen.

"Congratulations. Can I just grab an ID please?" I asked.

"What for?" the little old lady asked back.

"It's just a procedure for big wins."

"Oh?" the lady seemed completely unaware of her luck. "Did I win something?"

"Won?" I laughed, "You've won a hundred thousand dollars on the link!" I blurted excitedly.

"Oh. Did I?" she asked, still unsure of what was happening.

The woman collected her cheque and shuffled out again. She left no tip, and didn't notice the busload of angry gamblers on her way out.

Just like that, the room was empty again.

| 53 |

Were You Even Listening?

Luckily, I'd confirmed my start time the night before. I was rostered half an hour earlier than usual. Curious with the odd time, I popped into the office to find out why. That's right! Michelle did mention it! There was a function booked for lunch – an eightieth birthday for William, with two set courses and a cake.

Well of course the night managers hadn't set it up, so now I had to panic about moving tables and lifting the giant coffee urn.

As I was lugging the urn to the party room, there was Grace posing in the entry. William's wife wore stilettos and big designer shades. Her red lips scorched her face and that dress was certainly too short. Those fishnets were a hint of a former slut. She was mutton dressed as lamb. A snow leopard. A silver fox. A gran with a seduction plan.

"Here, let me take that for you," I offered, holding out my hands toward the cake box she'd dumped on the host desk.

"No," Grace told me, suspiciously, "It's rather heavy. Where is the cake table?"

I escorted Grace to the table, curious how a geriatric might possibly think it would be too heavy for *me*, a youthful ninja who ran around like a maniac most of the time. *Each to their own,* I thought, deciding I'd just let Grace call the shots; she seemed the decidedly type anyway.

Grace strutted over to the cake table dramatically, and dumped the cake down a bit clumsily, causing me to wince.

Instinctively, I fluttered over and turned it so it was on an attractive angle, and decoratively draped the twisted piles of napkins around it.

"Oh-" Grace hesitated, before realising I made the table look rather appealing. That shut her up. Looking around the room, Grace found plenty of other things to complain about. "There is no cutlery on the table. We're having two courses, so we'll need-"

"Yes, I'm still setting up, sorry," I told her, frustrated that this woman was so early. Why were the doors to that area even allowed to be open?

"Balloons aren't done either," Grace ticked off her mental list.

"As I explained, I'm still setting up. I have the run sheet here, so I'll just-"

"And where is the gift table?" Grace demanded.

I knew the longer I explained to Grace that it was all happening – and I had enough time to set up – that I would soon run out of time. Grace needed to go so I could work.

"Why don't we get you a wine and you can wait in the lounge while I set up. I'll let you look over it as soon as we're ready," I suggested.

"I need balloons! Michelle told me the room would be filled with balloons!" Grace whined. She was getting wound up over tiny fixable things, making a drama without a llama and just getting on my nerves. They're balloons - rainbow spheres of air enjoyed for an hour and then free to pollute the planet every minute after that. Why was it such a big deal? It's not like I was shooting dead her pet pony.

I looked at my watch, horrified that Grace had now wasted seven precious minutes. Get out, Grace, or there'll be no party at all.

Grace continued to pick and refused to let me do anything without suffocating supervision and careful instruction. I'd had enough. This would take a bit more force.

"I need you to wait outside to greet early arrivals please!" I snapped.

Grace was taken aback. She looked at me like a charity chugger deserving a good slap, so I smiled at her encouragingly to throw her off guard.

Right on cue, a couple of her friends pushed open the foyer doors and called out with open arms to embrace her.

"Darlings!" she crooned affectionately.

I shooed Grace out, locked the function doors behind her and zoomed around, throwing cutlery down, flicking napkins around and shifting tables into place. Amazingly, the party was ready to go. I breathed a sigh of relief. I could kill the night manager for not setting it up!

"Now I would like all the speeches after the main meal, then we sing happy birthday," Grace appeared again, and began speaking to me as if we were mid-conversation still. So she managed to get through my locked doors. I'd better add the dodgy doors to the maintenance list, at the off chance Dean felt like doing his job ever.

"Can I make a suggestion?" I inquired, "Perhaps we sing first, then while the speeches are going, I can take the cake out the back to get cut. It will take some time and you won't want everyone to wait."

Grace looked at me, puzzled.

"So as soon as the speeches are finished, the cake will be ready to serve," I repeated, nodding.

Grace blinked and allowed this suggestion to process.

"So the chefs will be cutting the cake while you're speaking, then it'll be ready as soon as speeches are finished," I repeated.

Blank look.

"If you wait until the end of speeches, you'll have to wait for the cake. There'll be lots of waiting. If you cut the cake during speeches, there'll be no waiting," I said one more time.

Blank face.

"Grace? Trust me, it's a good idea."

Grace was deep in thought, pondering the suggestion. It must have been approved, because she slapped my arm excitedly, exclaiming, "What a wonderful idea! So we don't have to wait!"

"Er... Yes. It is a good idea," I agreed. I fakely chuckled nervously, unsure of whether this was a test.

Grace seemed pleased, and chatted with her friends. It must actually have been a decent suggestion.

More guests arrive and Grace bossed me around again. Guests sat down and Grace told me how to seat them. Food was ready and Grace taught me how to give people food. Thank goodness Grace was here, for otherwise I would have had no idea how to serve!

I began to clear the dinner plates. I took as many as I could carry – up to six - depending on leftovers – but they all continued to 'help' by picking up and shoving their plates in my face. It was only after I leant forward and offered that they put them on my head that they laughed and stopped. "I've only got three hands!" I called, causing them to laugh.

Toward the end of the last table, a kindly fellow stood up and began to boom his speech out, putting the guests into fits of more laughter! Well, there was no way I could finish clearing now, while he was talking!

What should I do? Finish clearing and make a heap of noise? Or stay still silently, but waste time?

I stood at the table dumbly, holding three plates but not daring to move for fear of being reprimanded. Clearing plates was noisy business.

What happened to the plan, Grace? I thought angrily. The plan was to clear plates, sing happy birthday, do speeches! Speeches had already commenced, and dirty plates were still dumped in front of guests. I took some deep breaths, stressing about the fiasco. The plan was being ruined!

I looked at the cake, which appeared to glare back at me. I blinked and the rosettes sat innocently, glittering under the sunlight. I blinked again, and the cake shot another angry look. I shook my head and the fondant sparkled once again.

An applause and an old lady squealed, "Oh, my hat!" while laughing, indicating that the speech was over.

Time to get the plan back on track!

I zipped across to the self-appointed MC and called for a word. "Sorry, I think we were going to do the cake first, *then* the speeches," I told him. "If you wouldn't mind just a second while I clear the rest of the plates, so that way you can do your speeches in peace, without me interrupting," I smiled and suggested, slightly forcefully.

"Of course, dear," he laughed. "And now time for William's son, Barry!" he boomed to the room.

No. No, that's not what the plan was!

"What?" I exclaimed, "We really need to do the cake *now. Before* William's son Barry speaks!" I hissed at the man. "I need to clear the plates, then we need to sing and do the cake, *then* we can do the speeches!"

"Yes, dear, you're very sweet thing," he laughed softly.

That wasn't even a sentence! He was not even listening!

William's son Barry stood and said some heartfelt thing that got the crowd hushed. He spoke softly and genuinely. It would have been a beautiful sentiment, had I not been so panicked about the plate-clearing and cake-cutting catastrophe.

I was panicking.

Grace specified that she wanted the cake served exactly at the end of dinner. No one to wait. There were still four dirty plates on the table that I couldn't clear while William's son Barry mumbled incessantly, and there was an enormous cake to deconstruct and serve.

Grace caught my eye, and exaggeratedly pointed to her watch.

I felt like she was trying to indicate something to me but I couldn't for the life of my figure out what. I tapped my watch exaggeratedly, and gave her a big smile and a thumbs up. As long as Grace and the guests thought all was under control, everything would be ok.

As William's son Barry concluded his speech, the self-appointed MC went to stand up and introduce someone else. "Lovely! Thank you, Barry!" he boomed. "And now..."

OH NO YOU DON'T!

"Wait!" I called to him. I whizzed over and whispered up at the tall MC man, "Sorry, but we have to do the cake and sing happy birthday *before* the next speech!"

"Of course, dear, you precious thing..." he brushed me off. He turned to introduce the next person. "Sorry about that," he crooned to the crowd. "We have some more people who have some nice words to say..."

I knew he wasn't listening! Too many elderly men have done the same thing to me in the past. Talking over me, instead of listening. I had to be more forceful to be taken seriously. "Did you hear me?" I demanded angrily.

"Sorry, did you need something, pet?" he asked me airily.

Pet?

"Yes. We have to do the cake *now*," I insisted. My stance indicated the little pet meant business. "*Cake*. Now."

The man concentrated briefly, then announced to the room in an embarrassingly loud tone, "Apparently we have to do the cake now, I'm being told."

I cringed. Thanks buddy. Just throw me in front of a bus then. I looked around and saw the faces of the inconveniently interrupted and felt like an idiot.

The MC begrudgingly helped William to his feet and over to the cake. William appeared unaware of the tension and stood with pride as his friends sang out to him.

The second the song concluded, it was, *"Cut it!"* Grace again popped out of thin air and barked orders at me. "I wanted it served by the end of the speeches – *weren't you listening?"*

I opened my mouth, but instead shot a glare, then a big smile to hide it. *Was I listening? WAS I LISTENING?! I suggested the whole process, lady!*

"Certainly, Grace, I'm just taking it to the kitchen now," I beamed professionally.

I went to lift the cake, and Grace started fussing, "Are you ok? It's heavy. Do you need help?"

"I've got it," I told her through a gritted smile.

Grace's arms flail toward me to 'help', just about knocking the darn thing out of my hands. Grace's 'help' was making things worse and slowing me down.

"I've got it!" I snapped, then quickly beamed sunshine so Grace couldn't tell that I had yelled at her. I was the master at this technique. A sharp flash so quick they're not sure if they've seen it followed by copious quantities of fair natured, good old fashioned customer service.

The cake wasn't even that heavy.

Grace chased after me, calling out instructions. "So you'll take it to the kitchen, where the chefs can cut it..."

I tried to rush, but was slow under the weight of the cake. Ok, it was a little heavy.

Grace caught up to me, desperate to explain to me how to cut it. She grabbed my forearm and pulled me to a stop.

I steadied my balance, and managed to stop the cake slipping. Flames shot across my face as my skin prickled. *Did she just grab me?* I yanked my arm away, jolting the cake. *Don't touch me!*

I murdered Grace with my eyes. Then smiled.

Grace looked horrified, concerned the cake might fall. "Now, I've worked out, if you cut it about a centimetre wide," she holds up her fingers, in case I didn't know what a centimetre was. "You should be able to cut exactly seventy two slices," Grace finished, nodding, concerned that I might eff this one up.

"Sorry, what?" I blurted accidently. "You're not actually suggesting we cut this cake into pie wedges?"

"Yes," Grace nodded intently, "seventy two will fit, but you'll have to measure *very* carefully." Grace displayed grave concern for the fate of the cake. She'd thought long and hard about how it would be cut, devising an expertly planned trigonometric strategy – one thing she hadn't counted on was this young girl taking over.

I shook my head, "Sorry Grace, that's not going to work."

Grace went to speak but I knew this would be a disaster.

"Look, our chefs are *professionals*. They've done this before. They know what they're doing. They'll cut it so it fits and looks good – trust them."

I barged toward the kitchen so Grace could say no more. As I reversed through the doors, I spied Grace panicking and worrying with her friend.

I broadly smiled and nodded, indicating to Grace that the next speech should begin, and shooed her out.

Ten minutes later, at the conclusion of the final speech, I appeared with a platter of seventy two perfect cubes of cake, each adorned with an intricate floral crown.

"Oh!" Grace spluttered, looking horrified.

What? What could possibly be wrong with this? I had had it. Grace had been riding my back all morning – first the table set-ups, the balloons, the gift table then the clearing, now the cake! Each time, I had exceeded expectations, but Grace kept nagging and controlling. Enough was enough! These cake cubes were effing perfect, and if she didn't like them, she should shove them up her effing-

"*It's beautiful!*" Grace squealed.

What?

"How did your chefs know how to do this?" she fawned.

"It's... ah.. not their first time," I suggested.

Grace picked up a cube of cake and admired the chef's craft. "Wow, and they've even decorated each one with a flower!"

The women in the group all cooed at the sight of the cake pieces, some fishing out their cameras (yes, cameras, not phones) to take photographs of them. I stood as the women poured over the cakes and carefully captured shots from every angle.

"Excuse me?"

I turned to see a tiny little old woman with blue-rinsed hair. "Yes, can I help you?"

"Can you take a look at my camera? It just won't work!" she fiddled with it dramatically, to show me exactly how much it was not working.

"Try turning it on first," I suggested.

The surrounding women cackled at the hilarity of such a simple mistake!

I imagined their visiting families being subjected to photo albums filled with pictures of cake. Then again, people make entire hashtags out of photos of cake, so maybe they were progressive in the time before social media.

I must have earnt Grace's trust, or the wine must have kicked in, for rather than being tormented and criticised, Grace began raving about what a wonderful job I was doing, introducing me to all of her friends.

I was especially impressed when Grace made a point of inviting her great-granddaughter over to say hello, because she and I were "about the same age." I explained that I was in my twenties – slightly older than the blossoming tween standing opposite me.

Later, the 'MC' came to settle the bill. Ah, this guy again. The geriatric with verbal diarrhoea who embarrassed me in front of everyone and called me 'pet'. I was not his darn 'pet', as much was I anyone's 'babe' or 'sweetheart'.

I assumed he must have a tight relationship with William and Grace to both MC the party and pay the bill. It seemed like a fairly safe topic for the mandatory small talk. One can not serve without making some sort of small talk. "So how long have you known William and Grace for?" I asked politely.

"Yes, it was all very good," he replied, completely ignoring what I'd said.

I clenched my teeth, then took a deep breath and counted in my head to five. I exhaled slowly.

The man didn't seem to notice, as he was reading over the invoice with great concentration, peering over his glasses and thrusting his arm out in front of him to make the wording clearer.

"The remainder is exactly two thousand dollars please," I stated.

The man frowned, flapping the sheet over, then back again, scanning the same words yet again. "I can't see it... How much is remaining after the deposit?"

I clenched my teeth, then took a deep breath and counted in my head to five. I exhaled slowly. "I just told you. The remainder is two thousand dollars please."

He raised his eyebrow, questioning whether to trust me. He'd have to – his arms weren't long enough to focus on the small type font clearly. He pulled out a card and pushed it toward me.

I took his card and inserted it into the machine.

"You can do that ah, 'tap and pay' thing they do now," he chuckled as if he were in with the cool kids.

"It doesn't work for that amount, sorry. It'll still ask for a pin anyway. Which account would you like, cheque, savings or credit?"

"I said just tap it, dear."

I corrected him by saying my name. I clenched my teeth, then took a deep breath and counted in my head to five. I exhaled slowly.

"Yes, very good, dear," he mentioned to no one.

"So, savings?" I breathed, punching in the numbers. "I'll just need your pin please," I said, pushing the terminal toward him.

"Oh, you just do it for me," he nodded.

"Very well, what's the number?" I asked.

"For?" the man asked.

"For your savings account pin?" I cringed.

"Oh, no, I said just 'tap and pay'," he replied.

"As I explained, you need to enter a pin regardless, because it's over the pin-free threshold."

I clenched my teeth, then took a deep breath and counted in my head to five. I exhaled slowly. Don't snap. Don't snap. He's probably just confused. Old people get confused sometimes. Don't snap.

"So I need to enter a pin?" he looked at me fishily.

"Yes please!" I forced a huge grin.

As he keys it in, he muttered, "Nowhere else needs one.."

I kept beaming, and confirmed he was free to go, by saying, "That's all been approved. Would you like a receipt?"

To which this man, who had been talking over me all day now, said, "Yes, yes," with a small chuckle, turning away from me, as if I told him a hilarious farewell joke.

I was perturbed. He is still treating me as if I am offering small talk! I offered the receipt slip, and he brushed it off, laughing, "No, no receipt! I'm sure I'll find you if it's wrong!"

"Have a lovely day, thank you!" I responded fakely, hoping he'd leave faster.

Some random I'd never seen approached me. I really hoped he didn't see me scream inside my head.

"How can I help you?" I asked, curious as to what he needed, as everyone else had left. If he was the MC's kid, I might lose the plot and become crazier than I already was.

"We wanted to give you this," he handed me a gift bag with a bottle of wine. Thank goodness! He was far too nice to be related to the last guy.

"We really appreciate all the effort you put into today, and we really think you went above and beyond in making our day special."

"Really?" I was pleasantly surprised. "That's so lovely! Thank you, you don't need to do that, that's my job!" I exclaimed happily.

"You deserve it. Thank you," he said before taking off.

Rule number two: You will never be able to guess who will tip, or how much.

I peered into the bag. Did he just re-gift me a gift they didn't want? It didn't matter though, I'd take free wine any day! Was it any good though? How much was this bottle worth exactly? I was no sommelier. If people asked for recommendations at the bar, I'd wing it, saying vague things like, "This pinot grigio is very popular," and offering small tastes to undecided guests. I knew the usual 'red goes with red meat and white goes with white meat' but not much else. As a drinker, I was no snob. If it tasted ok, I'd drink it. A gift for an eightieth birthday wouldn't be cheap though. If I were attending an eightieth party, a good fifty dollars would be the price point for a gift.

Maybe I'd scored a decent drop! If it were, I would keep it and take it to the next dinner party I went to. I giggled – what a silly idea. As if anyone would ever have a dinner party on a Monday when I was free!

Curiosity got the better of me, and I searched the net for the wine he gave me. It was worth ten dollars. Of course it was. Still, free alcohol was free alcohol so I wasn't complaining.

A young woman walked in and asked, "Do you have toilets here?"

I scrunched the gift bag closed, shoved it under the desk, and said the completely wrong thing to her.

I'd been ignored all day. I was put off from the second I walked in and saw the function wasn't set up. Without even looking at the roster, I knew it was Dean who closed, because he was just the kind of person who went out of his way for a stitch up. Another reason to hate him. Grace was high pressure, and that MC man was just painful. I'd been letting all my fury come to the surface, and I got a bit jumpy when she caught me looking in my wine gift bag at my ten dollar bottle of rubbish (that I was actually eternally grateful for). So when she asked me *if* we have toilets, the first thing to pop out of my mouth was, "Nah, we just shit on the streets."

There was about a three second delay before it registered. We both looked at each other in horror as we realised what I'd said!

"Oh my goodness, I'm so sorry! I didn't mean to say that!" It was too late. I blew it.

She walked straight back out in a huff - rightly so - to go pee in the sports bar.

Not long after that and Dean came in to remind me of my faux pas. Of course the woman who needed to pee tattled on me. All good for him to set me up for a bad day, but I get in trouble with one throwaway comment.

"Well?" he demanded. "Did you tell this customer that she should defecate on the street? She told me you said she couldn't use our toilets, and that she had to go outside!"

"Well, no, that's not what happened…" I protested, knowing I was in big trouble. To be fair, that wasn't what I'd said. I'd just told her a big lie - that we didn't have toilets, and *we* just went on the street. I never suggested that *she* go on the street.

Dean started lecturing me again so I decided a dignified silence was the best idea.

I'd had such a tough morning that I had to actively tell myself not to cry. I remembered a meme I once saw, that said, "Never cry over anyone who wouldn't cry over you." As if Dean would ever cry over me.

I was remorseful and the guilt was eating at me. Kind of like that time I told a customer to eff off. Actually, not like that time. Telling a customer to eff off when they deserve it is incredibly satisfying.

Dean left me with one final warning, "I'm onto you."

Yep. Never mind all the magic I'd created today. One stupid slip up, and he's trying to get rid of me. I wondered if I was being paranoid, but I honestly felt like he was the slimy kind of manager to do just that - get rid of people just to remind everyone of his power.

It turns out, I was right.

| 54 |

Fight Day

It was eight in the morning, and as I arrived, I answered the phone.

"Hey, are you guys showing the fight today?" some random person asked me.

"The fight?" I asked.

"Yeah the fight. Are you showing it?" he asked again, excitedly.

I had no idea. What fight? I was no sports enthusiast. I didn't have a clue about a fight being on, and couldn't care less.

"We sure are! See you soon!" I told the customer and hung up. What fight? There was nothing in the manager's diary, and nothing on the noticeboard. Nobody mentioned it at the manager's meeting. There was no artwork on the walls - nothing. I decided to risk sounding stupid, and sent a text to Dean.

Sure enough, it was fight day. Fight day meant it would be busy.

Sure enough, the doors opened, and patrons filed in, shoving to get to the seats with the best view of the screens. They were mostly younger, and mostly male, apart from a handful of girlfriends and the odd bulky tattooed men, who I all knew by name plus what they were drinking.

I groaned to myself as Old Mate took a seat. Great. He was here. He was always so much fun. I smiled and gave him a quick wave, because he was a local. I still hated him, but I was still nice, because, you know, hospo.

The pub was fairly silent during the telecast, apart from random cheers and groans. The bar staff all watched intently with nothing to do, for no patron would dare approach the bar and miss anything. I had to be on my game though. I knew as soon as the fight finished, the bar would be packed. Time to be prepared.

Silence then groans then cheers. Silence. The young men winced in unison as one guy got hit. Commentary and silence. Cheering. Abuse at the TV. Muttering among selves. Encouraging yell... go! Go! Go! Annnnnnd... the whole bar stood up and screamed happily, clapping, hugging and celebrating. The underdog took out the champion!

I blinked and a hundred faces ran toward me, vying for attention! The guy who clicked his fingers at me would be the last to be served.

"Oi, sweetheart, I was next!" he called out.

I ignored him.

"Bourbon and cola and three wet pussies," the next guy said.

"Please! Twenty eight dollars!" I reminded him.

"Oh. Please," he apologised as I made them.

Next person, "A vodka lime and soda and a vodka orange."

"Please! Fourteen dollars!" I reminded her.

"Oh. Please," apologised the girl as I made the drinks.

Next person, "Six scotch and cola."

"Sorry, mate, maximum is four per person," I replied.

"Aw what? But I got me mates o'there!" he whined.

"Go grab a mate, otherwise I can only serve you four, sorry," I said automatically. I felt like this has been said to hundreds of people, hundreds of times. How stupidwere some civilians? As if you could ever get six drinks at one time – anywhere!

"Nah, how about you serve me my six scotch cokes, love. You holdin' up tha line, look!" he bragged.

"No. Next waiting, please!" I called to the crowd.

Old Mate heard me, and crooned deeply, "Just a beer, Lexi."

I didn't need to ask which one; I knew which one. Old Mate was frequently a bit of a douche-canoe, and ordinarily, I'd snap at him for calling me Lexi. He only did it to get a rise out of me. Most of the time I'd get him to specify which beer, just to throw some shade back at him, but we were busy and I felt the pressure building. Speed up service time.

As I grabbed a glass out of the chiller, the kid with the scotch and cola's sweaty hand reached over and clutched mine, tightening his grip steadily.

I froze and a feeling of panic washed over me. This was not good. I ripped my hand from his, but he still yelled, waving a fifty-dollar note at my face, causing me to squint and lean away, intruded.

"Oi! Where ma drinks? I ask fur six scotch cola and you won't get em!" the young guy spat across the bar at me.

Just who the heck did he think he was?

JUST WAIT YOUR TURN!" I bellowed.

As I was serving Old Mate, I looked at the young scotch drinker to memorise his face so I could spend the rest of the shift turning him away. I never really looked at customers to see them until I needed to. They all seemed to blend into one. I remembered their orders, but couldn't tell you their hair colour. I knew their mannerisms, but wouldn't know what colour shirt they were wearing. For the first time that morning, I took a really good look at the young scotch drinker, while I poured Old Mate his beer.

Young Scotch had greasy hair, patchy bum fluff and a narrow face with acne scars. He was skinny, but had been working hard at the gym. He looked like a late bloomer, keen to prove himself as a man. He had gone about it the wrong way. If he were nicer, I would have never questioned him. He was rude though. Then he touched me. No one should ever touch me unless invited to - and let's be honest, I was usually way too generous with my invitations. I became intently focussed on Young Scotch. He had better watch out. I shouted Old Mate his drink (he was tolerable that day, and even grunted and waved a thanks) and turned back to Young Scotch.

"Six scotch and cola love!" he demanded condescendingly.

"You got ID?" I asked.

"What?"

"Do... you... have... identification?" I repeated, pausing slightly between words for an embarrassing jut.

"You bin servin' me all day."

Hundreds of people watched and fought for their place in the queue. I had better hurry up. He had better not be so rude. Last chance.

"I have not. This is the first time *I* have served you, and *I* have the right to request ID off *any* patron at any time. So, can I see your ID?" I demanded. I knew I'd got him.

He shouldn't have touched me. He should not have touched me.

I looked around, frantically searching for support. Being a Sunday day, there were no guards rostered on. The bar staff were mostly young females like myself. Tim was too scrawny to be of any help. *It's not the size of the dog in the fight*, I reminded myself. I would be in this alone. Here we go.

"Just gemme my drinks, bitch!" he spat at me.

Wrong answer.

I lunged toward his face scowling menacingly and bellowed at the top of my lungs, *"GET THE EFF OUT OF MY BAR! GET OUT! GET OUT RIGHT NOW OR I'LL CALL THE POLICE!"*

There was silence as the rest of the patrons turned to watch. Obviously the word 'eff' wasn't used. Surely by now you get the picture.

"You can't talk to me like that, you effing slut! I'll report you!" He retorted, side-glancing to find a mate who'd be on his team.

"GET OUT! EFF OFF OUT THE DOOR! *AND WHEN YOU GET THERE, EFF OFF SOME MORE!* EFF RIGHT OFF OUT OF HERE, NOW! GO ON! GET OUT!" I howed, clambering up over the bar to gain height. I was rigid, clammy and obviously threatening, for Young Scotch looked around again, searching for backup. There was none.

Young Scotch and I eyed each other off. The whole bar and the staff were watching. They'd got more than they'd come there to get. Who cared about a pay per view fight when there was real action right here! We were both fuming, breathing scattered, daring each other to make the next move.

He lunged toward me, arms outstretched, ready to make contact with my face. I ducked instinctively and fell a metre to the floor in a pile on the customer side. I jumped up, ready to defend myself, terrified of a punch coming at me, but aggressive enough to project that I was brave and a force to be reckoned with.

No need to worry.

There was no one there.

Scotch was gone.

I looked up and saw him being blocked by none other than the prickly thorn in my side, Old Mate.

Old Mate appeared from nowhere, and wedged himself between Scotch and I, protecting me. I was astonished and the crowd watched on, dying to know what would happen next.

Young Scotch still looked angry, but there was a hint of apprehension now too. Old Mate, though older, was a big guy. He was a man of habit, visiting the same pub every other day, sitting in the same chair, drinking the same beer. His blurred tattoos, however, hinted at a wilder past.

Old Mate offered his hand to the kid. "You ok, mate?" he asked him quietly.

Young Scotch looked at him suspiciously, then returned his hand. The idiot must have thought Old Mate was sticking up for him, as some customers did that thing and ganged up on hospos. He shook Old Mate's hand, "Yeah."

Old Mate pulled Scotch close.

Scotch's eyes widened, as he realised that he was actually in big trouble. If he wanted to pick a fight with me, he was going to get a real fight.

In a voice, so deathly quiet, Old Mate looked down at Young Scotch's hand, and squeezed it. He looked down to him, dead in the eye, and firmly told him "*Never* raise your hand to a lady."

Old Mate held Young Scotch's hand and kept freakishly intense eye contact. His grip seemed to tighten. I was certain I heard a crack.

Young Scotch eyed off Old Mate, challenging him to be the big guy, until he finally retreated, and Old Mate let go. No one would want to face Old Mate in a fight, and I was pretty certain Old Mate had just broken his hand.

"This bar is shit anyway," Young Scotch spat as he finally left

Old Mate walked back to his table without saying a word, sat down in his usual spot, took a sip of his usual beer, and focused on the horseracing as if nothing had happened.

I was shaking with fury and fear. That was a close call.

"Well I wouldn't want to meet you in a dark alley," Tim observed.

"What?!" My mind snapped back into reality. "Oh, yeah. Don't tell Dean about that one." My voice was raspy from the tirade. The line at the bar began to buzz again. I had to serve. Big smile. "What can I get for you?" I asked a young woman in my Customer Voice.

"Oh, can I please get a... a... *how did you do that?*" she asked.

"Do?" What on earth was she talking about?

"How did you scream like that? And not get attacked? And get him to leave without being scared? Then come back and serve like nothing happened? *How?*" the young lady asked, intrigued by my behaviour.

"You see I would cry, but working in hospitality destroyed my soul!" I laughed in a fake forced sort of way - there was far too much truth to that sentiment.

The woman I was serving laughed too, with a confused look, because she had no idea what I was joking about. She looked like a pharmaceutical rep, so she was probably a pharmaceutical rep.

Resilience was key to lasting in the hospitality industry. I had just turned off my emotion, as if it were nothing. Well, almost. According to the staff and the patrons, I had switched it off. In actual fact, I had deferred it. I still had five hours left in my shift. In six hours time, I'd process what had just happened, probably cry, and would drown my sorrows. Alcohol was the best way to handle a bad day. Tonight it would be bourbon. Right now, however, I was at work, and I was in charge. I needed to leave my emotions at the door and put on the performance of customer-ing.

"I just told myself that he was an arsehole, and that was something I had to deal with," I elaborated to the woman. "Some people are just arseholes. There's no point dwelling on it because they'll never change."

"Yeah, he was a bit of a tool," she agreed. "Any longer and I would have told him to eff off too. He was lucky he didn't get knocked out by that big guy."

I smiled, glad that this young girl was on the same wavelength. There are only very few patrons you can say those sort of things to and be real with. She was cool.

I looked over at Old Mate and saw his glass had only a third left. I poured another one and walked it over to him.

"Thank you," I said, putting the glass down.

"What?" he asked.

"For helping me back there. Really, I mean it. Thank you."

"You always look after us, Lexi. Keep up the good work."

| 55 |

A Meeting Regarding Performance

I've had some really fantastic GMs over the years and I've also had some really awful ones, but it's more fun to write about the awful ones.

One of the worst I had was Dean. Dean tried to do anything to get rid of me. He had been picking on me for months.

I don't know exactly why, but I do know that I'm one of those people you'd either get on with really well, or just clash horribly with. There was no middle ground. Nobody had a vague opinion on me - it's just love me or hate me.

The young bartenders suggested that he was probably jealous of me and was threatened by me. Dean hated me. He'd obviously been looking at getting rid of me for a while. I figured he was bullying me to try make me quit, that way he wouldn't cop any repercussions (no one ever complained about bullying in hospitality; everyone just moved to another venue).

Being the stubborn bitch that I was, instead of quitting, I just cried myself to sleep each night, then went back to work with an extra strong smug attitude just to piss him off.

One afternoon, he texted me to come in early the next day. I thought it sounded a bit suss, so I asked him why, and he told me there was a meeting and 'nothing to worry about'.

Of course, the fact that he told me there was a meeting and 'nothing to worry about' meant that I immediately worried and had lots to worry about. So I asked for an agenda to prepare myself.

He told me that it was just a performance review and 'nothing to worry about', then hung up on me.

I knew I was in trouble but I just couldn't think of why.

The next day, I met him and the area manager, John. Actually, let's call him Johnno, because it's more hospo-manager-y and less scary. Of course the area manager was there; it was a supermarket pub and they had compliance to uphold, such as area managers being present for written warnings - not that I had anything to worry about, according to Dean.

Well, would you believe it? It turned out Dean was trying to fire me! What a surprise. He was orchestrating this meeting as a means to get rid of me. He was clutching at straws, trying to find something – anything - which proved I could be terminated.

Unfortunately for him, I was not as stupid as he imagined, so I put up an excellent fight for my job.

After suggesting some really dumb things, he finally came up with a legitiment argument, "...swearing on several occasions, and, finally, failing to fill out the decibel register as part of your duties to comply with our liquor license," he finished reading.

"The *what?*" I asked.

"The – ahh – *decibel register*... which you're required to fill out every shift," he revealed craftily.

"*What* decibel register?" I demanded.

"Oh – so you admit to not filling it out then?" He trapped me!

"Well if I knew I had to – or what it was – I would!" I snapped back.

"The decibel register is where we record the level of noise in the venue via the decibel monitor. We can be breached should we not comply with noise restrictions. It is a legal requirement that it is filled out each shift," Dean read, scorning as he knew he'd finally got me for something.

He forgot, however, that I was yet to have my turn in speaking. I stared straight ahead, deciding it was best not to respond at this point. My chance at rebuttal was approaching. I reminded myself once more that he was a bully. He hated me because of my youthful looks and the one thing slowing me to a promotion: my vagina. Both of these things were against the anti-discrimination policies in the company manual, but it would be exceedingly difficult to prove they were the source of his poor behaviour. Therefore, I knew that I'd have to get him on general bullying.

I actually wasn't sure what he meant by 'decibel register'. I didn't want to seem silly in front of him, or Johnno, but I couldn't ever remember being shown it. Come to think of it, I'd hadn't ever heard *anyone* ever mention it at all. What should I do? Should I say I'd never been shown it? Should I ask where – or what – it was? What was the best approach to make me come up on top? I knew that a breach of the liquor license was serious. But I had no other option. I literally had no idea, before today, that it was a part of my job. I decided to be honest and just say I didn't know.

"Every shift, you are required to record the sound levels of the sports bar and write them on the register. But you have failed to do so on four hundred and ninety eight occasions," Dean read robotically. He shot a triumphant glare at me, knowing he'd finally got me for something.

Four hundred and ninety eight. I thought, *That's almost two years. The whole time I've worked here, and he never said anything... hang on.* It clicked. He never said anything until now.

"May I see it please?" I asked.

"Sure," Dean said, unaware he was about to be floored. "I just happen to have it right here." He half passed, but half threw a bright orange folder at me.

I snapped it up and flicked through it, comparing my roster with the pages in the folder. It took time, but I had it. I ignored my bladder panging, thankful that despite the heat, I hadn't touched the glass of water poured for me.

"So you're telling me that I've failed to complete a task four hundred and ninety eight times?" I asked.

"Yes," Dean smugly replied, "Four *hundred* and ninety eight times, you failed to complete this task."

"But you never trained me to do it. I have my job description here, and my diary notes, and it's never been mentioned. If I never did it, why wait until now to say something?"

Dean tried to speak, but I raised my voice, and my hand to hush him.

"There are more than four hundred and ninety eight reports missing. Some of the other managers have forgotten to fill it in on some days too. Did you tell them they'd forgotten too?" I asked.

"This meeting isn't about them, it's about you!" he snapped, losing character and causing Johnno the area manager to jump.

"Are they getting warnings too? Or just me?" I asked.

Dean had no response.

I continued. "On the 22nd of September, I have a roster that states *you* were the duty manager, but the decibel register hasn't been filled out. Do you get a warning too?"

"I swapped that shift out," Dean tried to say.

"I have a legal document that says you were rostered and responsible," I said simply.

"Ok, that's enough!" Johnno interrupted, "I've seen enough!" He pointed at me. "You will receive a written warning for failing to fill out the decibel register – and *only* failing to fill out the decibel register. Dean you will conduct a documented training session with *all* of the management team, teaching them the importance of the decibel register. This meeting is now adjourned."

Dean disappeared before anyone else could get the chance to move. Johnno the area manager thanked me for attending, before excusing himself.

It was over.

| 56 |

Epilogue: Knock-offs

On a bustling Friday evening, diners chatted and laughed happily over the blaring music. There was the usual crowd in that night - not that anyone would *ever* stereotype a customer.

There were the boys overdrinking the beers so they didn't get called 'soft'. They were half watching the game, every so often yelling at the screen, then discussing what the ref did to screw them this time.

The girls were posing, wearing just the right balance between slutty and sexy. They took photos of their food, their boobs and their faces, captioning each picture with things like 'besties', 'girls' night out' or something about love to the moon and back.

Speckled around the bar were the office workers who had overstayed and would end up doing something they'd regret, whilst hiding in the corners were the awkward singles waiting for first dates.

Old Mate was spewing that some random stole 'his' seat, while the full-timers told him that's tough and he'd have to deal. It was petty revenge because he never said please or thank you. Even though he's a tool, they'd still serve him first, because locals always took priority. If the new girl served him by accident, he'd roast her, and teach her how to pour a beer the proper way. There's no need; Tim who'd been there for years will scold her, then retrain her.

The chinking of cutlery scraping plates clean and the chiming of glasses during toasts enhanced the loud fun, as friends cheered, dates impressed and woo-girls squealed. Happy Friday indeed.

Then there's Nicki.

Nicki was shoving her way through the crowd, rage-glaring at the idiots who didn't keep left. She said, "Excuse me," then a bit louder, "*Excuse me!*" then violently bellowed, "*EXCUSE ME!!!*" at the top of her lungs to try get the suits to move out of the way. They give her rude looks for yelling and would definitely include that in their online review.

She was already in a mood, but how dare they have a drink and unwind while she needed to shove her way through.

She barged out the back sobbing, and went to hide and have a smoke huddled on a milk crate.

We were still getting slammed, but I could acknowledge she needed a time out, so I ran around on the floor as fast as I could to help get it clean. I understood what's wrong with her; sometimes we all just needed to remove ourselves from the situation to get better.

Nicki came in via the bar to sneak in a shot of vodka, which I of course, definitely did not see. She saw the man who made her rage; he was walking toward the door, so Nicki, being the good hospo girl she was, did the right thing and farewelled him.

"Eff you! Have a great evening! See you next time!"

He turned to her, with confused anger.

I really hoped he wouldn't cotton on. Pretty daring for Nicki, but if he made her cry, he probably deserved it. I pretended she said the right thing all along.

She smiled and repeated the exact same thing, just like I thought she did. "Thank you! Have a great night! See you soon!"

See? I told you Nicki was good. She's resilient, and obviously knew some things about working in hospitality. Resilience is key when you're on the front line.

Hospitality staff can conjure a protective shield out of nothing, deflecting all further insults and bickering, only to be removed by copious quantities of alcohol at the end of shift.

The customers eventually trickled out, the floor got cleaned and reset and the beers got poured. They're only allowed one 'knock-off' drink each, but as per unspoken protocol, one went through the till, one got wasted by accident, and a third one mysteriously disappeared. After the third one, it was easy for a few shots to disappear too, depending on if it was a Sunday (start of the weekend) or a Thursday (the beginning of the work week).

Staff knock-offs were a time for venting, philosophy and solving all the world's problems.

I loved my job, and spent a lot of time training my staff on the importance of customer service and customer retention. Without customers, we didn't have jobs. It was true. There's no service industry without people to provide a service to.

Still, my knowledge provided a veteran insight into the industry that newbies failed to see. Customer service isn't just about kissing butts and sucking up. It's not about being walked all over, and it's not about entitlement. It's about finding that sweet soft spot between 'the customer is always right' and 'the customer is an arsehole, but we still need to run a business, so we need to make them *feel* like they're right'.

Most customers are nice. Some are a bit thick. Some are scum who are out to pick fights and belittle another person just to go on a power trip, because they can.

These scumbags think because we work in service, we are servants. They think because they pay for our service, they are entitled to sordid behaviour and cruel words.

Abuse doesn't have to be physical, for words can shatter a soul. Too much of that can break a person's spirit. It's one of the reasons hospitality has such a high turnover: staff leave after customers attack them, too embarrassed and too upset to fight back.

Some people are just arseholes. These arseholes are a different breed. They aren't the usual bob-haircut wearing, mini-van driving, ignoring child making messes bitches who order gluten free to be fashionable and whinge about us not smiling enough. They aren't the old people who turn their nose down at us for not having a 'real' job and boss us around because they 'know better'. They aren't the gambling addicts who glue themselves to the pokies and demand that we owe them the world because our jobs rely on them.

A true arsehole could walk into *any* restaurant. He could be served by *any* staff member. He could order *any* dish. And you know what? He would complain! He just wants to make someone feel inferior! Because you're getting paid to provide a service, he feels the need to take advantage of the fact that you can't yell back, and he tears you down! He's an arsehole! There's nothing else to it. He's just an arsehole. It's not your fault.

Once I understood and accepted that some people are just arseholes, I became better at my job. A weight lifted off my shoulders, and suddenly I found it easier to fake a smile, and find that happy borderline between being sickly sweet and outright rude.

I stopped trying to excuse their foul disposition. I stopped being upset about it for the rest of the shift. I stopped caring if they whined to their friends and spoke behind my back. I just stopped caring. It is possible to exude a perfect disposition without actual emotion behind it.

They are everywhere.

Some staff are arseholes. There are the Laurens at the Rutherford, and Deli Ham Susans. Mavises and Misogynist Deans were more upfront about it.

I have also served so many over the years. There were the gluttonous buffet hoarders of the Rutherford. The creepy guy who'd asked to see my boobs at Clarkson. The crazy woman who ripped up the plants at The Woody. Old Mate in general (well, actually, he turned out to be not so bad) and the thousands of gluten-free, fussy, snappy entitled tossers who just thought they were better than everyone else. Arseholes. All arseholes, and some people are just arseholes.

Respect goes both ways, and working in customer service is not an excuse to endure rotten behaviour from people who somehow believe we are beneath them.

Being a successful human being is about lifting others up, not tearing them down. Therefore, one rule I live by is: *Be nice to everyone* (to an extent - some people are just beyond help).

Paying for service does not entitle one to be arseholey, for you are still being served by *people*. Scream at machines, but don't you dare take your mood out on us.

Since coming to this realisation, I rarely let customers get to me. I just think, 'He's an arsehole,' and continue on my merry way. It's not worth letting them make me stew over them in fury. At the end of the day, they've gone home, and I need to be able to come to work the next day.

It is never worth crying over these people. These people are not regular civilians. They do not have legitimate complaints – they're simply searching for someone to yell at. Working in hospitality is one of the hardest jobs in the world. If you let it get to you, it'll eat you up. If you brush off the arseholes and never worry about the tips, it can be the most rewarding.

To anyone wanting to start in the industry, whether it be pulling a few pints whilst studying, or slaving away full time for the love, there are a few things I learnt about working in hospitality:

- It's not a job; it's a lifestyle
- You cannot guess who will tip or how much
- Cover your own butt
- If they say they're never coming back, don't try get them to stay
- Be nice to everyone
- Some people are just arseholes

Once you've got these, you'll be sweet, and although you may not love it as much as me, you might survive it. Best of luck and kick arse.

CHEERS & BEERS

Heya!

If you're reading this, please do me a HUGE favour and leave me some online reviews for this book.

If you think it's great, or you think it's awful, any bit of online attention is a gift!

Cheers and beers,

Emma

CPSIA information can be obtained
at www.ICGtesting.com
Printed in the USA
LVHW022109110521
687091LV00012B/2710